OF FRANCE) (1553–1610)

(1573–1642)
Regent, 1610–1614; thereafter
much in exile

Gaston d'Orléans
(1608–1660)
("Monsieur")

Elizabeth
(1602–1644)

Henrietta-Maria
(1605–1666)

Philip IV of Spain

Charles I
of England

Marguerite
de Lorraine
("Madame")

Louison Roger,
a bourgeois
girl of Tours;
(later, Mother Louise)

Maria-Theresa
(1638–1683)
Queen of France

Mademoiselle's
several half-
sisters; and
one half-brother,
dead in infancy

Louis,
Chevalier
(later
Comte)
de Charny

Charles II
of
England

James,
Duke
of
York,
later
James II
of England

Henriette
d'Angleterre,
(1644–1670)
("Madame")

(by secret marriage)
Françoise d'Aubigné,
created Marquise de
Maintenon; formerly Mme.
Scarron, governess
of Madame de
Montespan's children
by the king

Henriette
d'Angleterre
(1644–1670)
("Madame")

Elizabeth-
Charlotte
of Bavaria
(the younger
"Princess
Palatine")

1 son, 2
daughters

2 sons, 1
daughter

*A Partial Family Tree of the Bourbons,
showing The Grand Mademoiselle
among some of her relations.*

THE GRAND MADEMOISELLE

Books by FRANCIS STEEGMULLER

The Grand Mademoiselle
The Two Lives of James Jackson Jarves
Maupassant, A Lion in the Path
Flaubert and Madame Bovary: A Double Portrait
The Selected Letters of Gustave Flaubert (*translator and editor*)
States of Grace
French Follies and Other Follies
The Musicale

(*Under the name Byron Steel*)
O Rare Ben Jonson
Java-Java
Sir Francis Bacon

(*Under the name David Keith*)
A Matter of Iodine
A Matter of Accent
Blue Harpsichord

J. Bulloz

The Grand Mademoiselle, *after a portrait by* Mignard

THE GRAND
MADEMOISELLE

BY

FRANCIS STEEGMULLER

❧❧❧

FARRAR, STRAUS AND CUDAHY

NEW YORK

CONTENTS

PART ONE
THE UNTOUCHED HEART
Page 1

PART TWO
INTERLUDE: MADEMOISELLE FINDS HER KING
Page 99

PART THREE
LOVE UNDER AN ABSOLUTE MONARCH
Page 177

PART FOUR
MADEMOISELLE OR MADAME?
Page 269

APPENDIX
A SELF-PORTRAIT OF MADEMOISELLE
Page 303

NOTE
Page 307

Part One

THE UNTOUCHED HEART

1627–1652

1

MADEMOISELLE IS TWENTY-FIVE as she begins her memoirs. Twenty-five: incredibly old still to be Mademoiselle, and not Madame!

In those days scarcely a girl at court remained single at twenty. Mademoiselle's own stepmother was fourteen when she married Mademoiselle's father. Mademoiselle de Brézé, the cardinal's niece, was sent to convent school to learn reading and writing immediately *after* she married the duc d'Enghien (later the prince de Condé), and for the next two years she continued to play with dolls. When there were reasons of politics or fortune, marriage came early—except for Mademoiselle.

Mademoiselle is rich—she is the richest woman in France, "the richest private princess in Europe." She is the most Parisian member of the court. She is the king's first cousin. She is even handsome. "Not beautiful," she tells us. But her portrait by Mignard, a court painter who made most of his sitters heavy, as though oppressed by their own grandeur and finery, is alive not only with French elegance, but with French humor: it is the likeness of someone spirited, someone with "looks."

And yet, instead of dancing the courante or the tricotets with her friends in the Louvre or the Tuileries, Mademoiselle isn't in Paris at all. She is writing her memoirs in an isolated country château a hundred miles away. Mademoiselle is in exile.

The spinsterhood and the exile are not unrelated—far from it.

No one knows the details better than Mademoiselle; and as the days of exile lengthen, the sheets of manuscript fall from her writing table thick and fast. Her handwriting is the most dashing, the most difficult, in the world. Only Préfontaine, her faithful secretary, can transcribe it.

2

S HE WAS NOT the richest woman in France when she came
into the world in the Louvre on May 29, 1627, but she became so a few days later when her mother died. For under
the terms of her parents' marriage contract she inherited her
mother's entire dowry, and this included "the principalities of
Dombes and La Roche-sur-Yon, the duchies of Montpensier,
Châtellerault, and Saint-Fargeau, also numerous other fine properties carrying the titles of marquisates, counties, viscounties, and
baronies, together with other possessions, the whole bringing a
total annual income of about 400,000 livres"—about as many dollars today.

Not only wealth but rank made her a baby of almost incon-
ceivable importance. Her wealthy mother had been Marie de
Bourbon, duchesse de Montpensier; her father, Gaston d'Orléans,
a Bourbon also, was younger brother of the king himself—and
heir presumptive, because the royal couple was childless, to the
throne of France. The king, Louis XIII, was Mademoiselle's
uncle; his Spanish-born queen, Anne of Austria, sister of the
king of Spain (just as the queen of Spain was Louis XIII's
sister) was Mademoiselle's aunt and her godmother. Louis XIII
and Gaston d'Orléans were sons of the *Vert Galant,* king Henri
IV, whose statue has been standing on the Pont-Neuf in Paris
for three hundred years; Mademoiselle was Henri IV's granddaughter. Henri IV's widow, Mademoiselle's grandmother, Marie

de Médicis, now lived much of the time in exile because of her quarrels with the king her son and with his prime minister, cardinal Richelieu. When in Paris, she lived in the palais d'Orléans —often called then, as it is called today, the Luxembourg—decorated by Rubens and his pupils with the famous series of panels glorifying her that now hang in the Louvre. Mademoiselle's other grandmother, nee Joyeuse, married first to Henri de Bourbon, duc de Montpensier, had become by her second marriage duchesse de Guise. Bourbon twice over, Mademoiselle was a *petite-fille de France*—granddaughter of a king; and *fille de France*—daughter of the royal blood—was always her proudest title. Anne-Marie-Louise d'Orléans, duchesse de Montpensier, was a portion of her name; as her father's daughter, as inheritor of her mother's dowry, she was princess, duchess, countess many times over; but from her earliest days nobody ever thought of calling her anything but "Mademoiselle." As the king's younger brother, her father was known simply as "Monsieur"; her mother had been "Madame"; no more detailed tags were needed to identify these exalted beings.

Exalted, but not all of them in good odor. A few years after Mademoiselle's birth old Marie de Médicis intrigued once too often; Richelieu tricked her into self-exile and forbade the king her son to let her return to France; she wandered from one foreign court to another and died in Cologne—in a house that had belonged to Rubens, her glorifier—when Mademoiselle was fifteen. And Monsieur, Marie's favorite child, was all too much his mother's son. Discontented, weathervanish, rattlebrained, impatient to be king, he was always taking up arms in doomed conspiracies against the king his brother—or rather, as he always insisted, *for* the king but against the cardinal prime-minister, whom he considered the king's evil genius. Monsieur hated Richelieu, his mother's enemy. From time to time after Richelieu had plunged France into war with Germany and Spain, Monsieur didn't hesitate to fight him by joining forces with France's enemies: at such moments Monsieur persuaded himself that they weren't France's enemies, but only the cardinal's.

In these traitorous enterprises Monsieur customarily enrolled young French nobles as his accomplices. It was easy to recruit them, for many of them hated the cardinal as much as Monsieur did: they knew that just as it was the cardinal's aim to curb the power of the Spanish and Austrian Hapsburgs abroad, so at home he was committed to make the king—in other words, himself— absolute by destroying all important remnants of the nobles' old feudal power. And in his traitorous enterprises Monsieur always, at a certain moment, turned chicken-hearted: he always gave up; he always sued for pardon. "He entered into the conspiracies because of lack of will," Richelieu put it, "and he always crept shamefully out of them because of lack of courage." He was too close to the throne to be executed for treason, too exalted ever to be punished by anything more serious than temporary banishment; but he habitually betrayed to the cardinal and the cardinal's executioners the nobles he had enlisted. Monsieur's pattern of living might be given as: revolt, surrender, betrayal, banishment, return. Monsieur always returned. But in France under Richelieu it was dangerous to be Monsieur's follower or friend.

It was in obedience to the cardinal, following the failure of one of the conspiracies, that Monsieur had married Mademoiselle's mother. The decapitation resulting from this plot was a more than usually bloody one; the victim was Monsieur's friend and follower the young marquis de Chalais. In the hope of at least delaying the execution, the marquis' mother had bribed the two professional headsmen of the town to disappear, but as a result she had to watch the destruction of her son by an amateur: after the twentieth stroke Chalais was still groaning, and only after the thirty-fourth was everything over. The blood of Chalais, people said, spurted as far as the steps of Monsieur's marriage altar. (Once in later life when Monsieur gave a hand to a fellow courtier who was descending from a grandstand erected for some public function, he received memorable words of thanks: "I'm the first man you've ever helped *off* a scaffold.")

Monsieur being as he was, it was not considered wise to give him full charge of his very important daughter. He was perforce made her guardian, but officials were appointed to administer her estate. Even at the moment of Mademoiselle's birth, when like all royal babies she had received immediate informal baptism, the cardinal had determined, for the greater protection of the child and of the realm, to consider himself her godfather, though this was a role he could not actually assume until her later, formal christening. And when, after a few days, she was left motherless, she was installed in her own apartments—a suite that had been prepared for her in the Tuileries. Here she grew up under the care of a governess and with her own household staff numbering about sixty, "a greater staff than any one of my three aunts—the queen of Spain, the queen of England, or the duchess of Savoy—had before marriage." Down the immensely long corridor connecting the Tuileries with the Louvre—today the Grand Gallery of the Louvre Museum—the king and queen of France often walked to call on their rich little niece: she was a distraction for one of the gloomiest childless couples in history.

The governess, Madame de Saint-Georges, was a worthy, long-widowed marquise who had spent much of her life supervising the education of a series of princesses: by the time she came to Mademoiselle she had dropped from her curriculum, whether out of wisdom, weariness, or convinced awe of her betters, any element of compulsion. "Young women of my birth so rarely fear anyone of lower rank," says Mademoiselle, "that those charged with our education really need the support of some superior authority. Which makes me hazard the belief that if I possess some good qualities, it is because they were inborn; they cannot be attributed to my upbringing, excellent though it was, for I never had to fear the slightest punishment." And she casts further light on royal childhood: "Children who are the object of great respect, who hear nothing spoken of except their high birth and their great wealth, usually become horribly puffed up. I myself had those things so constantly dinned into my ears that I became convinced they were all that mattered, and the vanity I displayed at that time can scarcely have been agreeable to those around me. Eventually my reason told me that the true greatness of a highborn princess consists in going beyond such grounds for vulgar flattery. But when I was a child and anyone mentioned my grandmother Guise, I used to say: 'She's a very distant grandmother; she's not a queen.' "

"The true greatness of a highborn princess consists in going beyond"—going beyond mere considerations of birth and wealth. Mademoiselle, for all her "reason," never got totally beyond those things, of course: her birth and her wealth were the underlying, if not the immediate, causes of her long spinsterhood, her exile, and her later fate. It is the extent to which she did and the extent to which, at the same time, she didn't get beyond them that make her so interesting.

Her father's frequent "distance from the court"—it is her expression for his repeated banishments—made it impossible for her not to know, as the years passed, that he was constantly in disgrace; she knew better than to breathe his name before the king and queen, whom she called *"petit papa"* and *"petite maman"*; and yet the often-absent figure—the "dangerous mischiefmaker," as Larousse calls him, the "utter mediocrity"—became the object of her worship. At a ceremony at Fontainebleau, when the little girl heard two nobles read out of the Order of the Saint-Esprit before the assembled court and saw their armorial bearings defaced and was told it was "because they had followed Monsieur," she wept and insisted on leaving, saying that it would be "undignified" for her to stay; when more kindly courtiers explained her father's absence by telling her he was "with the army," she knew vaguely that "the army" was his own body of troops, fighting against the army of the king, but she trembled for the peril he was in.

What a joy to see him, the few times she was allowed to! When she was five and a half she went to meet him at his château at Limours; he had removed his distinguishing decoration, the *cordon bleu* of the Order of the Saint-Esprit (*he* hadn't been read out of it!), to see whether without it his daughter would recognize him, for he had been in Flanders for more than a year; she picked him out at once, and flew to his arms. In Paris, to let her show him the dances she had learned, he commanded her and her friends to perform a "ballet of pygmies"; as the tiny blue-bloods pirouetted, a flock of birds was let loose in the room; one became entangled in the ruff of the cardinal's niece; the pygmy wept, the grownups laughed; it was "much more amusing than the king's ballet." And he made her sing to him songs that to his delight he found she had been learning secretly while he was away—"songs that people were singing against the cardinal."

Five years later, after another "absence," he again returned to France; but this time, on Richelieu's order, he kept away from Paris. He wrote his daughter to meet him at his château of Chambord. (On his marriage Monsieur had received from the crown as his *apanage*—an endowment, that is, his to enjoy for life, but reverting to the crown on his death in the absence of a male heir—a pension, the duchies of Orléans and Chartres, and the county of Blois. Chambord, in its forest alive with pheasant, deer, and wild boar, formed part of the county of Blois.) "Dear Papa," Mademoiselle wrote him, "I'm dying of joy at the thought of obeying the order you honor me with, and I'll leave Monday, and assure you, dear Papa, that I am your very humble and obedient daughter and servant Anne-Marie d'Orléans." In the château she found him waiting for her on the famous trick staircase; when he saw her, he started down toward her; she ran up toward him; to her bewilderment, he disappeared as though by magic: the staircase was double! They met at the bottom in a gale of laughter.

In the château of Blois, they played battledore and shuttlecock, and he let her win game after game of forfeits, giving her as penalties the watches and jewels that Blois was famous for.

This visit to the region of the Loire was enchanting; everyone and everything conspired to please her. At the great convent-monastery of Fontevrault, the abbess was her aunt—Jeanne-Baptiste de Bourbon, illegitimate daughter of Henry IV: *bâtardes de la maison royale* were much sought after as reverend mothers of such establishments. The abbess delighted her niece by showing her, on two successive days, two different madwomen, shut up half-naked and screaming in convent outbuildings; "and since there wasn't a third for the third day, I got bored and went away, though my aunt urged me to stay." At another abbey, Bourgueuil, situated amid forests, it was disappointing to see the stag escape from the hounds and swim away across a pond; but what a thrill later, when the frantic animal came crashing into the very courtyard of the abbey itself, followed by the pack, as though on purpose to let Mademoiselle watch the kill from the window of her room!

At Tours there was Louison Roger, a local "favorite" of Monsieur's, a sixteen-year-old bourgeois girl with whom he spent much of his time, but who was so virtuous, he swore to Madame de Saint-Georges, as to be absolutely uncontaminating to little princesses. Mademoiselle, who was going through a prudish phase that caused her to smile as she wrote about it later in her memoirs, demanded reassurance. *"Maman,"* she said—it was her name for her governess—"if Louison's not a good girl I won't see her even if Papa loves her; or if he insists on my seeing her, I won't be nice to her." Madame de Saint-Georges placed the seal of her approval on Louison. Presumably this was before Louison's son by Monsieur was born or even conceived; but even so Madame de Saint-Georges must have been skeptical. For the whole court knew that Monsieur was scarcely one to leave a sixteen-year-old "virtuous" if he could help it. His *galanteries* were famous. The

day of Mademoiselle's birth, when a fawning courtier had assured him that his daughter was "just like" him, he had laughed.
"Don't say that. If she were just like me she'd be in the streets
by now."

But at Tours daughter and favorite played happily together;
Louison was pretty, Mademoiselle thought, "and witty, too, for
a girl of her station, who had never been at court." And when
she wasn't playing with Louison, she was asking Monsieur a
thousand questions about his new wife, her stepmother. For while
still "absent with the army" he had married in Nancy the fourteen-
year-old princess Marguerite, sister of the duc de Lorraine. He
had left her in Nancy until some of the anger the match had
stirred up in Paris should die down. Mademoiselle found it easy
to understand that the cardinal should be infuriated—everything
about Monsieur invariably infuriated the cardinal for reasons of
state—but that the queen, too, should be angry. . . . There was
some mystery there: the queen was known to think differently
from the cardinal about everything. Powerless as she was, and
snubbed by everyone, including her husband, the queen was Monsieur's ally against the cardinal. But gradually, during the gossipy
days at Tours, Monsieur let the story—his version of it, at least—
slip out. The queen herself was more than a little in love with
him, her own brother-in-law. The king's health was not brilliant,
and was not improving; who knew but that, in time. . . . Married
to Monsieur, Anne of Austria might even have children, bear an
heir to the throne of France. But Monsieur was not interested.
Once, some time ago, "for two or three months," he couldn't
deny that he had returned the queen's passion; but now he claimed
he loved only his Lorraine princess. (Perhaps it was this bridegroom's sigh that decided Madame de Saint-Georges to give
Louison the benefit of the doubt.) Mademoiselle was not at all
jealous of her stepmother; she was entranced by her father's tales
of how he had had to leave his bride at the altar and rejoin his
army, and how she had crossed enemy lines to be reunited with

him, disguising herself as a man and traveling twenty leagues on horseback.

All those varied pleasures of the trip to Blois and beyond—it seems to have been the high spot of her childhood—were associated with her father: at both Blois and at Tours he hired troops of actors for her, and at Chenonceaux and Amboise there were other gaieties. And associated with Monsieur, too, was something else: the attentiveness of the comte de Soissons, a nobleman twenty-three years older than herself, who, like Monsieur, was often "with the army." For some reason, even before the trip to Blois, while Mademoiselle was not yet ten, Soissons kept sending one of his retainers, a gentleman named Campion, to call on her in Paris, to ask for her news and bring her his compliments. "The better to succeed in impressing me with the count's attentions," Mademoiselle records, "Campion used to bring me candy." Only afterwards did she discover that the comte de Soissons had been her first fiancé, that Monsieur had promised him her hand. (She probably discovered also—courtiers would scarcely keep from her a fact so interesting even if, in those times, not particularly remarkable—that a decade earlier Soissons had tried to marry her mother.) Soissons was handsome, rich, and a Bourbon; like Monsieur, he was a hot-headed dissident; he scornfully refused to marry the cardinal's niece; instead, he plotted against the cardinal himself and had to flee; he entered into a treaty with the Hapsburgs; and in the battle of La Marfée, near Sedan, he led the Spanish troops to victory against the army of the king and cardinal. But alas for his and Monsieur's plans! The moment of victory was the moment of death for Soissons. He was just opening the visor of his helmet with the barrel of his pistol; whether he was careless with the trigger or whether, as many thought, one of the cardinal's agents chose that moment to shoot him, there was a report, and he fell dead on the spot. At that very same instant, in her château near Paris, 150 miles away, his mother, the comtesse de Soissons, was passing from one room to another when suddenly two bits of wall-covering became detached and fell to the floor at her feet. She was startled, but then merely ordered that they be put back in place. Later, when the news from Sedan reached her, how clearly the old countess recognized—so Mademoiselle tells us—that she had been vouchsafed, without knowing it at the time, *"Un présage de la funeste nouvelle!"*

3

B UT SHORTLY after that trip with Monsieur, and several years before Mademoiselle learned how matters stood in Monsieur's mind between her and the comte de Soissons, there was a crucial event at court that dramatized the entire interesting subject of her marriage. After twenty-three years of childlessness the queen of France astonished Europe by announcing her pregnancy. The king, who gave the impression of being astonished almost to the point of stupor, was nevertheless unquestionably responsible—court life was too public to allow the slightest doubt. The queen was certain that she would bear a son, and she used to point to herself, when Mademoiselle was present, and say, "You'll be my daughter-in-law."

Mademoiselle was enchanted by her aunt's condition and by those words—it was all almost as much fun as traveling; and when, in the queen's bedchamber in the suburban palace of Saint-Germain-en-Laye, a royal son and heir, Louis-Dieudonné—Louis the God-given—did indeed come into the world, the presence of her new first cousin in his cradle quite excited her, and she visited him every day, referring to him freely as *"mon petit mari."* Mademoiselle was not quite eleven at the time, and so "innocent," as she put it later, that in her joy she quite lost sight of an important fact: as a consequence of the birth of "Monseigneur le Dauphin," as the first-born would be called during the lifetime of the king his father, Monsieur was no longer next in line for the throne.

Monsieur had been permitted—even ordered—to come to Saint-Germain for the event; he had been present as an eyewitness; it was deemed imperative that he be convinced, beyond possibility of future dispute, that there had been no hocus-pocus, no false pregnancy, no stillbirth, no switching of babies: that a real, live royal boy had emerged from the womb of the queen. Monsieur was understandably made melancholy, rather than joyful, by the event.

If God were to allow the child to thrive, the cardinal would be relieved of one of his nightmares—the prospect of the irresponsible Monsieur on the throne of France. Now the cardinal had always taken a grave view not only of Monsieur, but also, in a different way, of Monsieur's daughter. It had been on his order that father and daughter were kept largely apart: her birth and her wealth made her not a pawn, but one of the principal pieces, on the chessboard of Europe, and the manipulation of such pieces was the cardinal's life work. He had recently been in the habit of reminding the little girl that as her godfather he had certain responsibilities; he would "take care of her," he said; he would see to her marriage when the time came. He had not been at all sure that the company of this daughter of a troublemaker was the best thing for the queen during her pregnancy; this was only the most recent, and one of the slightest, of the countless differences between Richelieu and Anne of Austria; and only reluctantly, lest the thwarting of the royal will be even more prejudicial to the birth than the girl's presence, had he allowed Mademoiselle to stay at Saint-Germain. Now, with the Dauphin safely arrived, he saw no reason to suppress his anger when he was told of the term, learned from the queen herself, that the child was employing toward her new cousin. "*Mon petit mari*" indeed! Who knew, when the time would come to choose a bride for the Dauphin, what princess from what country of Europe would bring France the greatest advantage? Similarly, who could tell, as yet, as whose wife Mademoiselle herself might be most valuable to the realm? Perhaps it would be decided that her vast revenues should remain in France;

or perhaps her dowry would make an ally of some foreign sovereign. It was too early to know. But the badinage was deplorable. Prime-ministerial intervention was imperative. Mademoiselle must be recalled from Saint-Germain.

"Cardinal Richelieu ordered me to return to Paris. I wept and sobbed when I said good-by to the king and queen; their majesties were sweet with me, especially the queen, who was kindness itself to me as I left. And after this parting I had to endure something else: on my way to Paris I had to stop at Rueil, where the cardinal lived when the king was at Saint-Germain. He was so displeased that I should have called the Dauphin 'mon petit mari' that he gave me a terrible scolding; he said that I was too big a girl to use such language, that I was guilty of dreadful impropriety. He spoke to me so solemnly, exactly as he might have spoken to an older person, that I began to cry without answering a word. He gave me lunch, hoping to quiet me, but for a long time thereafter I was furious whenever I thought of the way he'd talked to me. During the next two months I went to court but once; and that time I was driven back to Paris to sleep after dining alone with the queen."

The queen, dining alone with her niece, didn't conceal that she, too, was annoyed with Richelieu for his behavior; and she spoke soothing words: "It's true that my son is too little for you," she said. "You shall marry my brother instead." It was fortunate that the two ladies were dining alone—that the king, and especially Richelieu, weren't present: this new remark of the queen's was perhaps as irresponsible as her earlier words, but it was scarcely pointless. For the brother she meant, Ferdinand, cardinal-infante of Spain, was commander-in-chief of the Spanish troops in Flanders, precisely the troops that Richelieu and the king were engaged in fighting, precisely the troops to which Monsieur and the comte de Soissons were lending treasonable support. The queen of France remained Spanish at heart; the little girl having dinner with her was only vaguely aware of the political overtones. Ecclesiastically, marriage to the queen's brother the Spanish cardinal would have been quite possible. Like many another bachelor grandee of the time, he enjoyed a princely church title and the revenue it brought without ever having taken priestly vows: to make himself eligible for marriage, he would only have had to have himself "de-cardinalized" (it was the word used in such cases) in Rome. But: "Marriage had no meaning for me," Mademoiselle tells us. "I gave little thought to the various projects I heard mentioned; my head was full of dancing, and the fun I'd have in Paris during the winter."

4

THUS IT WAS that Mademoiselle, glittering matrimonial bait of a faction-ridden court, had already been spoken of, before she could properly be called anything but a child, as the wife of three different grandees, each of them a political symbol. The talk about *mon petit mari* may well have been, at the time, the mere deplorable badinage the cardinal branded it; but, as we shall see, of Mademoiselle's three earliest marriage projects, the one frivolously linking her to the unborn and just-born Dauphin was the only one that had a sequel.

Death put a quick finish to the others. By the time the news of the comte de Soissons' fatal shooting reached court, the fourteen-year-old Mademoiselle knew enough about his closeness to Monsieur and his intentions concerning herself to weep for him, despite the king's stern order forbidding mourning; shortly before his death he had asked Monsieur to consent to his elopement with Mademoiselle—probably the only way so notorious a rebel could circumvent the cardinal—but Monsieur, who was just then in one of his prudent periods, had demurred. As for the queen's brother, Ferdinand, the cardinal-infante, he was carried off by a sudden fever in Brussels—poisoned, many thought, by his fellow Spaniards, suspicious that he was zealous in their cause only in order to make himself master of Flanders and then, once in power, conclude an alliance with France by marrying Mademoiselle. "Your brother is dead"—the king broke the news to the queen with those dry, abrupt words; she had recently borne a second son, Philippe, duc d'Anjou—a further cause of melancholy for Monsieur—but her husband couldn't forgive her her Spanish relations, and from long habit spoke harshly of any of them, even one just deceased and perhaps pro-French in secret. It was the weeping queen who told Mademoiselle.

The bursting of this second marriage bubble caused Mademoiselle, now fifteen, to indulge in a certain amount of candid self-examination. Already on the death of the comte de Soissons she had recognized, amid her tears, that for some reason which she couldn't fathom, she still didn't feel the slightest inclination to marry—not only the comte de Soissons, but anybody. And with the disappearance of the cardinal-infante, she took further stock of herself. The cardinal-infante had been a prince of many fine qualities, she had been told—"well proportioned even if a little short, very handsome, and with an admirable character." She was very sorry he was dead. But why? She knew the answer, and admitted it without hesitation. Because of the perfect "establishment" she would have had as his wife. It would have been *"du monde le plus agréable."* The Low Countries were beautiful; they were close to France; ways of life were similar to French ways. But "as to his personal qualities, though I regarded him very highly, they were the last things I thought of."

From now on, for quite an incredible number of years, it is the question of an "establishment" that will be the chief matrimonial interest of Mademoiselle; or at least she will long believe, beginning at this moment, that such is the case. There is a certain interest for us, perhaps, in the fact that this realization, or belief, should have dawned on her at this particular time; for it was just now, also, that she was beginning to see Monsieur with new eyes.

Almost simultaneously with the death of the Spanish cardinal-infante, two other events were shaking the court.

Monsieur was involved in a new betrayal, of the usual sordid and sickening sort. A young nobleman from Touraine, the marquis de Cinq-Mars, had been presented to the king by Richelieu, who had been a friend of Cinq-Mars' late father, the marquis d'Effiat, a maréchal de France who had died in the king's service. Cinq-Mars rapidly became a royal favorite; he was made captain of the royal guard and grand equerry of France. But he was ambitious for even greater glory; tacitly encouraged by the king himself, he plotted the overthrow of the cardinal; he made the mistake of associating himself with Monsieur; they formed a party and despatched an emissary to Spain to conclude a treaty that would send Spanish forces to help them rid France of the hated prime minister. But the cardinal's agents uncovered the existence of a plot; Monsieur penitently, eagerly, identified his accomplices; and the cardinal ordered the king to arrest his own favorite. In one of the most famous and pathetic episodes of French history, Cinq-Mars and his boyhood friend François-Auguste de Thou were ordered aboard a boat on the river Rhône at Tarascon, where Richelieu had been lying mortally ill. In their prison-boat the two young romantics were towed up the river by another boat—that in which the cardinal, unable to leave his bed, was having himself transported toward Paris. At Lyons the cardinal's boat paused; the prison-boat was detached. The two friends were taken to the château of Pierre-Encise, royal prison and place of execution. Cinq-Mars was the first to go to the block. His hair was cut; then: "What are you waiting for?" he asked the executioner; and during his last moments his friend called out to him, in a voice "clear and pure as that of an angel," * the words of the *Ave maris stella.* Then de Thou, mounting the scaffold, knelt and kissed the blood of Cinq-Mars; the executioner's first blow glanced off the top of his head; the second knocked him to the scaffold floor; then the executioner "leapt upon him" and the massacre was over. Monsieur had achieved a new record—a *double* decapitation. The cardinal continued his way. This liquidation of de Thou, son of a famous historian, and of the twenty-one-year-old favorite

* So says Alfred de Vigny, in that best of historical novels, *Cinq-Mars.*

Cinq-Mars, called *"cher ami"* by the king himself, was like a defiant, final boast by the dying Richelieu that it was he, and not Louis XIII, who ruled France. In the Louvre, the story runs, as the hour of the execution at Lyons approached, the king glanced at his watch and murmured to his courtiers: "I'm afraid *cher ami* isn't looking his best at the moment."

The cardinal, reaching Paris a few days later, continued even on his deathbed to pronounce new banishments; then, a few months after de Thou and Cinq-Mars, he too was gone.

The enormity of Monsieur's role in the destruction of those two young men seems not to have dawned on Mademoiselle at once. It took a few weeks or months. On learning of Richelieu's death, she immediately begged the king to allow her father to return from his exile, but it was some little while before he was told he might live in Paris. His wife was still in the north, and on his arrival he came straight to Mademoiselle in the Tuileries. It was now, in her very joy at the reunion, that the change began to make itself felt. A member of Monsieur's household, the abbé de la Rivière, who had been in Paris negotiating Monsieur's return, had said something unfavorable about Mademoiselle to the king; as always happened at court his remark had "got back" to her; and now she told Monsieur she had found the abbé's words improper. To her dismay the father she had not seen for so long promptly took the abbé's side against her. "This did not, of course, spoil the happiness I had in seeing him," she says. "He had supper with me. My twenty-four violins were playing"—it was the king's orchestra, often placed at Mademoiselle's disposal—"and he was as gay as though Cinq-Mars and de Thou hadn't perished by the way. I confess that I found I couldn't look at him without thinking of them; and in the midst of my joy at being with him, his own utter joyousness depressed me."

It is a slight reproach, still gentle, still respectful; and, indeed, even when her reproaches will become louder and graver, her loyalty will persist, even flourish. But it is now, when the defects in her idol begin to be visible to her, that she begins to have a clear view of herself as well, or to think that she has; and she speaks with complacency of the results of her self-probing. "By nature I am directly opposed to the occupation known as *galanterie*," she says, as factually as she might say, "I am tall, neither fat nor thin." And the lack of *galanterie* and the love of an establishment go hand in hand. To have become the wife of the comte de Soissons, Bourbon though he was, would scarcely have *improved* her station. Whereas to have married the cardinal-infante, a son and brother of kings of Spain, the near ruler of the Low Countries . . . Even though the talk of the cardinal-infante's murder may have ~~be~~en mere gossip, the thought that she could be spoken of as one ~~of~~ its reasons must have given a princess of fifteen a dizzying view ~~of~~ her own importance. She had been born, she reflected, every-~~th~~ing except archduchess, queen, and empress: those were the only ~~s~~teps still to be mounted, the only establishments she didn't pos-~~se~~ss in her own right.

The quest of the proper husband was thus narrowed consid-~~er~~ably.

Conditioned to take orders from a cardinal, Louis XIII appointed another as Richelieu's successor—the Italian Mazarin, ~~b~~orn Mazarini or Mazzarino, who had come to France on a diplo-~~m~~atic mission and remained in Richelieu's employ. Richelieu, in ~~h~~is dealings, had been stern, imperious, uncompromising; Mazarin ~~w~~as outwardly obsequious and cringing. He was a fawner and flat-~~te~~rer, suavest of tricksters, incapable of forthright acts or straight ~~an~~swers. He was deviousness incarnate; his "fine Italian hand" ~~ha~~s become a household word. Such was France's new prime min-~~is~~ter; the new godfather, in a sense, of Mademoiselle.

5

TOWARD THE END of that winter of Monsieur's return, during which Mademoiselle attended "more dances than ever before" (there were factions and subfactions in ba ballets as in everything else; entertainments in certain princi houses were shunned by the habitués of others; Paris swarm with Montagus and Capulets), Mademoiselle, at fifteen, had other first experience: her first grief. She lost *maman,* Madame Saint-Georges.

The old lady had been ill, and then had had an attack of a plexy; Mademoiselle was told of the stroke one morning on awa ing, and she rushed to *maman's* bedside in time to see her bein given the last rites. "She called her children to give them her bless ing, and she asked my permission to bless me as well; she told m that the honor she had always had in being with me since my bi made her dare take this liberty. I felt a tenderness for her seemed like a response to the tender care she had always given upbringing; I knelt beside her bed, my eyes bathed in tears. I w so moved by the thought of losing her and by the thought o thousand kind things she had said to me that I didn't wan leave her before the end. But she asked that I be taken away, her children too; she was too affected, she said, by our tears a sobs, and she told me that to take leave of me was her only regr in dying. I went to my room; a quarter of an hour later she w dead."

Despite the naïveté with which the scene is presented (Made-

moiselle suspected as she wrote her memoirs that readers would
find them "naïve"—she used the very word), the sentences carry
a hint that Mademoiselle felt a certain surprise at finding herself
so affected. *Maman* was the closest to a real mother she had ever
known; but still. . . . Was it proper, was it even natural, that a
princess on whose account a grandee had recently perhaps been
murdered should be so shaken by the death of an old marquise
who had been her paid governess?

In any case, Monsieur quickly interrupted the first sobbing
misery. Mademoiselle must spend the night outside the Tuileries,
he said; she must not sleep "in a building containing a dead body,
beee _lly the body of someone whose loss was so painful"; and
o_demoiselle spent the next week in a Carmelite convent—only
o_ residence for a princess temporarily without a governess.

th_*Maman's* successor, Madame la comtesse de Fiesque, had been
st_ress of the robes to Mademoiselle's mother, and had recently
se_n asking Monsieur to give her the same position with his new
__, due shortly to arrive in Paris. But Monsieur knew better than
er_ake Madame de Fiesque back into his household. She was an
_triguer, with the specialty of intriguing against those under
_hose roof she lived. So he shunted her onto Mademoiselle.

_. For a time all went well. Madame de Fiesque was delighted to be
b_n charge of so important a household. She displayed her best
m__. She was sprightly, effervescent, one of the best storytellers at
his_; she enthralled Mademoiselle with "a thousand tales about
w_times." But witty though her talk might be, she hadn't the wit
te_void falling from grace. "She began by making an inventory
ans_y jewels, in order to prevent me from giving any away with-
ha_her permission. Then she locked my writing desk, which had
is _ays stood open, and kept the key, so that I had to ask for it
_h time I wanted it: it was her duty, she said, to know every-
__g I wrote, and to whom. I was very much displeased by this; _
wasn't accustomed to such supervision, and hated it, but I put up
with it in silence. However, I was unable to keep quiet on another

occasion, which happened soon after, when she acted offensively to Madame de Saint-Georges' children. Very respectfully, I told her what I thought I had to complain of; she replied sharply; from then on I never enjoyed her company, and we quarreled constantly. One day I had a heavy cold; my doctor prescribed a certain medicine, which as usual I didn't want to take. She thought she could treat me like a child—I was almost sixteen; she locked me in my room and told me through the door that no one would be allowed to see me because I was ill. I managed to escape, and went to her room, where I knew she was; I locked *her* in, and took away the key. The next few hours weren't the most agreeable in her life. No one could find a locksmith, and what upset her particularly was that I had locked her grandson in another room, and he was screaming as though I were torturing him. I took the intensest pleasure in her predicament. . . ."

In her struggles with this fiendish charge, whom old Madame de Saint-Georges had known how to manage without managing, Madame de Fiesque appealed to the authority of Monsieur. She asked him to approve the "book of conduct" she had composed, a list of rules governing every detail of Mademoiselle's life—sign of the cross the first thing on waking, and "other such things suitable for babies." She insisted that his permission be sought each time Mademoiselle wanted to go for an evening drive in the Cours-la-Reine instead of retiring to early dreams as a girl of her age should. "It was just because she liked to go to bed early herself," Mademoiselle tells us indignantly. Monsieur, impatient of Madame de Fiesque, carelessly gave permission whenever Mademoiselle's messenger reached him in time. But there were evenings when he couldn't be found, and Mademoiselle was "deprived of the outing I wanted." One is almost sorry for Madame de Fiesque on such evenings as those.

Such was the personal situation in Mademoiselle's apartments in the Tuileries when, from the palace of Saint-Germain, came the great public news, on May 14, 1643, that Louis XIII was dead. During his last illness he had made excellent preparation for the next world simply by gazing out his window: the view made him reflective, for it included a portion of the road leading to Saint-Denis, where French kings had been buried for centuries. One spot in the road worried the king: it seemed always to be muddy; and one of his last acts was to order its repair, lest his hearse be bogged down. He made other preparation, too: on his deathbed he composed his own musical setting for the *De Profundis,* which according to royal custom would be sung in his room just after he drew his last breath. Fresh from his official baptism on April 21, the little Dauphin had come and sat on his dying father's bed. "Well, what's your name?" the king demanded.

"My name is Louis XIV."

"Not quite yet, son, but soon."

Louis XIV was not yet five, and in Paris, the Parlement deliberately set aside the late king's order—really an order of the dying Richelieu—that the queen, as regent, share her powers with a council, one of whose members was to be Mazarin; defiantly, Parlement named the queen untrammeled regent, and appointed Monsieur lieutenant-general of the realm during the king's minority, under her authority. The Parlement of Paris had always played a lesser role in politics than its great namesake in London; inherent differences made it a vastly inferior political institution; and particularly under Richelieu it had been snubbed into impotence. Now, in giving the queen "free, absolute and entire authority," it felt proud of itself, confident like everyone else that the queen, whom Richelieu had treated with as much contempt as he had treated Parlement, would cast out Richelieu's successor. Monsieur, Anne of Austria's former *galant,* her fellow sufferer at the hands of Richelieu, had every expectation that his new title would now make him her chief adviser; and other nobles, expecting to fill high posts in the new regime, formed themselves openly into a party, calling themselves *Les Importants.* How surprised everyone was when the queen promptly appointed as her prime minister and sole adviser none other than Mazarin, who according to Richelieu's and the late king's order was to have been only one of her councilors! How surprised several of the most self-important *Importants* were to be thrown into jail or exiled! Courtiers gasped, then wondered why they had been so deluded. The explanation was soon clear: it was, like most matters, a matter of sentiment. For all her Spanish piety, the queen was well known to be susceptible. Monsieur had not been the only man to attract her attention. As every reader of *The Three Musketeers* knows, the duke of Buckingham, too, had enjoyed with Anne of Austria a brief amorous passage. Mazarin was wily: he had been quick to perceive what kind of approach to the queen as woman would win him the support of the queen as regent. *Les Importants* were, as Mademoiselle puts it, "dissipated in an instant," and once again Monsieur found himself at odds with a cardinal.

Monsieur did not share in the punishment meted out to *Les Importants,* except in one particular. He was allowed to remain in Paris. He was even allowed, finally, to send for his wife. But the new cardinal prime minister subjected him to one humiliation. He pretended to believe that Monsieur and his bride, who had been living apart all the ten years of their marriage, had never been properly married at all, or at least that their marriage was invalid from disuse; and well knowing what would appeal to the sense of the ridiculous that was always lively at court, he obliged the fuming groom and weeping bride to be married again, by the archbishop of Paris, before they could cohabit.

Monsieur could think of only one bit of revenge for the moment. He suspected that the queen had not been totally unconnected with the absurd second marriage ceremony that caused so many grins at court, and—perhaps for purposes of dissemination— he confided to Mademoiselle an anecdote concerning her mother. "Brother," he claimed the late king had once feelingly said to him many years before, "I should dearly love to exchange wives with you; but you'd never consent—you'd be the loser."

By now Mademoiselle was less disposed to love the stepmother who had so long been lurking offstage in the provinces. "She no longer possessed the great beauty that had once charmed Monsieur," she writes of the new Madame's appearance at the marriage ceremony, "and the manner in which she was dressed did nothing to make up for the ravages of so many unhappy years." As time went on, she found that she didn't get along well with her—but then nobody did, except Monsieur. The new Madame had indeed sadly changed since her early, adventurous days: she was now a tiresome hypochondriac, eating almost incessantly to "cure her vapors," dragging herself about, complaining and unamiable. "I did everything possible to stay in her good graces," says Mademoiselle, "and I'd never have got out of them if she hadn't given me reason to grow careless."

6

MUCH OF THE YEAR that followed the king's death the queen spent praying in the churches of Paris. There were well over a hundred of them, and during that first year of mourning she was careful to visit each at least once, timing every arrival to coincide with the feast day of the church's patron saint.

Unlike the queen, Mademoiselle was not an old Spanish widow of forty-two, but a sixteen-year-old French girl, crazy about dancing—"There was dancing everywhere in Paris that winter," she tells us, "especially in my apartments, though I suppose violins shouldn't have been playing when the walls were hung with black." And yet at this moment she entered into a period of piety herself. The queen, since becoming regent and snubbing Monsieur, had been less cordial to her niece as well, and there is something touching in the spectacle of Mademoiselle, who had so recently lost *maman,* wistfully patterning herself on her royal aunt, *petite-maman,* and trailing behind her in her pious explorations of Paris shrines. She often fell asleep when the queen prayed too long— "I was never a girl for long prayers or meditations"—but she was always there. "At that time I felt such an attachment to the queen, out of inclination as well as out of duty, that I followed her everywhere; I gave up outings that I would have enjoyed in order to accompany her wherever she went; and though she scarcely noticed my attentions and never confided in me, I was happy in my fidel-

ity, and the strong affection I felt for her made me put up with
her new treatment of me."

Before long, Mademoiselle's wave of churchgoing took on the
aspect of a course of training, luckily embarked upon.

Eighteen months after Louis XIII's death came the news of the
death of his sister Elizabeth, queen of Spain; and the courtiers'
condolences to Mademoiselle on the loss of her aunt in Madrid
were strongly interlarded with hints that soon she would be re-
ceiving congratulations as the bride of her aunt's widower, Philip
IV of Spain, the oblong-headed monarch so often painted by Ve-
lásquez. Even the queen and Mazarin spoke to Mademoiselle about
it, raising her hopes, telling her that the match was being seriously
suggested in Spanish despatches. How appropriate, how necessary,
even, the long hours of church visits now appeared, invaluable
practice for the ceaseless court devotions practiced in Holy Spain!
Invaluable, too, the refuge of prayer for any wife of Philip IV:
Mademoiselle's aunt Elizabeth (although much of her refuge had
been in the pleasures of the *corrida*) had always been spoken of
at the French court as a "saint" for what she had had to put up
with in Madrid. Philip IV's affair with his preferred mistress, the
beautiful actress Maria Calderon, was only normal (indeed, everyone found the story touching: after bearing him his favorite son,
Don Juan of Austria, she pleaded that she had reached the peak of
this world's felicity, and retired, as abbess, to a remote country
convent); but the rapid turnover of his other mistresses, and the
number of his known illegitimate children (between thirty and
forty; eight recognized) was considered ostentatious even by the
French court. Then, abruptly, Mademoiselle's marriage to her
Spanish uncle was talked of no more. Mazarin told Monsieur that
the Spanish suggestion of the match had been a lure, intended to
entice Monsieur, flattered by his daughter's queenship, into the
service of Spain; indeed, a wretched Spaniard, picked up in Paris
and suspected of being sent on such a mission to Monsieur, was
thrown into the Bastille. Monsieur believed the story. "But some

people think there was no such intention," Mademoiselle tells us, "and that the gentleman had been charged to make solid and sincere proposals for the marriage of his king and myself, and that he had thought he should speak of the matter to Monsieur first, before approaching the court." In any case, the *pauvre misérable* stayed in the Bastille several years; and instead of Mademoiselle, Philip IV took as his second wife his own niece, an Austrian Hapsburg, Mariana, the emperor's daughter. It was, after all, scarcely the moment for the marriage of a *fille de France* to a Hapsburg of Spain. The two countries were still at war: France had recently won a splendid victory at Rocroi, but Spain showed no sign of seeking peace by marital or other alliance.

Would an Austrian Hapsburg be more suitable for Mademoiselle? The question soon arose; for a year or so later the queen was mourning *her* sister, another Mariana, empress of Germany— mother of the new queen of Spain. Along with the new condolences came new sepeculations: who, if not Mademoiselle, should be the new bride of the emperor, Ferdinand III? Once again, this time even more optimistically, the queen and Mazarin spoke to her: the queen, warmer now to a niece who might be Holy Roman empress, hoped "passionately" for the match; Mazarin was "working hard" at it. Mademoiselle caught fire: "the thought of the empire filled my mind."

Monsieur was against it. He was living in the Luxembourg now, inherited from his mother, and in the two years following their second marriage-service Madame had borne him two daughters, half sisters to Mademoiselle. Mademoiselle saw him fairly often: he picked as many of his favorites from among her maids of honor and ladies in waiting as from among his wife's. "They tell me the idea of marrying the emperor appeals to you," he said to her one day, more amiably than usual. "If that's really so, I'll do all I can to help. But I'm persuaded you'll never be happy in that country. They observe all the tiresome Spanish etiquette. The emperor is an older man than I am. The only places you'd be happy are England, if conditions improve, or maybe Savoy."

But Mademoiselle knew her mind. "I told him that I *wanted* to marry the emperor; it was a match of my own choosing. I begged him to consent. I told him politely that I agreed with him: I knew the emperor was neither young nor attractive—from which, I pointed out, the truth must be obvious: that I was thinking more of the establishment than of the person."

To prepare herself for her new glory, Mademoiselle now embarked on what we would call a cramming course—with a strange result. "The desire to be empress, which never left me, and which seemed close to fulfillment, made me think it would be a good thing if I were to adopt in advance ways of living that would be in conformity with the emperor's tastes. I had heard that he was pious; and following his example I became so very pious myself, after a little period of merely seeming to be, that for about a week I actually yearned to become a Carmelite nun—a longing I confided to no one. I was so obsessed by this desire that I neither ate nor slept. Every time the queen visited a convent (which was often), I stayed alone in the church weeping for those who loved me—because of their grief at my taking the veil. This strange state of mind, seemingly the effect of a detachment from myself, a kind of alienation, was in fact directly due to the strong affections of my nature: I can truthfully say that during that week the empire meant nothing to me. Mixed up in it all was a certain vanity in leaving the world at that particular juncture: everyone would say admiringly that with a perfect establishment just within my grasp I turned my back on the world because I knew it too well; no one could suggest that I did it out of frustration."

Engrossed by the idea of a vocation, she sought her father's counsel. This time she found him too busy gambling to listen to her (he spent much time losing large sums at cards), and a few days later, when she was finally able to tell him of her wish, and to ask his permission to go ahead, he laughed. The only thing troubling her, he said, was that nobody was working hard enough at getting her married to the emperor. And when she said that that couldn't be the case, since she no longer cared about the marriage and would rather "serve God than wear all the crowns in the world," he flew into a rage: "It's those bigots at court that put this into your head! Keep away from them! And I'll tell the queen not to take you to any more convents!" It was all she needed: "When I saw how he took it, my fear that he'd turn the thing into a scandal made me beg him not to speak of it, and I promised him that I would do nothing against his orders. Nobody was ever more obedient than I on that occasion: within three days the whole thing had faded from my mind."

What had evaporated was the by-product of the course of piety: the training itself continued. "Although I no longer planned to become a nun, the piety remained, and I was so strict in my observances that I no longer went driving in the Cours-la-Reine, no longer wore beauty spots, no longer powdered my hair. My coiffure was so neglected that nobody recognized me; I muffled my neck in three kerchiefs that stifled me in summer, and I wore not a single colored ribbon, as though I wanted to look like a woman of forty—and I truly think that I'd have felt complimented if anyone had taken me for such. My only pleasure was in reading the life of St. Theresa, and in listening to talk about Germany or talking about it myself. There was such a change in my way of living and dressing that it will surprise no one to learn that it didn't last. Gradually I abandoned all those new features of my life. The last to go was my habit of thinking about Germany. . . ."

That is Mademoiselle's way of preparing us for the end—the end for the time being—of the mirage of herself as empress. Ashamed to break the unwelcome news to her themselves after negotiations had—so, at least, they claimed—been underway for two years, the queen and Mazarin employed the kindness and tact usual at court by entrusting the task to the abbé de la Rivière, Monsieur's *domestique* whom Mademoiselle particularly disliked.

It was he who announced to her, with ill-disguised pleasure, that the emperor would marry one of his own Hapsburg cousins, Maria, archduchess of Tyrol. It was, of course, purely a matter of political timing: the peace of Westphalia, ending hostilities between France and Germany, was still a year away.

Now shortly before this, a marriage by proxy had been arranged, and brilliantly celebrated in the chapel of the Palais-Royal, between the princess Marie de Gonzague, daughter of the duc de Nevers, and Ladislas IV, king of Poland. Princess Marie was a lovely girl—she had been wooed by the ill-starred Cinq-Mars—but she was far from being equal in rank or wealth to Mademoiselle, who had taken precedence over her as a matter of course all her life. But after the ceremony, which Mademoiselle described as "a magnificent masquerade" (for the Poles, including the ambassador who wed the bride in the name of his king, appeared with shaved heads and jeweled Slavic robes such as Paris had never seen), the queen of France, who had given herself no end of trouble about the match, did not even invite Mademoiselle to sit at the same table with herself and the new, upstart queen, and Mademoiselle was severely scolded for absenting herself from court rather than accept a place below the "queen of a day," or "that royalty," as she dubbed her.

So that Mademoiselle, although she had accepted meekly enough the bad news from Spain, was in no mood to react the same way to the bad news from Germany, in no mood to listen to political explanation. This time she was angry—angry and suspicious. One by one, she saw establishments to which she felt herself entitled falling to other, far less worthy candidates. Mazarin, she was convinced, was acting in bad faith. The queen, infatuated with Mazarin, was no longer *petite-maman,* no longer even a friend. Who could hope to win an establishment with such negotiators as those?

There was another establishment vacant. The emperor's brother, the archduke Leopold, seemed about to be made what the cardinal-infante had so nearly become: sovereign of the Low Countries. Indeed, the archduke had been mentioned as a marital possibility for Mademoiselle at the same time as the emperor; Mademoiselle had, she says, been given her choice. She had preferred the emperor, naturally; but now if he was no longer available as a husband, his brother still was. This time no one of any importance spoke to Mademoiselle about the vacancy. The queen, Mazarin, Monsieur —all were silent.

But there was, at court, a young man, brother of one of Madame's maids of honor, who fancied himself as a go-between and was devoted to Mademoiselle. His name was Saujon; he was a simple gentleman of provincial upbringing, too lowly to be considered anything but a servitor, but there was something charmingly moody and visionary in his character, something *songe-creux* (a delightful word, implying the very essence of dreaminess) that appealed to Mademoiselle. "I like crazy people, both the gay kind and the melancholy kind," she tells us; and she liked Saujon. He had first won her favor by conveying to her a compliment from Flanders, where he had been fighting—a compliment coming in a roundabout way from an Italian general in the Austrian service, Ottavio Piccolomini, duke of Amalfi, whom Mademoiselle had never met but who was "well known to be one of the finest and most chivalrous men of the century." "Tell her that we have the highest opinion of her in the Low Countries and should be proud to have a princess like her" had been the Italian serenade from Flanders, and it had pleased Mademoiselle. Now Saujon told Mademoiselle of letters he himself had received from important officials in Flanders close to the archduke, saying that they and he wanted nothing more than to have her as his wife. If he could only treat directly with those high-placed people, Saujon said, he himself could probably negotiate the affair in no time. It seemed to be a "chimera" with him, Mademoiselle says; she gave him no encouragement, never dreaming that he was serious; nor did she think it necessary to tell him to desist. She was utterly amazed when she learned one day on returning to Paris from Saint-Denis, where she had been spending Holy Week with the Carmelites, that Saujon had been arrested for "treating with the enemy"—corresponding, that is, with Hapsburg officials in Flanders about her marriage. Questioned in prison, he swore that Mademoiselle had known nothing of his doings; and to Mademoiselle he sent an apology, begging her to believe that he had "meant well." As Mademoiselle says, "This affair should have taught me to keep away from visionaries for the rest of my life."

The scene that followed, the solemn royal and ministerial interview in the Palais-Royal to which Mademoiselle was inevitably summoned, shows us a princess at twenty, no longer deluded concerning the good will of those about her, fearless, contemptuous of discretion. It was the first of the great scenes of her life: all the previous violences done to the "strong affections of her nature" had prepared her for it.

She entered the council chamber "very calmly"; she knew she was innocent. The queen, awaiting her with Mazarin, greeted her with a look of anger. Deliberately, Mademoiselle chose as her place "a window alcove, raised above the level of the rest of the gallery; from there I listened with all the pride one can have when pride is in the right—a considerable advantage when dealing with persons who have advantages over you in other ways." Monsieur joined them: he had recently, against his habit, been winning military victories *for* the court, and was furious with Mademoiselle for jeopardizing his unaccustomed favor. The queen opened the attack. "Your father and I know all about your dealings with Saujon," she began sharply. "We know all about his great schemes."

"I replied," Mademoiselle says, "that I myself knew nothing about them, that I was very curious to know what Her Majesty meant, and that she would do me an honor to tell me. She then said it was impossible I should be ignorant: Saujon was in prison because of his devotion to me; I was the very cause of his predicament. I replied that devotion to me did not necessarily imply either prudence or good fortune, and that although Saujon was indeed devoted, he could very well be lacking in both qualities without my being responsible."

"We know that Saujon is trying to arrange a marriage between you and the archduke. We know he has told you the archduke will be the ruler of the Low Countries, and a thousand other absurdities that you let yourself believe. The archduke is the vilest of men —the most unsuitable candidate for your hand that could be imagined."

Mademoiselle said nothing.

"Answer me!" the queen commanded.

"I obeyed her. I replied that if Saujon was really capable of embarking on such a scheme, she was doing him too much honor to put him in prison like a rational being: an insane asylum would be more appropriate. If he had done what they accused him of, he had taken upon himself a role that belonged only to Her Majesty's brother the king of Spain; that was pure madness. I myself had never been considered a madwoman, and yet that was what I would have to label myself if I had ever given Saujon charge of my affairs."

And then Mademoiselle struck hard. "Considering how indefatigable Her Majesty has been in establishing, as queen of Poland, a young woman far beneath me in rank and other qualities, how foolish I would be not to trust Her Majesty herself, rather than anyone else, to find a suitable establishment for me! Especially now that she has reason to be grateful to Monsieur for his recent services, what complete confidence I know I can repose in her!"

The sarcasm stung the queen to a fury. "A fine thing, when someone shows the devotion that Saujon shows you, to send him to the scaffold!"

Mademoiselle paused, looking at her accusers. How many heads had rolled for Monsieur and the queen, back in the days when they had been allies against Richelieu! "In my case, at least," she said suavely, "Saujon would be the first."

And when she grew "tired of answering preposterous questions" and the queen again commanded, "Answer me!" Mademoiselle retorted: "I've had no practice at answering: I've never been interrogated." It was a reference to one of the queen's most humiliating ordeals under Richelieu—the merciless interrogation he had subjected her to on a famous occasion when she had been found to be in secret correspondence with the court of Spain.

Little wonder that after the interview had dragged on for "an hour and a half," the queen and Monsieur wrangling with her, trying to extract a confession and not succeeding, Mazarin looking on with sangfroid, even laughing at some of Mademoiselle's sallies, and after Mademoiselle, against all rules of etiquette, herself brought the scene to a close by saying, "Your Majesty has nothing more to say to me, I think,"—little wonder that when it was all over, the queen, unable to admit that she had allowed *herself* to be so spoken to by a subject, cried to her first lady in waiting, Madame de Motteville: "If I had a daughter who treated me the way Mademoiselle treats *her father,* I'd banish her from court forever and shut her up in a convent!"

As for Mademoiselle, she swept out of the room, after the usual deep curtsy, feeling "victorious but furious." The courtiers waiting in the antechamber noticed that she looked "far more haughty than ashamed." The abbé de la Rivière alone among them had the imprudence to approach her; she "discharged her anger on him" and went home to bed with a fever.

She knew what she had incurred, of course: disgrace. And to forestall measures she knew would be taken against her, she barred her door to all visitors, saying she was ill—"which was indeed the case." She was unrepentant, only worried as to what effect reports of her behavior might have in foreign countries, and, despite long experience, depressed by the hostility of Monsieur. As she had foreseen, he stayed away from her. He ordered

Madame de Fiesque to keep her imprisoned in her room; he demanded that she dismiss one of her ladies in waiting who was a friend of Saujon's, but on this Mademoiselle defied him. She could not exclude his emissary, the abbé, who kept coming to spy and "did nothing to diminish the fever."

Gradually her health improved; one day the abbé brought Monsieur's order that she begin to see people. "I was visited by the whole court, who were all on my side. Everyone blamed the queen and Monsieur, and couldn't understand why they had treated me as they had." Mademoiselle was still heavy-hearted. Another father would have afforded his daughter some protection if she had made a mistake. "The sadness I felt was caused by one thing: Monsieur's lack of affection for me, which he made apparent to all. Sincere though his indifference might be, he should have hidden it from others." When she could go out, she called on him at the Luxembourg. He was in his library. Madame de Fiesque and Mademoiselle's equerry—Mademoiselle never went out unaccompanied—remained in an antechamber; Mademoiselle entered the library alone. "My father's expression changed as he saw me. He seemed abashed. He tried to reprimand me, and began in that tone; but it was clear that he knew he should apologize rather than scold, and he actually did so without realizing it: I recognized, as anyone else would have who heard it, that the disapproval he was expressing was really a kind of apology. I wept bitterly, I don't know whether out of distress or affection—I hope the latter. Tears came to his eyes too. . . ."

From the Luxembourg she went to the Palais-Royal. Everyone stared and whispered as she appeared, but: "My manner was proud: pride is natural to me, and has never been lessened by adversity. The queen was just getting out of bed. Instead of going up to her as usual, I stood at the door. The duc d'Anjou" —he was eight years old—"ran up to me and kissed me and said, 'I've been for you all along, cousin; I've been taking your side against everybody.'

"At first the queen said nothing, and then: 'Sit down; you must be weak after being so ill.' I replied that my illness hadn't weakened me, that I was quite strong enough to stand on my feet." The queen flushed: by now she was ready to find a barbed double meaning in Mademoiselle's words whether it was intended or not. Her Majesty dressed for Mass; Mademoiselle handed her her gloves—it was the privilege of the highest-ranking lady present—there were a few polite words, and Mademoiselle withdrew.

The next day Mazarin called on Mademoiselle. He regretted the affair, he said, and assured her that he had played no part in it. Mademoiselle let him think that she believed him: "He always enjoyed thinking he'd hookwinked someone." From then on Mademoiselle called on the queen less often than formerly: "I didn't think that the presence of someone she had treated so badly could be agreeable to her."

The affair died down. And let it be said for Mademoiselle that, unlike Monsieur, she did not abandon even the first victim of her indiscretion. She was indefatigable in seeking Saujon's release. Mazarin kept him locked up for about a year in a place calculated to inspire dread—the same château of Pierre-Encise at Lyons where Cinq-Mars and de Thou had perished: apparently his aim was to warn Mademoiselle from ever again meddling in matters that concerned her. The order for Saujon's release that Mademoiselle finally secured relieved her, but made her smile. It directed that he retire to one of his estates—"a difficult order for him to follow," Mademoiselle says, "since he was a gentleman with only a cape and sword to his name." And she records that his release caused her one regret: she had to be grateful to the cardinal and the queen.

The affair of Saujon and the archduke was followed by another brief flare-up. The cardinal spoke of marrying Mademoiselle's particular friend, Mademoiselle d'Epernon, to Prince Casimir, the

king of Poland's brother and heir presumptive to the Polish
throne. Mademoiselle had a moment of hope. The newly remar-
ried German emperor had, by his first marriage, an unmarried
son, Ferdinand, called king of Hungary, who was about Mademoiselle's own age. Germany and Poland were so close together!
How wonderful if Mademoiselle and her *bonne amie* d'Epernon
could spend the rest of their lives in such proximity, as the spouses
of adjacent monarchs! This time it wasn't Mazarin and politics
that spoiled the scheme, but the proposed bride herself. Mademoiselle d'Epernon's fiancé, the young chevalier de Fiesque,
whom she loved, had recently been killed at the siege of Mardyck;
and now, as Mademoiselle puts it, "she preferred the crown of
thorns to the crown of Poland." In other words, she did what
Mademoiselle had once briefly thought of doing: she became a
Carmelite nun. She turned her back on the court—she literally
ran away from home—and in a convent at Bourges she became
Soeur Anne-Marie de Jésus. After taking her vows, she was transferred to the Carmelite house in Paris, and asked Mademoiselle
to visit her. The emotional violence of Mademoiselle's reunion
with her new-conditioned *bonne amie* is worthy of record: "I went
in a spirit of anger, beside myself with violent grief, and fully
resolved to express my resentment concerning everything I had to
complain of about her. But when I saw her, I found myself moved
only by affection; and all my other feelings so gave way before
it that I could not hide it from her, since my tears and my extreme grief made it impossible for me even to speak; for the
entire two hours I was with her I could not say a word. She was
very severe with me. . . . Two days later I paid her another visit;
it was the same thing all over again, and I think that if I hadn't
left Paris to follow the court there would always have been the
same grief in me and the same severity in her. . . ."

Afterwards, when Mademoiselle was writing her memoirs, she
claimed that she had come, with time, to realize that her behavior
during those convent visits should have been different. She should

have been joyful over her friend's new condition. It was the nun who could more properly have wept "to see me out in the world, and so little touched by any thought of God." But one suspects that even at the time she had some sense that her tears were not entirely for her friend's claustration: Mademoiselle d'Epernon's new robes represented for Mademoiselle not only this newest of the marital disappointments, but all of them, and other things as well; and there is hysteria in the violence of the resentment and the grief.

It is scarcely surprising, perhaps, that by the time Mademoiselle reaches this point in her memoir-writing, her manuscript should begin to contain touches of asperity and puzzlement about other people's marriages, and about marriage in general. How glad she is, at twenty-one, that the Spanish match fell through: "I should hate to be queen if I had to be as miserable as the queen of Spain!" How monstrous, and yet how comical and suitable, was the alli- ance between the daughter of Monsieur de Joyeuse and the son of Madame de Carignan: the bride insane and the groom all but dumb! But it is Monsieur, her own father, who gives her the great- est pause in this matter of marriage, as in all other matters. Mon- sieur's marriage is the most puzzling of all. "I will mention here something that I have noticed myself and that has been confirmed by Monsieur," she writes; "namely, that it is impossible to be friendly with both him and Madame at the same time, even though he expresses and indeed has the friendliest feelings for her, and lives with her just as calmly and pleasantly as a good bourgeois lives with his family." And Mademoiselle finally dismissed, after all, the very lady in waiting whom, after the affair of Saujon and the archduke, she had defiantly kept despite Monsieur's order. The young woman married for love—how could Mademoiselle keep her?

7

CROSSING THE PERIOD of the Spanish, German, Flemish, and Hungarian fiascos, and continuing for some little while thereafter, there was something more constant in Mademoiselle's life, something that ran through it like a thread: her prolonged wooing by—it would be more accurate to say *for*—her first cousin Charles Stuart, prince of Wales, later Charles II of England. It was a comedy in three acts—a comedy that might be called *The Indifferent Lovers*.

In 1644, at the moment of the talk about Mademoiselle's Spanish marriage, Charles I of England, his subjects increasingly turbulent, bade his queen farewell and sent her to safety with her own people across the channel. She was Henrietta-Maria of France, daughter of Henri IV—Monsieur's own sister, Mademoiselle's aunt; and Mademoiselle went with the queen-regent and the seven-year-old king to meet the royal refugee as she approached Paris. "Though she had tried her best to repair her strength and her health, she was in every way in so deplorable a state that everyone pitied her. She was given lodgings in the Louvre, and the next day was paid all the honors due a queen, a queen who was also *fille de France*. For several months she appeared in all a queen's pomp; she had with her many ladies of quality, maids of honor, carriages, guards, footmen. All this gradually diminished, and within a short time her retinue and the very food she ate were far indeed beneath her dignity."

Memoirs of the times—to say nothing of the novels of Dumas —are full of details of how the English refugees, although allowed to live in the Louvre, were neglected, by order of the parsimonious Mazarin, as long as the English royal cause seemed hopeless: how they were indeed kept on short rations, how they sometimes stayed in bed to keep warm for lack of firewood. But in the midst of privations Henrietta-Maria remained devoted to the cause of her husband and her son. Much money was needed. On the very first visit her niece paid her in the Louvre, she showed her hand: "She took pleasure in emphasizing all her past prosperities, the pleasantness of the life she had led in England, the beauty and goodness of the country, the entertainments she had had; especially the good qualities of the prince of Wales her son. She said she wished I might see him: it was easy to guess what she had in mind. . . ."

Two years later the sixteen-year-old Prince Charles arrived in France, sent to safety like his mother before him. He was presented to the king, the queen-regent, and Mademoiselle in the forest of Fontainebleau as he approached the palace; Mademoiselle found him "rather tall for his age, with a fine head, black hair, a swarthy complexion and quite agreeable presence," but she found it *incommode* that he neither spoke nor understood a word of French: British fear of foreign intrigue had caused that language to be banned at his father's court, and even his mother, on arriving in Paris, had had some difficulty with her native tongue.

Mazarin allowed Charles to stay at court only three days, during which he was taken hunting and given other fitting entertainment; and during those three days his mother conducted a campaign quite devoid of subtlety. "She did her best to persuade me that he was in love with me, that he spoke of me constantly; that if she hadn't forbidden it, he would have come into my bedroom at all hours; that he found me much to his liking, that he was desperate at hearing of the empress's death, lest I be married to the emperor."

Back in Paris other people, obviously primed by Henrietta-

Maria, spoke similarly about Charles to Mademoiselle. But she couldn't forgive him his lack of French; it immensely deepened her skepticism about his true feelings: "I don't know what success he might have had if he himself had spoken to me; but I do know that I can never put much stock in what others tell me on behalf of a man who can say nothing for himself." One suspects that Mademoiselle sensed the truth: that Charles was the possessor of budding animal qualities which were beginning to enable him, even at sixteen, to make contact with any woman he really wanted, despite language or other barriers.

But Henrietta-Maria persisted. She saw to it that Charles sat beside Mademoiselle at the plays in the Palais-Royal, that, bare-headed whatever the weather, he escorted her to her carriage. One evening, before a ball, she told Mademoiselle that she herself would come and arrange her hair and her gown; she brought Charles straight into Mademoiselle's boudoir that evening, and he held the light for the ladies while they attended to the intimacies of Mademoiselle's toilette: especially if Mademoiselle did have an inkling of his nature, his unperturbed politeness during so provocative an inspection can scarcely have been flattering. But his mother had decked him in the same colors as Mademoiselle— crimson, white, and black. At the ball everyone noticed it, even the queen-regent. All evening Charles scarcely left Mademoiselle's side, and he saw her home to her very door.

Later that winter, at "a famous fête at the Palais-Royal, with a magnificent Italian comedy with machines and music, and with a dance afterward," Mademoiselle was again accompanied by Charles; but this time he can scarcely have realized what was passing in her mind, how very much more than equal to his own lack of interest was Mademoiselle's. "The queen-regent took a special interest in my costume that night. Three whole days went to the arranging of my ornaments; my gown was trimmed with diamonds and with bows of crimson, white, and black ribbon; I was wearing all the French crown jewels and the few that the queen of England still possessed. No one has ever been dressed with greater taste or magnificence than I was that night, and there were plenty who remarked, quite truthfully, that my fine figure, handsome face, white skin, and blonde hair were not the least of my ornaments. Everything combined to show me off. The dancing was on a large stage, specially constructed for the occasion, decorated and brilliantly lit; in the center of this stage, at the back, there was a throne, approached by three steps and covered with a canopy. All the rest of the room was arranged like an amphitheater; those of us on the stage were in full view. Neither the king nor the prince of Wales cared to mount the throne; I went and sat on it myself; at my feet were the two princes, and all the princesses of the court. I felt utterly at home on that throne; everyone who saw me there told me that they had never seen me look so easy and unconstrained, and assured me that, being born for a throne, I should be even more completely in my element when I found one that would last longer than a ball. Not only with my eyes, but with my whole heart, I looked down at the prince below me; my mind was full of my marriage to the emperor; I no longer thought of the prince of Wales as anything except an object of pity."

During the next five years, as the English royalist cause grew more and more desperate, and as Mademoiselle lived through her series of marital hopes and disappointments, even Henrietta-Maria seems to have recognized the futility of pursuing her. Early in 1649, when the headsman's ax had finally fallen at Whitehall, Mademoiselle paid a condolence call in the cheerless apartment in the Louvre. It was more than many another did; because of "lack of money"—a shabby excuse, Mademoiselle thought—the French court, which was having its own troubles, had gone into only partial mourning for the royal British victim. Charles was in Holland; with the widowed queen was now her second son, the duke of York (later James II). He was only thirteen or fourteen, but Mademoiselle found him preferable to his brother: he spoke

French very well. "Nothing so disfigures a person, to my taste, as inability to *talk*," was her immediate thought about Charles; to Mademoiselle, talking and talking French were synonymous. Henrietta-Maria sent James and Mademoiselle out driving together.

But it was Charles who was now king—proclaimed in Edinburgh, if not in London; the air over the channel was heavy with political subtleties; and just as the queen-regent and Mazarin had spoken to Mademoiselle about the king of Spain and about the emperor, now they spoke to her about Charles. "The cardinal assured me that France would give him powerful aid; he had many loyal partisans in England; whole countries were still for him; he was master of all Ireland." As for the queen-regent, "She told me that she loved me as her own daughter; that she wouldn't urge me to marry the king of England if she didn't think the match a good one from my point of view; that all she wanted was my happiness." And somebody—Mademoiselle never knew who; she didn't think it was Monsieur—sent the abbé de la Rivière to needle her: she shouldn't forget, he said, that if she married Charles, she would have the exquisite pleasure, according to court etiquette, of taking precedence once, as a queen-bride, over Anne of Austria herself. And she would also do well to reflect that there was no other husband for her in all Europe; by now everybody was married except minor German and Italian royalty whom she wouldn't have anyway, and the king of France and his brother, who were both too young.

Mademoiselle spoke her mind without committing herself. If she did marry Charles, she told the abbé, her one aim would be to get him back his throne. She would consider it unfitting to continue to live luxuriously in Paris: she would either accompany her husband to Ireland and fight by his side, or she would wait for him in some quiet corner of France, economizing violently, even selling her possessions, and sending him every available penny for his cause. And, frankly, she said, such prospects frightened her:

was Charles's crown worth such a change in her habits? "If my father wants me to marry the king of England," she said, "and if he is convinced that the marriage is inevitable, I should rather marry him now, while he is in difficulties, because that will put him under obligation to me. Then when he regains his kingdom I can be sure he will treat me properly—he will recognize that he owes his restoration to me." And she said one other thing: she would never turn Protestant.

The queen-regent thought it appropriate to be sugary. "Your sweetheart's coming," she said coyly to Mademoiselle at Compiègne when they learned that Charles, returning from Holland, would be there for dinner.

Mademoiselle was merciless. "I do so hope he says sweet little loverlike things to me," she said, pretending to address the abbé de la Rivière. "Nobody has ever dared say sweet little loverlike things to me so far. It can't be because of my rank: plenty of people have said them to queens I know."

It was a reference to Anne's dalliance with Buckingham. Undaunted, the queen-regent called on the courtiers to notice that Mademoiselle had had her hair curled. "It's easy to see who's expecting her sweetheart! How carefully she's got up!"

This time Mademoiselle bit back her words: "People who have had sweethearts know what they're talking about!"

That day at Compiègne Mademoiselle found Charles much better-looking than she remembered him: "If his intelligence had seemed to me to match his looks, I might have liked him." But although he replied readily enough when the king asked him about Dutch dogs, Dutch horses, Dutch hunting, and the health of the prince of Orange, questions about more important matters brought from him only the plea that his French was inadequate. It was incredible: he still couldn't talk! "I confess that I decided then and there not to go through with the marriage. I conceived a very low opinion of him: to be king at his age, and to have no knowledge of affairs! I admit I should have recognized my own blood in his behavior: the Bourbons aren't very serious-minded; they care only for bagatelles—I among them, perhaps, since I'm a Bourbon twice over. As soon as he arrived, we dined. He refused ortolans, and flung himself on a piece of beef and a shoulder of mutton, as though they were the only things worth eating. His taste didn't seem very refined."

During a quarter of an hour following dinner, when everyone left them alone, he didn't address Mademoiselle a single word. "I should like to think that his silence was due rather to respect than to lack of passion, but I confess I could have done with less of it in either case." Finally, by calling in others, she induced him to open his mouth; but "sweet little loverlike things" didn't come out of it. His wooing that day consisted of a few farewell words chiefly about his mother's major-domo, Lord Jermyn: "Lord Jermyn talks better than I do. I think Lord Jermyn must have told you my feelings and wishes. I am your very obedient servant."

"I replied," Mademoiselle reports, "that I was his."

From Holland the eighteen-year-old Charles had brought with him his mistress, Lucy Barlow, who had just borne him a son, the future duke of Monmouth; and during the next three months, which he spent with his mother at Saint-Germain, Lucy was openly one of the party. When the time approached for his departure from France and Mademoiselle felt that courtesy to his mother demanded that she go to Saint-Germain and bid him good-by, Henrietta-Maria pointed the pretty Lucy out to her. "He's frightfully worried lest you find out he's in love with her," the queen said. "See how ashamed he is that she should be here where you are: he's afraid I'll tell you about her." Charles would be a perfect husband, Henrietta-Maria assured Mademoiselle. "He would love only his wife. He has told me so himself. He can't understand how a man who has a good wife can love anybody else. Whoever he might be attached to before marriage, after marriage it would be all over."

"I think," writes Mademoiselle with heavy irony, "that her little speech had a purpose."

By this time Charles had so impressed Mazarin with his indolence and carelessness that his political future seemed a poor financial risk, and all pressure except Henrietta-Maria's had been taken off Mademoiselle. Besides, there was interesting news from central Europe: the emperor's second wife, the Tyrolean archduchess, had died in childbirth; and once again the queen-regent and Mazarin had spoken to Mademoiselle about that establishment. That afternoon at Saint-Germain Henrietta-Maria congratulated Mademoiselle on the empress's death: "the business" wouldn't fall through this time, she supposed, the way it had before. "However," she said, indefatigably, "here's a young man who is persuaded that a king of eighteen is better than an emperor of fifty with four children. I know the truth, though: my son is too poor and wretched for you."

Mademoiselle didn't deny it.

"I agree with you," Henrietta-Maria then said. "You would have been miserable with him, and I love you too much to wish for that, even though it would have been his good fortune to have you as his companion in his bad times. All I can hope is that his expedition will be successful and that on his return you will want him."

When Mademoiselle took her leave, Charles spoke to her politely, but that was all. "Anything else would have been useless, for once again I had fallen into the trap of dreaming about the empire, and I could think of nothing else."

Those first two acts of *The Indifferent Lovers* had taken place before Charles II's career, properly speaking, had begun. But during the succeeding intermission, the two years that elapsed between his cool farewell to Mademoiselle in 1649 and his final return to France in 1651 to begin the third act of the comedy, he forged the most romantic part of his legend. He betrayed Mon-

trose; he crossed to Scotland and was crowned at Perth; he fought
Cromwell at Worcester; and then, in the famous "Worcester
flight," he made his escape, unbetrayed, through a country swarm-
ing with soldiers eager to earn the reward of a thousand pounds
posted for his capture. Finally he crossed to France. His mother
met him on the road between Paris and Rouen; once again they
were together in the Louvre; once again Mademoiselle paid the
visit that etiquette demanded.

"You'll find my son looking rather odd," Henrietta-Maria
warned her. "In order to escape he cut his hair, and his clothes are
extraordinary."

But Mademoiselle found him still better-looking than the last
time, despite his round-head and his beard; and—greatest of im-
provements—he now seemed to talk French very well. "He told
us that after losing the battle he passed with forty or fifty cavaliers
through the enemy army and through the city near which the fight
had taken place; that he had then dismissed them all, and remained
alone with a single *milord;* that for a long time he had hidden in
a tree, then in the house of a peasant, where he had cut his hair;
that a nobleman he met on the road had recognized him and taken
him to his house, where he stayed; and that he had gone to London with the nobleman's brother, riding behind him on the same
horse; that he had spent one night in London, sleeping ten hours
perfectly calmly; that he boarded a boat in London which took
him to the port where he embarked, and that the ship's captain
had recognized him. And so," Mademoiselle concludes, "he arrived in Dieppe." Since it was really at Fécamp that Charles arrived, there may be other slips, too, in her remembrance of his
adventures; but she found them impressive.

At the end of her visit he accompanied her down the corridor
to the Tuileries. "He told me of the wretched life he had led in
Scotland. There hadn't been a woman there; the people were so
brutish, they thought it a sin to listen to music; he had been furiously bored. The loss of the battle had distressed him less than it

might have if it hadn't given him the hope of coming to France, where there were so many charming people whom he liked. He asked me if we mightn't have a dance one day soon."

During that walk down the corridor to the Tuileries, Mademoiselle records, she had the impression that Charles was "a timid, fearful lover, who didn't dare tell me everything he felt, and who preferred that I think him insensible to his misfortunes rather than bore me with complaints." And she admits: "This time he didn't displease me." The uncertainty of her feelings is betrayed by a conflict in her account: only a few lines after saying that Charles now "seemed to talk French very well," she declares that "his French was quite poor." For a little while that winter she seems to have been touched and troubled by the tall, dark young king. In her mind, perhaps, was the recently received news that the emperor was once again not available: he had just married, as his third wife, the princess Eleanora of Mantua, whose North Italian principality was of crucial political importance. ("I can say without vanity," is Mademoiselle's comment on that event, "that God, who is just, did not wish to give a wife such as I to a man who did not deserve me.") And as to Charles, the "timid fearful lover"— in a way her intuition was not wholly wrong; quite apart from his immediate situation in regard to her, there is little evidence that the animally magnetic Charles, by now well advanced in easy rakery, ever took the trouble to do any courting at all.

That winter, as the king's twenty-four violins played for Mademoiselle every other day and her rooms in the Tuileries were crowded from five or six o'clock to nine with the dancing of "all the young men and pretty girls of Paris," Charles, always in attendance, "talked as much as he could." He even forced himself to the point of saying "sweet little loverlike things" to Mademoiselle—"at least, people who overheard them told me that's what they were. He spoke such good French at those moments that there is no doubt that Cupid is French rather than of any other nationality. When the king spoke my tongue, he forgot his own.

This happened only with me; no one else understood his French as well as I did."

Henrietta-Maria continued her pressure and often came to the dances: Mademoiselle was never in any doubt as to the source of Charles's assiduity. But she enjoyed it; she enjoyed having him act toward her "the way they say all lovers act." And she enjoyed it particularly when she learned that the queen-regent and Mazarin now disapproved. They did not summon her personally—the court was spending the winter in Saint-Germain—but they let her know through others how gravely they had come to oppose the match. As a result, Mademoiselle was so responsive to Charles that Henrietta-Maria spoke to her directly.

"She told me that the way in which she and her son had always lived with me didn't allow them to speak of it to Monsieur without first knowing whether I was favorably inclined. Were the king her son in better circumstances, he would have made the proposal to Monsieur without asking me, since he was convinced there was nothing I disliked about his person. As it was, my acceptance of him would so improve his condition, that he preferred his good fortune to come from my generosity rather than from Monsieur. I replied that I was too happy as I was to think of marrying; I was content with my present rank and my present fortune; I had nothing to wish for. I received her proposal with all the respect it deserved, I said, but needed time to think about it. She told me she would give me a week, and she begged me to consider that I would always be mistress of my own fortune, even though married. Her son would live on the 200,000 écus a year that would come to him either from England or from the king of France; I would be a queen, and the happiest person in the world because of her son's affection for me. There were several princes in Germany who were promising him great help; he had a strong faction in England, and so excellent a marriage would impress everyone in his favor; with that, and with the help he hoped for, he could soon get his throne back. So ended our conversation."

Mademoiselle found Henrietta-Maria's openness "very civil," and she gave her permission to speak to Monsieur: she knew how he would answer. He was polite but cautious; the English did him and his daughter great honor, he said; still, it was his duty to point out that his daughter belonged not to him, but to the king and to the state; the king's consent would be necessary. He was so affectionate and courteous with his sister, however, that Henrietta-Maria was naïvely optimistic at having surmounted all obstacles except the last. She sent Charles to Mademoiselle. "He told me of his joy in the favorable answer that Monsieur had given his mother. This made him dare speak to me openly for the first time, he said; so far he had allowed his mother to speak for him. And he made me a fine speech: now he was more eager than ever to mount his throne, he said, since he would be sharing his good fortune with me; that would increase the pleasure it would give him. I told him that if he didn't go seek his throne himself, he might not have it very soon.

" 'What!' he said. 'As soon as we're married you'd send me away?'

" 'Yes,' I said. 'If we marry I'll have a greater interest in your affairs than I have now; I'd hate to see you here in Paris dancing the tricotets and amusing yourself, when you ought to be where you would either be getting your head broken or having it crowned.' And I added that he would be unworthy of wearing a crown if he didn't go after it with his sword, at the risk of his life."

But the comedy was almost over. The culminating step, Henrietta-Maria's or Charles's or Lord Jermyn's formal request at court for the hand of Mademoiselle, was never taken. Whether Mademoiselle did or did not stand ready to marry Charles is a question that scarcely enters into play: a mere personal consideration, of no concern to Mazarin, who was deep in negotiations with Cromwell that combined with other reasons to make the marriage impossible. She herself suggests that she had decided against it:

she felt that Monsieur disapproved; England was in a bad way and Charles was indolent—there might never be a throne; besides, the Protestant issue was insurmountable. The situation was misty both personally and politically. Mademoiselle seems never fully to have understood Mazarin's devices for ending it, but they can nevertheless be deduced from her own account. People began to call on Mademoiselle. They all had something to tell her about the affair. But they all beat around the bush; they all spoke obliquely. Gradually the meaning of their hints began to dawn on her: Mazarin and the queen-regent really *wanted* her to marry Charles! And why? Precisely because the marriage *would* be a political mistake. Responsibility they planned to shift onto Monsieur; and he, guilty of negotiating for his daughter a match so seriously disadvantageous to France, would be dishonored forever. She was to be the instrument of her father's disgrace.

Confirmation came from Monsieur's secretary, Goulas. However directly his words may have been inspired by Mazarin, however much Monsieur may have connived in his being sent, Goulas visited her and told her how things stood. Of course the queen-regent and Mazarin wanted her to marry Charles. Wasn't it the surest way to ruin her as well as Monsieur? Wealthy though she was, did she think even her riches sufficient to finance the kind of war that Charles would have to wage against Cromwell? Stripped of everything she owned, her husband's throne as far from recovered as ever, she would starve. Charles himself might die; and then where and what would she be? The most wretched queen in the world, a burden on Monsieur instead of a help to him. The whole proposition was clear evidence of just how concerned the court was for her welfare.

That, of course, was the *coup de grâce* to the affair: Mazarin had well known how to administer it.

Lord Jermyn, calling on Mademoiselle, all but rubbing his hands at the approaching climax of negotiations, was dumbfounded by her cool request that Charles come to see her less often: people, she said, were talking. Charles stayed away three weeks: Mademoiselle knew he must be missing her dances. "He was bored and annoyed, I think: he was having no entertainment; everyone could see that I wasn't dependent for mine on his conversation and his company." Mazarin's agents continued active: rumors, sure to be distasteful to Mademoiselle, were carefully spread. Everyone knew, for example, that she was desperately in love with Charles; Lord Jermyn was saying privately that the English would still have her, and that once they had, they would "cut down her expenses, sell her lands." Reports of such talk as that confirmed Mademoiselle in considering the affair at an end. "I made up my mind very definitely. I was a little brusque about it, I fear, but such is my nature."

When finally Mademoiselle and Henrietta-Maria met, the queen covered her with a thousand reproaches. How could it have been otherwise? Frustrated Henrietta-Maria, heavy-handed campaigner that she was, saw before her only a self-willed and mercurial young princess: the princess with whom Madame de Fiesque had had to deal, a princess mistress in a haughty way of her destiny—politics permitting—just as she was mistress of her household in the Tuileries. Henrietta-Maria was not subtle enough to sense the peculiar yearning, tremulous, almost breathless, of the Tuileries for the favor of the Luxembourg. "The abbé de la Rivière often told me that if I wanted to be loved by Monsieur, I could be; I should just be careful to avoid doing certain unimportant little things that displeased him. I asked him what they were; he answered that I should try to find out for myself. . . . I have always known that Monsieur had an aversion to seeing me established. . . . It has always been easy for anyone to do me a disservice in Monsieur's opinion: all anyone has to do is mention my name, and Monsieur is off. . . ." Those constant, almost ceaseless broodings of the proud princess were not apparent to Henrietta-Maria. But they were no secret from Mazarin. The cardinal knew everything; and he well knew how very secondary, in the Tuileries, was Charles of

England's crown to the welfare, and especially the good opinion, of Monsieur.

As his mother scolded, Charles entered. Hitherto he had always made a respectful point of sitting, in Mademoiselle's presence, on a simple stool or chair—the hierarchial significance of stools, straight chairs, and armchairs was acute at court; they were a veritable language. This time he demanded a large chair and sat defiantly in it before her. "I think he intended to cause me great offense," Mademoiselle tells us, "and he caused me none whatever."

Charles never did fight for his throne, as Mademoiselle had said he must. He waited in France, in Germany, in the Low Countries, in Spain, for eight more years, until Cromwell was dead and General Monk made ready the way: then, in 1660, he crossed the Channel and received the allegiance of his kingdom. Toward the end of his exile he made another attempt to marry in France, but the cardinal thwarted him again: this time it was Hortense Mancini, one of the cardinal's own nieces, whom Charles—or rather Henrietta-Maria—had chosen. In this instance, too, Charles seems to have obeyed his mother with the same ungraciousness as in the case of Mademoiselle—an ungraciousness as notable as the passion with which Mademoiselle obeyed *her* parent. Only after his restoration did Charles find a bride, the Portugese Catherine of Braganza; and the degree to which he "loved only his wife," as forecast by Henrietta-Maria to Mademoiselle, is a matter of history.

It is tantalizing to think of Mademoiselle as queen of Restoration England, queen of Congreve and Wycherley, of Nell Gwynn and Pepys and Evelyn: she would have counted for more on the throne, one suspects—counted for more in the English scene in general—than meek little Catherine of Braganza. But by the time of the Restoration Mademoiselle was up to other things. Our pre-Restoration comedy, *The Indifferent Lovers,* had been, after all, a Restoration kind of play, a stylized and stylish one. The rake was royal, and his very existence posited a legion of cuckolds. There had been nothing below-stairs in the comedy of Mademoiselle's wooing. And there hadn't been much realism, either. How could there have been? For realism was up to Mazarin; and Mazarin was considering Mademoiselle for another role.

8

MADEMOISELLE WAS the most Parisian member of the court. Unlike the king and his brother, she was Paris-born; and from the age of a few days she had lived continuously in the Tuileries, absent far less often than the rest of the royal family at the outlying palaces of Saint-Germain and Fontainebleau. She adored riding in the Cours-la-Reine and stopping for refreshments, in fine weather, at Renard's outdoor restaurant beside the Seine. She was constantly passing through the streets to the Palais-Royal and the Luxembourg; everyone knew her coach and her livery; her defiance of the unpopular Spanish queen and Italian cardinal in the council chamber had spread as a legend far beyond court circles; in a special fond way Parisians of all classes regarded her as *their* princess, almost a mascot. *"C'est Mademoiselle!" "Voilà Mademoiselle!"* She was accustomed to such street greetings from her babyhood.

Not that Mademoiselle had, in the normal course of events, much contact with the citizenry beyond accepting their homage. Her life was a court life, and it is easy to forget, reading many of her pages, that all around her a cityful of artisans and professionals was working more or less hard and talking more or less continuously.

The loudest, the most insistent, talking in Paris was done by the famous *harengères,* the fishwives who shouted their wares and their opinions from stalls in the public market. These ladies extended a ferocious affection to anyone, of any class, who happened to charm them; and they were just as ferociously defensive of their own rights. Their parish church, Saint-Eustache (it is still the parish church of the market quarter), had for generations been administered by a series of curés named Merlin. When an archbishop of Paris appointed as successor to a deceased Merlin, not Merlin's nephew named Merlin but an unknown named Poncet, the fishwives rioted; when soldiery arrived to disperse them, they locked themselves inside the market halls and inside the church itself, sounding the tocsin; they sent a deputation to the queen-regent, and the fishwife spokeswoman, carried away by the righteousness of her cause, pleaded before Her Majesty that they had "always had Merlins as curés, from father to son." All Paris laughed,* and the archbishop withdrew Poncet.

Monsieur's friend the duc de Beaufort was long the fishwives' darling among the nobility. He was the grandson of Henri IV and the beautiful Gabrielle d'Estrées; but somewhere he had learned to speak the fishwives' language, and they adored him for it and called him the "king of the markets"; to them and to many others he had stood as the very symbol of feudal resistance to the tyrannical Richelieu. He was the greatest and most hot-headed of the *Importants* imprisoned by the queen-regent and Mazarin, and when he escaped after five years in the dungeon of Vincennes, the enthusiasm of the fishwives was vociferous; and a little later, when he was back in Paris and seemed on the point of fighting a duel, the encounter was prudently scheduled to take place beyond the city walls—for if his opponent were to walk off the field within Paris, it was feared, the fishwives would tear him to pieces.

During Mademoiselle's first two decades, and for a little longer, it was the fishwives, the shrillest and most picturesque of the citizenry, whom she chiefly had occasion to notice. But then came a change, and for several years large numbers of *les bourgeois* and *les Parisiens* were to force themselves on Mademoiselle's attention.

* All the more so because Merlin sounds like *merlan*—whiting.

It was Mazarin's fault, and Richelieu's before him. Both cardinals accumulated huge private fortunes from public funds, and spent even more of the public funds on foreign wars. The French state was desperate for money. Not only the royal English refugees lived shabbily; the young king of France himself sometimes slept in torn sheets and wore old clothes, although there is no record that Mazarin ever did so. Mazarin's financial experts, searching through old statutes, discovered the *toisé,* a tax on newly built houses, forgotten for a hundred years. The *toisé* was revived and made retroactive; and like the fishwives before them, Parisian house-owners staged a riot, marching in the streets with drums and banners. Then Mazarin attacked the Parlement with a decree revoking the members' right to bequeath their offices to their heirs —unless they agreed to serve four years without pay. This was even more provocative: the London Parliament had recently been giving the world all too vivid a lesson in the art of active protest, and the Paris Parlement seized the occasion to imitate its example and demand a constitution. They insisted that they were loyal to the king, but that the royal power was being abused by the cardinal and the queen-regent. Mazarin at once arrested three of the most prominent members, gentlemen with the middle-class names of Charton, Blancmesnil, and Broussel; but Broussel was much loved by Parisians, and the streets again filled with rioters and barricades; a mob armed with stones and slings (*frondes*) besieged the Palais-Royal; Parlement forced the release of the prisoners and exacted a royal declaration promising reforms. The bourgeois hastily donned swords, and Mademoiselle laughed at the gracelessness with which they wore them.

The cardinal and the queen-regent found the air of Paris unhealthy; and for a time, "because the Palais-Royal needed a housecleaning," the court moved to Rueil, where Richelieu had scolded the ten-year-old Mademoiselle. There was a brief return to Paris, but clean though the Palais-Royal now was, "the court wasn't as happy there as it might be," as Mademoiselle puts it, and before dawn on the morning of January 6, 1649, while Paris was sleeping off its celebration of Epiphany Eve, the chief royal and princely personages, Mademoiselle among them, stole out of the city and encamped, shivering, in the ill-equipped summer palace of Saint-Germain. Mademoiselle spent the first night with one of her half sisters, "who kept seeing the bogeyman," on a mattress on the floor of "a beautiful bedroom under the eaves, handsomely painted and gilded, with almost no fire and no panes in the windows—not very comfortable for January." But the next night Monsieur, in good humor, gave her his room and moved in with Madame. It was a game of bivouac: "Those who had beds had no bedcovers, and those who had bedcovers had no clothes. I had no change of linen: my nightgown was washed during the day and my underslip at night. I had no one to dress my hair or attend to my clothes —it was very inconvenient. I ate with Monsieur; the food was very bad. But I was in high spirits nevertheless, and Monsieur admired me for not complaining. I am not one to let such things trouble me; I'm above bagatelles."

The move to Saint-German was the cardinal's way of making contact with the army—more precisely, with its dazzling, hawk-like commander, the prince de Condé, who had been winning brilliant victories for France in Germany, Flanders, and Spain; and although Condé's soldiers were slow to arrive, the great general proceeded now to direct, from Saint-Germain, what was called "the war of Paris." This was a siege of the city, complete with skirmishes, designed to starve into repentance the insolent citizenry and those rebellious nobles—among them the duc de Beaufort, the hero of the fishwives, untamed by his years of imprisonment—who out of ambition and hatred for Mazarin had made themselves Frondeurs alongside Parlement and the bourgeois.

The war of Paris wasn't the proudest episode in Condé's career. The winter was a ridiculous one. Whenever a few Paris-bound cattle or bread carts were captured, heralds rushed the news of victory to Saint-Germain. The besieged Parisians, who made occasional sorties waving flags inscribed "We seek our king," returned from one such sortie bearing not the king, but a drove of pigs, which they herded triumphantly into the city. There were few casualties, chief among them the duc de Châtillon, whose duchess mourned him as much as she could considering that at the moment he fell he was wearing on his arm one of the blue garters of his mistress, Mademoiselle de Guerchy, and considering also that with him disappeared the only obstacle to the duchess's own amorous escapades. It was that kind of a war: a French-farce version of the grim drama of the Commonwealth.

For Mademoiselle, at twenty-one, it was a merry time. All those around her at Saint-Germain were so harmonious, so united! The queen-regent was relieved to be out of the restless city. "She couldn't have been gayer if she had won a battle, taken Paris, and hanged everyone who displeased her," Mademoiselle says. Monsieur, despite an attack of gout, was behaving well, displaying his devotion to the king not only in words but by sharing military responsibility with Condé, who was a Bourbon like himself. Everyone agreed that the declaration extracted by Parlement was a shame. "Since the king has to account for his actions only to God," Mademoiselle later wrote, "it came hard that he should be asked to account to Parlement. The rank to which I was born puts any approval by me of this sort of thing so far out of the question that I can see how people of inferior rank might feel the opposite, due to their natural inclination to want to be master. It seems to me that a single authority is so close to God's divinity that one should willingly submit to it with joy and respect if God has not willed that one be born that authority oneself. As for me, I know perfectly well that had I been born in a republic I should do my best to bring about a revolution; but not to put *myself* at the head of things—I esteem the monarchy too highly." On another occasion she put it differently: "I don't say I love the monarchy—that would be saying I love myself, for monarchy in France began with my family."

Mademoiselle enjoyed making herself useful during that winter at Saint-Germain. In those days, when French grandees traveled from one palace to another, they took much of their furniture with them: no one had yet had the idea of keeping several palaces fully furnished at the same time. But the surreptitious Epiphany departure from Paris had forced the court to leave its effects behind, and now the Frondeurs were so unwilling to contribute to the comfort of the cardinal that they refused to allow any furniture, clothing or bedding to leave the city lest it be destined for his use. As a result, the entire court suffered: so rare were mattresses at Saint-Germain that there was a black market in straw. But Mademoiselle knew how to profit from the Parisians' affection. She despatched one of her pages, a boy of fourteen or fifteen, who went straight to Parlement and coolly said she had sent him to fetch some of her things; the members assured him that Mademoiselle could take anything she wanted, and they asked the page to convey her their respectful greetings. Passports and escorts were provided; and the entire court shared in Mademoiselle's wagonloads of comforts—especially a trunkful of highly scented Spanish gloves, which caused the prying bourgeois customs inspectors at the "frontier," unaccustomed to heady court perfumes, to suffer well-deserved attacks of sneezing; everyone at court praised Mademoiselle's clever page and addressed him thenceforth as "ambassador."

Yes, for Mademoiselle the war of Paris was a lark. She was almost sorry when it ended. But it had to end: it was too hard on the court. As Mademoiselle puts it: "We at Saint-Germain were in the predicament we had wanted to put Paris in. The intention had been to starve the city, but the citizens had an abundance of everything, whereas at Saint-Germain there was often not enough to eat—the troops took everything." And if the troops took, the peasants smuggled, selling their produce at black-market prices in Paris rather than to the court. But the Frondeurs, too, were uneasy and weary of the deadlock, and in March "peace" was signed,

both sides making vague concessions. Except for the duc de Beaufort and a few others too proud to bow, the principal Frondeurs
flocked to Saint-Germain to thank the king—not the cardinal, they
made clear—for bestowing peace on his kingdom; and on the sur-
face all was forgiven.

Mademoiselle, among the first, visited Paris for a few days. (It
was on this occasion that she paid her condolence call on the
Queen of England.) In the city the duc de Beaufort was charming to her: he even loaned her his musicians, since the king's
were not at the moment available, to play serenades in the Tuileries gardens. His politeness was better-placed than he knew. He
and the other Frondeurs who were attentive to Monsieur's daughter could, at that moment, have no complete idea of what fruit-
ful ground Mademoiselle was for their sowing of courtesies.
For Mademoiselle confided to no one what she later confided
to her memoirs: her intuition, from the very beginning, that
everything the court did—the arrest of the members of Parlement,
the signing of the declaration, the flight to Saint-Germain, the war
of Paris—that everything was a mistake. A mistake that would be
costly to the court itself. And, entertaining though the stay in
Saint-Germain turned out to be, Mademoiselle had gone there
filled with a troubling yet joyous feeling that now, by being a
spectator of the court's mistakes, she would at last be getting a
little revenge—revenge for what she had neither forgotten nor
forgiven: her marriage fiascos in general, and, in particular, the
queen's tirade on the subject of Saujon and the archduke. But even
Mademoiselle herself didn't realize, quite yet, how very much
more "advantageous a situation"—the words, written later, are
her own—she was soon to be in: a situation in which she could
both "do her duty and at the same time achieve her revenge."

Louis de Bourbon, prince de Condé, was not someone Mademoiselle had ever liked. The branch of the house of Bourbon to
which he belonged was a "younger" branch, regarded by the

others with a mixture of condescension and distrust. Condé's mother had been tactless enough, when Mademoiselle was younger, to treat her like a little girl at dances. "I *was* a little girl," Mademoiselle admits, "but I never came away from her house without a deadly rage in my heart." And Condé himself, while still the duc d'Enghien, had married Richelieu's niece, Mademoiselle de Brézé. Everyone knew that he had wed her only reluctantly, forced by his father and the cardinal; and everyone remembered what had happened to the comte de Soissons, who had refused another of the cardinal's nieces; still, such close alliance to the cardinal had made Condé *persona non grata* to Monsieur and Mademoiselle. The glory he had won by his dazzling and debonair behavior on the battlefield—at Lerida twenty-four violins had played for his regiment, as though the battle were a ballet at the Louvre—had caused Mademoiselle nothing but rage. She had wept at the news of his victories—"I was less a Frenchwoman than Condé's enemy"—and when she heard that at Mardyck his face had been burned by a grenade, she hoped that he would be disfigured forever. Furthermore, Condé had been almost the only person at court so impolite as not to leave best wishes at the Tuileries when Mademoiselle came down with smallpox. So she was not too displeased, nine months after the end of the war of Paris—and Monsieur did not object in the slightest—when Mazarin, finding Condé unbearably self-important and full of political ambition, arrested him, his brother, and his brother-in-law (known collectively as "the princes") in the Palais-Royal, where they had been summoned by the queen on "special business," and sent them to the prison of Vincennes.

Almost at once, however, Monsieur began to waver. The ladies of the Condé family showed such diligence in petitioning Parlement against the illegality of the arrests, in rallying for Condé's defense the troops who had fought under him, and in securing the promise of Spanish troops, too, to fight against the cardinal if need be, that it began to look as though the moment might be approach-

ing, at last, to rid France of the hated Italian. The king would
soon reach the age of thirteen years and a day, the age of ma-
jority: how very desirable it was that the reign begin under new
auspices! The cardinal grew nervous. He began to woo Monsieur;
and he began to woo Mademoiselle, who was skeptical of every
move he made. The cardinal offered to send Saujon, of all people,
to see what might be arranged between Mademoiselle and the emperor (it was when the second empress had just died). Mademoiselle recognized the offer as an apology for past behavior: and
yet, wasn't it also a trick? A trick to make sure that once again
nothing would happen with the emperor, since Saujon was so
addlepated? Time and again, these days, the cardinal assured
Mademoiselle that he had always had her welfare at heart; the
queen-regent also; it was Monsieur who, for reasons of his own,
had always kept the truth from her. Mademoiselle listened coolly:
it was true, she replied, that she had ever had any *evidence* of the
court's good will. The cardinal smiled. "This breeze blowing in
your window seems to come from Bordeaux"—Bordeaux was
Condé country—"it may turn you into a *Frondeuse* if it blows
long enough."

The breeze blew stronger and stronger; Mazarin was hung in
effigy on Paris street corners; for greater security he had Condé
and the other two princes transferred to a prison in Le Havre;
Parlement demanded that they be freed. Mazarin, furious at such
impertinence, lost his temper one evening in the Palais-Royal before Monsieur and the queen-regent; the Parlement was as bad as
the British Parliament, he shouted; the leading Frondeurs were no
better than the regicides Cromwell and Fairfax. Monsieur, who
had finally made up his mind, retorted in a rage: loyal Frenchman
that he was, he screamed, he could not tolerate—and from a
foreigner!—such an insult to France. Never again, he swore, ad-
dressing the queen and pointing to the cardinal, would he sit at
the king's council table as long as *"ce personnage-là"* was present.
The queen sided, as always, with her beloved minister, and Mon-

sieur rushed out of the Palais-Royal, fearing arrest. A few days later he proclaimed himself an ally of Condé. Mademoiselle was delighted, if disquieted. "Although I didn't like Condé, I so loved Monsieur that I was thrilled that he should undertake two such large responsibilities: to get Condé out of prison and Mazarin out of office. But I was frightfully worried lest he weary of the affair, and not carry it through to its conclusion. At that moment I resolved to surmount the unreasonable aversion I had for Condé."

And now Mademoiselle began to savor her revenge. For the cardinal began to woo her more strongly; and this time—so he pretended, at least—for someone closer to home than the emperor. He revived the earliest and the most glorious of Mademoiselle's marriage projects—the question of *mon petit mari*.

Mademoiselle de Neuillant, one of the queen-regent's maids of honor, called on Mademoiselle. She had been ordered by the cardinal, she announced flatly, to say that if Mademoiselle would detach Monsieur from the Frondeurs, the cardinal would promise that Mademoiselle would be queen of France. For so grandiose an offer, it was made with such grotesque abruptness and casualness (the cardinal's promises were notoriously worthless anyway —"I'm not the slave of my word," he was accustomed to say) that Mademoiselle burst out laughing. Both Monsieur and she herself, she said, were pledged to right the wrong done Condé and the others, and they would not go back on their word. Mademoiselle de Neuillant was incredulous: not even for the hand of the king? "For heaven's sake, Mademoiselle, first make yourself queen; *then* release the princes!" But Mademoiselle was incredulous too: she knew better than to listen to such preposterousness.

And there was further revenge. In the Palais-Royal, scene of the royal tirade concerning Saujon and the archduke, the queen-regent, now badgered and resentful, challenged her about Monsieur. "Well, Mademoiselle, aren't you amazed that your father should persecute me? That he should try to ruin the cardinal, whom he always protested he loved with a passion?"

"Monsieur does not hate the cardinal," Mademoiselle replied. "He loves the king and the state, as he should. But he knows how affairs stand, and he thinks the cardinal does not serve the king; that's why he thinks he should be removed."

"Why didn't he say so sooner, then?"

"Out of respect for Your Majesty he endured things as long as he could, in the hope that the cardinal would profit from his advice. Now he has had to speak out, lest one day he himself be accused of disloyalty to the king."

Mazarin, bowing to the storm, fled Paris one moonlight night and went to Le Havre, where he personally released the princes, hoping in this way to win their allegiance. When Condé, scorning the cardinal—who thereupon fled to Cologne—came to Paris in glory and attended an evening fête at the Luxembourg after he and Monsieur had together paid a triumphant call on the downcast queen-regent, Mademoiselle and Condé had a scene of reconciliation. Amid the laughter of their partisans she confessed how she had always rejoiced in his misfortunes; he retorted that when she had had smallpox he had prayed that it might leave her scarred (it hadn't done so: all smallpox did to Mademoiselle was to cure her rosacea, leaving her handsomer than ever). Now they swore eternal friendship. Condé—a Bourbon, her cousin, Monsieur's ally—became Mademoiselle's hero. Indeed, the following week, when Condé's wife came down with erysipelas, and Condé called on Mademoiselle daily at the Tuileries, Mademoiselle had serious talks with her secretary, Préfontaine, as to the advisability of becoming the princess's successor. But the princess recovered.

No one thought for an instant that the flight of the cardinal meant the end of what people were calling a new Fronde, *"la Fronde des princes."* The queen-regent, unswervingly loyal to her prime minister, was in constant communication with him: many believed them to be husband and wife, united in secret marriage —Mazarin was thought to be one of those cardinals who had never been priest. One night the rumor spread through Paris that the queen-regent was about to abduct the king. For once rumor happened to be true—the king was already in his traveling clothes. Thousands of Parisians besieged the Palais-Royal, shouting "The king! The king! We must see the king!" Hastily undressing her son and putting him to bed, Anne of Austria ordered him to pretend to be asleep; then the gates of the palace were flung open. Everyone who desired to enter the king's bedroom should be admitted, she commanded; but she asked the citizens to be quiet, as His Majesty was sleeping. Into the Palais-Royal swarmed the Paris *canaille*. All but holding their breath, they tiptoed down the corridors. Beside her son's bed stood the queen-regent, holding back the velvet curtains so that all could see their "sleeping" king. To pretend to be asleep while the unwashed mob filed through his bedroom was one of the most striking of Louis XIV's early royal acts; until three in the morning the stream never slackened; the odor was indescribable. Louis XIV never forgot that night as long as he lived. On the nights that followed, sometimes twice a night, his presence in bed was ascertained by one of Monsieur's gentlemen.

Not only was the queen-regent loyal to her minister, but also, all royal troops that had not gone over to Condé were, in effect, under his command. Mazarin's position was not desperate: he was well able to treat, from his exile, with the Frondeurs.

And treat he did. Once again he put forward the matter of *mon petit mari*.

This time the maneuver was more roundabout.

This time it was Madame de Choisy who came to Mademoiselle. She was an amusing court gossip, the wife of Monsieur's chancellor; one never knew what she would say next. Today she declared that she had something important to say, and in an inner room she said it: "I've come to make your fortune."

Mademoiselle laughed: it was a quaint thing, she found, to say to someone who had such a fortune already.

But Madame de Choisy persisted. Just yesterday, she said, she had been approached by a gentleman named Bartet, the king of Poland's resident in Paris. "Tell me about Mademoiselle," Bartet had said to her. "What are her plans? What kind of person is she?"

"A straightforward, good person," Madame de Choisy said she had replied. "And cleverer than most people think."

"I want to make her queen of France," Bartet had announced flatly.

"If you do," Madame de Choisy had cried, enraptured, "I promise you Bois-le-Vicomte!"

Now Bois-le-Vicomte, a country house a few miles outside Paris, was scarcely Madame de Choisy's to promise. It belonged to Mademoiselle. Hearing it so enthusiastically awarded to someone she barely knew, and hearing why, Mademoiselle "listened carefully and did not interrupt."

But Madame de Choisy said little more that day, except to add significantly that she had confidence in Bartet, since he was "close to the cardinal."

A few days later Madame de Choisy came again. Bartet was not the person to handle the affair after all, she said. The princess Palatine, the queen of Poland's sister, was much cleverer. She would take charge. She was poor as a church mouse, though: Mademoiselle would have to promise her 300,000 écus if she succeeded. An écu was three livres—about three dollars today. Mademoiselle agreed at once: she was listening more carefully than ever; for the princess Palatine, she knew, really *was* close to the cardinal. Perhaps the cardinal really was persisting; perhaps persistence might even mean sincerity. Between them, the princess Palatine and Madame de Choisy had worked everything out in extraordinary detail. "My husband will be your chancellor," Madame de Choisy said. "We'll all make a good thing of it. The princess Palatine will be your chief lady in waiting, with 20,000 écus a year; she'll sell all your household positions—that will bring her in a tidy sum, so you see you can count on her to work

for you. We'll have a new play every day at the Louvre. The princess Palatine will manage the king."

How kind of the princess Palatine to take over the bridegroom!
Mademoiselle had that sarcastic thought; but she said not a word.

"The king will come of age in two weeks," Madame de Choisy
said. "A week later, you'll be married."

Mademoiselle didn't know what to think.

"The princess Palatine will propose the affair to Monsieur,"
Madame de Choisy said, "and at the same time she'll propose the
cardinal's return. Monsieur will consent to the latter because he'll
be so overjoyed about the other."

"I told her," Mademoiselle records, "that I doubted it; that I
knew the oath Monsieur had taken against the cardinal's return,
and how hostile he always was to me whenever there was a question of my being established."

"Monsieur would be crazy not to agree to the cardinal's return
on this condition," Madame de Choisy said. "And even if he
didn't agree, the princess Palatine would have such a personal advantage from the marriage that she would tell the cardinal the
marriage was necessary from *his* point of view, and he'd believe
her."

Mademoiselle said she didn't believe a word of it.

She seems to have said nothing to Monsieur. The whole thing
probably still sounded too preposterous, too unlikely: anything
coming from the cardinal was almost certainly a trick. Besides,
there was another suspicious sign. Several times, during the next
week or two, Mademoiselle and her new, pretty friend Madame
de Frontenac, a young lady living apart from her husband, went
riding with the king; he seemed delighted to be with them; then
suddenly he rode with them no more. The queen-regent had noticed that he was getting too fond of Madame de Frontenac—
such was the explanation given Mademoiselle. But she suspected
something else: "I think that the most likely reason for her prohibition was her fear lest the king become too attached to *me;*

lest with time he come to love me—either as a result of what
Madame de Frontenac might tell him about me or merely from
his own constant seeing of me; and lest, coming to love me, he
realize that I was the best marriage partner he could possibly be
offered, except the infanta of Spain." Despite the prohibition,
Mademoiselle and Madame de Frontenac set out boldly one day
on their horses to where they knew the king was riding; he came
up to neither of them, and whenever he passed them he looked
the other way. "I confess I was displeased," Mademoiselle says.
"I had put more hope in the way the king had been behaving
with me, and in the pleasure he had been taking in my company,
than in the negotiations of Madame de Choisy: that way of becoming queen was more to my taste than the other."

Surely those are notable words in the story of Mademoiselle:
of all the candidates for her hand, her king is the only one she
has hoped might love her!

Now the king came of age. In his first appearance before Parlement the thirteen-year-old monarch named his mother, hitherto
regent, his chief councilor; and, bowing to the Frondeurs, he
declared Mazarin banished forever from the kingdom.

With the king's minority had expired also Monsieur's appointment as lieutenant-general of the realm; he no longer had the
slightest authority over the king's movements; and the court left
Paris for Fontainebleau, and left Fontainebleau for a trip in the
direction of Bourges and Poitiers. Mademoiselle, for the first time
in her life, was not invited. Still, the princess Palatine kept assuring her that her queenship was a certainty; and now the princess
sent word by Madame de Choisy that she needed money—200,-
000 écus in advance. Mademoiselle stalled: were the "negotiators"
trying to dupe her?

A few days later she thought she had her answer. Mazarin,
"banished forever," was back in France! He recrossed the border
about Christmas, 1651, with an army of six thousand men—foreign mercenaries in his own personal pay, so vast was the fortune

he had amassed while in office. He joined the court at Poitiers. The court's departure from Paris had been an escape from the Frondeurs; its trip to Poitiers had been a rendezvous with Mazarin. The king's proclamation of Mazarin's banishment had been one of the cardinal's tricks: the cardinal had hoodwinked the Frondeurs.

Now the cardinal and the court gathered their troops about them and moved to Blois; Condé gathered *his* army near Bordeaux: the new civil war, the *Fronde des princes*—far graver than the war of Paris—was on for fair. The rumor that Mademoiselle was being considered as queen of France began to spread; Condé let her know he hoped it was true. Mademoiselle knew how to answer the princess Palatine. "You may tell the princess Palatine," she said to Madame de Choisy, "that I thank her for her offers of service; that if she thinks she has some commitment with me, I beg her to understand that I want none with her; and that as for the 200,000 écus—I'll spend them helping Monsieur make war on cardinal Mazarin: that will be my best way of becoming queen of France."

Such was Mademoiselle's reasoning. And now, in the two great public adventures of her life, she acted in accordance with it. She had attained, in her opinion, that "advantageous situation" in which she could "do her duty"—her duty, of course, to Monsieur —and at the same time "achieve her revenge." Alas! "In taking this kind of revenge," Mademoiselle was to write later in sober discovery, "one takes a fierce revenge against oneself." But first came six months of glory.

The first of Mademoiselle's great adventures was in March.

Thirty-five miles from Blois, where the king and cardinal had established headquarters, stood the walled city of Orléans, chief jewel of the *apanage* of Monsieur, Gaston d'Orléans—the city to which, of all cities, he owed his protection. It was filled with grain and valuables, stored there for safekeeping by the nobility from miles around, for the royal army had been pillaging the countryside. To the governor of Orléans the king sent a message from Blois, asking that the city declare itself for him and the cardinal by admitting them peaceably. The governor respectfully declined; the king must not ask Orléans to be disloyal to Monsieur, its duke; and yet, to show his respect for the king, the governor refused, at the same time, to admit within the city a company of Monsieur's musketeers, who were encamped without. By some of the Orléanais the governor was suspected of being a Mazarine—as any supporter of the cardinal was now called—awaiting only the right opportunity to deliver the city to the cardinal's troops. The factions of the population loyal to Monsieur sent to him in Paris, begging him, as their patron, to come down and take charge.

But Monsieur didn't want to. Monsieur's enthusiasm for his cause was running out, as it always did. He grew nervous and irritable when he heard the word "duty": why couldn't people leave him alone? How happy were the people in this world who didn't meddle in politics! And he expressed the wish that he could go and live quietly in—of all places, at the moment—Blois! The Orléanais, impatient, sent further word: If Monsieur couldn't come himself, wouldn't he send Mademoiselle? And from Monsieur's followers in Paris there came a veritable chorus of urging: Mademoiselle must go to Orléans! "It's the finest thing you could do," they told her. "Condé will thank you."

But what made Mademoiselle happy to go was an order—an order from Monsieur: "I received it as I always received orders from Monsieur—with joy in being obedient. This time I felt a special joy—I felt that this was a glorious enterprise."

It was *"le jour de la Notre-Dame de mars"*—March 25, the feast of the Annunciation; after praying at Notre Dame, Mademoiselle set out. "Don't let the royal army cross the Loire," were Monsieur's farewell words to his daughter; and he showed his

bonté naturelle—a quality Mademoiselle was obstinately persuaded he possessed—by standing at a window of the Luxembourg to watch her departure. Crowds of Parisians in the streets
blessed her as she passed, her gray traveling costume trimmed
with gold. Madame de Fiesque went with her—her governess;
and Madame de Fiesque's daughter, and Madame de Frontenac;
it was a well-chaperoned military expedition. And of course they
were accompanied by Mademoiselle's secretary Préfontaine, servants, and a body of soldiery. The first night they spent in Arpa-
jon; the next day, beyond Étampes, they were met by five hundred
of Monsieur's musketeers sent from Orléans to greet them; and on
the plains of Beauce Mademoiselle transferred to horseback because the weather was so fine. At Toury there was a council of
war; Mademoiselle smiled at the word, but Monsieur de Nemours
told her she must accustom herself to military language.

The timid governor of Orléans, the marquis de Sourdis, sent
her an anguished message which reached her early on the morning of March 27 at Artenay, twelve miles from the city. Was
Mademoiselle determined to embarrass him? Wouldn't she, instead of presenting herself at the city gate, lie low somewhere in
the environs, pretending to be ill? Then, when the king or his
representatives arrived before Orléans, the governor could with
justice claim that he had forbidden Monsieur's emissary to enter;
the king would almost certainly respect such proof of neutrality,
and pass on; and then Mademoiselle would be admitted quietly.

Mademoiselle was disdainful. "I'll go straight to Orléans," she
announced to those around her. "The sight of a person of my
quality exposing himself to danger always does wonders for a
population: the people almost always give way willy-nilly to anyone with a little resolution. If the Mazarin party is too strong, I'll
hold on as long as I can; if I finally have to leave, I'll go to the
army—there's no safety for me anywhere else. At the very worst
I'll fall into the hands of people who speak my language, who
know me, who'll show me even in captivity the respect due my

birth. The occasion will probably inspire them with veneration for me. Surely there is no reason for me to be *ashamed* of having so exposed myself in Monsieur's service!"

At eleven o'clock that same morning Mademoiselle arrived before the great gate of Orléans, the Porte Bannier, with only her personal escort—she had left the musketeers a quarter of a league away. The gate was closed and barricaded. She waited there three hours in her carriage. Then she rested for a while at a nearby inn called the Port de Salut; and then, the weather being fine, she set out for a stroll. Someone handed her a jar of preserves—all the timid governor dared send her as a token of respect. The ramparts were crowded with Orléanais who cheered at the sight of her: "Long live the king and the princes! Down with Mazarin!"

"Go to the Hotel de Ville! Tell them to open the gate!" Mademoiselle called back.

Her walk took her to another gate: here the captain of the guard drew his men to attention in her honor, but when she called to him to open, he gestured that he had no keys. "Break down the door!" Mademoiselle cried. "Obey me, not the officials—I'm the daughter of their master!" She grew furious and threatened him, but he replied only with low bows.

But Mademoiselle had reason to know she would succeed. Before she had left Paris, the marquis de Vilène, the cleverest astrologer alive, had told her that anything she undertook between twelve o'clock noon on Wednesday, March 27, and the following Friday, would turn out well: "During that period I even predict you'll do something extraordinary," he had said. It was now well after noon on Wednesday, March 27. Standing beside the moat of Orléans, Mademoiselle turned to her governess and the other ladies—her "brigadier-generals," as she called them: "Something extraordinary is going to happen to me today. I have the prediction in my pocket. I'll break down the gates, or I'll climb the walls." They laughed at her: there was no sign of anything extraordinary.

But Mademoiselle approached some of the boatmen on the Loire. They crowded around her; she harangued them, appealed to their loyalty: would they row her around the ramparts to the Porte de la Faux, one of the water gates? They suggested something more practical: Why not break down the Porte Brûlée, which was nearer and gave on a quay? If she wanted, they said, they'd get to work. "Hurry!" she ordered. She tipped them well, and they set out at once. Now she sent away even the few armed guards who were with her: the Orléanais must see how utterly she trusted them. To watch and encourage her boatmen, she "clambered like a cat" up a nearby earthwork, pulling herself up on thorns and brambles. For a time she stood there—"it was great fun"—looking down at the battering boatmen and laughing at her ladies, who were wringing their hands at her rashness. But though she was in full view of hundreds, no one fired on her, and when she clambered down, other boatman made a two-boat bridge for her to cross the moat. From the second boat they raised a ladder against the wall of the quay, and once again, she climbed: "The ladder was quite high; I didn't count the number of rungs; I only remember that one of them was broken, which made it rather hard." Her presence encouraged the batterers to new efforts; as they weakened the gate from without, loyal bourgeois helped them from within; the city guards stood by, doing nothing to help, but nothing to hinder either; finally two planks in the Porte Brûlée gave way. There was so much dirt and debris around, and by now so much shouting and excitement, that one of Mademoiselle's footmen gathered her up in his arms and thrust her through the breach between the iron bars. "No sooner was my head inside the city than the drums began to beat." And with a regal gesture Mademoiselle extended her hand to the captain of the guard, who was waiting within. "You will be proud to be able to boast," she told him graciously, "that you admitted me."

"The cries of *'vive le Roi, les princes! et point de Mazarin!'* redoubled; two men picked me up and put me on a wooden chair. I don't know whether I was on the seat or on the arms, I was so beside myself with joy to be where I was; everybody was kissing my hands; and I was dying with laughter to find myself in so comical a situation. After they carried me in triumph a little way I told them that I was able to walk, and asked them to put me down; they did so, and I waited for the other ladies, who arrived a few minutes later, as dirty and happy as I. A company of the city guard marched before me, clearing the way and beating their drums; halfway between the gate and the house where I was to stay, I met the governor. He was rather embarrassed (others have been, for much less) and with him were his staff. They greeted me. . . ."

With the dignitaries Mademoiselle was less gracious, at first, than with the captain of the guard; she disdainfully absolved them of any disloyalty toward the court: she had "grown impatient at the Porte Bannier and had found the Porte Brûlée open," she said; no one could ever reproach them with having connived in her entry; besides, from now on they were not responsible for Orléans —she was. "When people of my quality are in a place, they are its mistresses: and I have a particular right to be mistress here— Orléans belongs to Monsieur." Then, thinking them sufficiently rebuked, she chatted with them as though nothing had happened. Her first thought, on arriving at her lodging, was to send Monsieur a despatch.

She had come to Orléans just in time. The next day, Holy Thursday, representatives of the court arrived outside the walls. But they found Monsieur's musketeers garrisoning the now impregnable city; from the ramparts the citizens greeted them derisively: *"Vive le Roi! les princes! et point de Mazarin!"* As the court emissaries retired from the scene, the guards on the bridge that crossed the Loire fired equally derisive salvos: Monsieur's parting words to Mademoiselle had been obeyed.

On Holy Saturday came Mademoiselle's reward:

My Daughter:
You can imagine my joy in the action you
have just performed: you have saved my Orléans and insured the
safety of Paris. It is an occasion of public rejoicing, and all declare your deed worthy of the granddaughter of Henri IV. I never
doubted the stoutness of your heart, but by this action you have
shown that you have an even better head. I say it again: I am
delighted by what you have done—delighted as much for your
sake as for my own. From now on, have your secretary write me
important things in his own hand, for the reason that you know.

Gaston

It wasn't an Easter that Mademoiselle ever forgot, or a letter
she ever threw away. "The 'reason' Monsieur mentions," she
explains, "is that my handwriting is so wretched that almost no
one can read it." Condé, too, sent her a letter of thanks.

In the Orléans city hall Mademoiselle made her first public
speech—it was one of the few moments of *embarras* she ever
experienced—and then for several weeks she administered the
city and served as mascot-patroness of Monsieur's and Condé's
troops in the surrounding district.

In May she returned to Paris. For a league outside the city
she found the road lined with carriages: half Paris, including
Condé, Beaufort, and other noble Frondeurs, had come out to
greet her; but Monsieur she found in bed in the Luxembourg.
He scolded her for having come back so soon. "I tried to tell
him about my trip, but he said he was ill; he couldn't bear to hear
anything about business—some other time, he said." In the streets,
though, people hailed her so enthusiastically that she was
"ashamed." The Cours-la-Reine was so full of those come to see
her that she could scarcely find room herself. Mademoiselle was
queen of Paris. Of all the people who crowded around her only
one spoke sourly—the queen of England, still smarting from
Mademoiselle's rejection of Charles. Henrietta-Maria said sarcastically that Mademoiselle resembled the other savior of Orléans,

Joan of Arc: like Joan, she had begun her work by chasing the English. But then no one expected poor Henrietta-Maria, widowed by Parliament, to be much of a *Frondeuse*.

All during the Orléans campaign, *mon petit mari,* still in the careful guard of the cardinal and the queen, had never been very far away from the army that Mademoiselle had been heartening against his own.

And then, in Paris, on July 2, came Mademoiselle's second great adventure: an adventure that has put her among the most picturesque, the most eccentric, heroines of French history, an adventure that was to make Anne of Austria want to "strangle" her, an adventure that was to determine the course of her life for years to come.

Throughout the early summer, units of the rival armies had been fighting many engagements, and things were not going too brilliantly for the Frondeurs. Turenne, Mazarin's general, was as clever a fighter as Condé; and the cardinal's entourage was less plagued by internal dissension than the Frondeurs. Condé was overweening and Monsieur shifting as the sands; the duc de Beaufort, the cardinal de Retz, and the others were constantly quarreling; and Parlement and the bourgeois were tiring of a war in which they seemed to have been forgotten by their betters, their supposed defenders. Everyone accused everyone else of seeking a truce; Monsieur, especially, was constantly suspected of being in secret touch with the enemy. But when Mademoiselle worried, Condé rallied her. He would see her established; everything looked more favorable than ever. "I promise you," he swore, "that no peace treaty will be signed in which you are not included"—included, he meant, as queen. The stronger the Frondeurs, the better the peace. If Mademoiselle had wavered for a moment—as many another Frondeur was now beginning to waver —Condé's words kept her to the belief she had acted on at

Orléans, the belief she had expressed to Madame de Choisy: that helping Monsieur make war on cardinal Mazarin was the best way of becoming queen of France.

In June there was a Mazarinist victory at Étampes, and Condé withdrew his soldiers almost to Paris—to Saint-Cloud. Then even Saint-Cloud had to be abandoned, and throughout the night of July 1 Mademoiselle heard drums and trumpets almost under her windows: the municipality of Paris had forbidden Condé's army to enter the city, but its new position was just outside the walls. Mademoiselle had intended to "take medicine" the next morning, but that night she told Préfontaine she had decided against it: "I have a feeling," she told him, "that I'm on the point of doing something unexpected, as at Orléans." And indeed, at six there came a knocking on her door and it was the comte de Fiesque, who told her that Condé had sent a message to Monsieur that he had been attacked at dawn between Montmartre and La Chapelle, that he had tried to enter the city by the Porte Saint-Denis to report to Monsieur, but that he had been refused admittance. Now he was continuing to fight; he begged Monsieur to get on a horse and come to his aid: what he wanted, among other things, was permission to withdraw his army into the city should it be too hard-pressed. But Monsieur was ill again. And Condé, suspecting that he might be, had sent further word: he hoped that Mademoiselle, at least, would not fail him.

At the Luxembourg, where she rushed as quickly as she could, Mademoiselle was amazed to find Monsieur up and dressed. "I expected to find you in bed!" she cried. "The comte de Fiesque told me you were ill!"

"I am not ill enough to be in bed," Monsieur replied. "But I am too ill to go out."

Mademoiselle burst into tears of shame; she begged him to get either onto a horse or into bed; but Monsieur shrugged; he seemed carefree, almost jaunty, indifferent to Condé's fate: Mademoiselle told him to his face that his behavior was comprehensible only if he had signed a treaty with the court. But other gentlemen arrived, more concerned than he, and made him write a letter to the city council. They told him how to word it, and they made him send Mademoiselle to deliver it to the Hôtel de Ville.

She set off at once—escorted, of course, by Madame de Fiesque and other ladies. In the streets there were signs of crisis: worried citizens recognized Mademoiselle and begged her for orders; the marquis de Jarzé, wounded and bleeding, passed them on his way to Monsieur with another message from Condé. At the Hôtel de Ville the clerk of the council read Monsieur's letter aloud. The council members readily agreed to send some municipal troops *out* of the city to help Condé, but they still demurred at opening the city gates to let his army *in*. After all, many of his soldiers were Spaniards: his enlistment of France's foreign enemies to help him win France's civil war gave the council pause.

"But if the enemy defeats the prince, they'll give Paris no quarter!" Mademoiselle cried. (By "the enemy" she meant, of course, the army Turenne was leading for the king and cardinal.) "And how can we better serve the king than by preserving his capital, the greatest, most beautiful city in his kingdom?"

"You know perfectly well, Mademoiselle," chided the governor of Paris, "that if your troops hadn't approached the city, the royal troops wouldn't have come here either."

"You're splitting hairs while the prince is in peril outside the walls! What a disgrace if Paris were to let him perish for want of help! You can give him help, so do it, and quickly!"

The council withdrew to deliberate. Mademoiselle went to a window and prayed: from a nearby church came the sounds of Mass, but "I didn't hear the whole Mass, since I kept trying to hurry the councilors and get their answer." The bourgeois were intolerably slow, but in the end her city did not fail her: the prince's army, the council decided, Spaniards and all, could enter Paris if it wished.

Mademoiselle despatched a messenger to take the news to

Condé, and hurried on herself to deliver the council's order to the captain of the guard at the Porte Saint-Antoine, outside which the fighting was now furious. As she approached, she came upon pitiful sights—wounded Frondeurs. The duc de la Rochefoucauld, shot through the head, blood pouring down his face and into his mouth, sat blinded on his horse, his son weeping beside him. Her friend Guitaut, pale as death from a musket wound through the body, was held on his horse by an aide: "Are you done for?" Mademoiselle called to him—*"Mourras-tu?"* He shook his head. Then her fat friend Vallon, battered and unable to walk; the handsome marquis de la Roche-Gaillard, mortally wounded in the head, carried on a ladder—for him, poor Protestant that he was, eternal damnation was only a few minutes away. They and other wounded had been admitted for humanity's sake; now, at the gate, Mademoiselle delivered the council's order admitting all. She took shelter in a house next to the Bastille; Condé, fighting just outside, was told she was there and rushed in to see her, "dust two fingers thick on his face, his hair tangled, his clothes bloody and torn even though he was unwounded, his naked sword in his hand." Even at such a moment the commander was observant of etiquette: entering Mademoiselle's presence, he handed his sword to her equerry. And then he burst into tears: how many friends he had seen fall! She must stay where she was, he said, controlling himself; her authority would be needed. She begged him to bring his army into the city at once. "What!" he cried. "Retreat from the Mazarines at noon?" And he dashed out.

For hours she stayed in the house next to the Bastille, watching the dead and wounded being brought in over the lowered drawbridge of the Porte Saint-Antoine: "I began to realize the truth of what soldiers say, that one feels less pity for the last than for the first, especially for those one doesn't know." The Parisian troops promised by the city council came; she posted them where the Mazarines could see that Parisians were helping defend themselves. Officers asked her for orders: Where should the wounded be sent? She felt she was at Orléans again, in command. Except that this time she was worried, uneasy: Monsieur's behavior of the morning had put her into a kind of despair. The day was frightfully hot; the combat outside the gate in the Faubourg Saint-Antoine was a desperate one: Condé, with five thousand troops, was resisting, "like a demon," Turenne with twelve thousand. The air was full of dust and noise.

As Mademoiselle waited, she was handed a message from the governor of the Bastille, Monsieur de la Louvière, who had been appointed to his post by the Frondeurs: if Monsieur would give him a written order, he said, he was at his or Mademoiselle's disposal. Mademoiselle sent the message to Monsieur at the Luxembourg: his signed order came back, and with it word that he would be with her later in the day.

During the afternoon, Condé came in again; he looked better, gay and laughing—he throve on fierce fighting. ("I didn't see one Condè," Turenne said of his antagonist that day, "I saw more than a dozen.") He thanked and praised Mademoiselle for her help, and she begged him to say nothing to Monsieur about Monsieur's cowardice. "I can only thank him," Condé said gallantly; "had it been otherwise, I shouldn't be here with you now." Mademoiselle laughed, then begged him not to joke: her father's behavior lay heavy on her heart. While he was there, Monsieur arrived and embraced Condé "as cheerfully as though he had done everything he could for him"; he complimented the prince on his bravery and lamented the loss of so many Frondeurs. When evening came, they agreed, the army would withdraw into the city. Monsieur went away: it had occurred to him that he might thank the gentlemen in the Hôtel de Ville. Condé returned to the fight.

Now Mademoiselle entered the Bastille, just next door. She had never been there before, though she knew—who didn't know?—people who had. Accompanied by Monsieur de la Louvière, she climbed to the top of the tower. Through a spyglass, she surveyed the view. On the heights of Charonne, she saw, many people were gathered, watching the fight. There were coaches there: it was probably the king, she surmised. Down below, she saw the opposing armies. As she watched, she saw an enemy cavalry maneuver beginning—a pincers movement, as she diagnosed it, that would, if it were allowed to continue, cut off Condé's withdrawal to the city. Impulsively, Mademoiselle gave an amazing order. Standing near her, atop the Bastille, were cannon. They were pointed inward, toward the city. They had always been pointed inward: it was what they were there for, to quelch any insurrection of the Paris *canaille*. Now Mademoiselle ordered that they be turned around—turned outward, toward Turenne's army—and loaded. The moment the pincers movement developed beyond a certain point, she ordered, the cannon were to be fired. And hastily descending from the tower of the Bastille, she sent word to Condé, by a page, of what she had seen. It confirmed what *he* had just seen from the top of the nearby tower of the abbey of Saint-Antoine; and he gave the order to retreat.

Back in the house where she had spent most of the day, Mademoiselle watched the retreating soldiers stream past into the city. All day they had been grateful to her; it was thanks to her, the word had gone round, that they could withdraw if hard-pressed. At Condé's suggestion, she had sent them wine. Now as they passed her window, they called out, "We've drunk your health! Health to our savior!" And as Mademoiselle sat there, accepting their homage, she heard the cannon of the Bastille roar. They roared several times. Turenne had pressed too far; and on Mademoiselle's order the cannon of the Bastille, symbol of the king's despotic power, had fired on the king's troops.

The king was, as Mademoiselle had surmised, on the heights of Charonne. Mazarin, too, and many another. Mazarin was delighted, at first, when the Bastille cannon went off. "Good! They're firing on the enemy!" Then they went off again.

"They seem to be firing on us!" someone cried.

"Perhaps it's just a salute to Mademoiselle," someone else suggested; runners had told the cardinal and his entourage all about Mademoiselle's mission to the Porte Saint-Antoine.

The maréchal de Villeroy, who knew Mademoiselle well, said, "If Mademoiselle is there, what's happened is that she has fired on us."

The king, the cardinal, the maréchal, and all the others on the heights of Charonne saw the balls from the Bastille cannon carry away a whole file of the royal cavalry—Paul Mancini, Mazarin's own nephew, was mortally wounded. They saw all of Condé's troops move safely into the city and the drawbridge outside the Porte Saint-Antoine open behind them. The cardinal summed up the situation in a few words. "Those cannon," he said, "have killed Mademoiselle's husband."

For Mademoiselle had been wrong. The joke was on Mademoiselle. The best way of becoming queen of France, of winning the one of her possible husbands she had hoped might love her, had not been to "help Monsieur make war on cardinal Mazarin" —not, at least, to help him to the extent of turning the cannon of the Bastille on the king. The confusions and contradictions of the Fronde were so incredible, the conflicts of loyalty and the reversals of values so chaotic, that even that *might* have been true. But it wasn't. "The stronger the Frondeurs, the stronger the peace"—perhaps so, but even for the Fronde pride and passion had curdled too hopelessly into bravado. Even in the Fronde, cannon salvos were not "sweet little loverlike things." In such matters, one might almost say, poor Mademoiselle was even more confused than the Fronde itself.

And it seems that she had been wrong about the cardinal, as well. He had been insincere about the emperor, perhaps; perhaps he had never had any intention of letting her marry him—or, more likely, he had let his intentions be guided by politics. But as for *mon petit mari*. . . . Those fantastic-seeming negotiations by Bartet, by Madame de Choisy, by the princess Palatine—what was fantastic about them, to one as devious as the cardinal? Why shouldn't the princess Palatine make some écus on the transaction? Why shouldn't she and Madame de Choisy, as the cardinal's negotiators, share in Mademoiselle's "fortune"? That was the way things were often done—even in France, and especially in Italy, where the cardinal came from. And as for the more direct offer, the one conveyed by Mademoiselle de Neuillant, which Mademoiselle had found so preposterous: isn't it significant, perhaps, that that little episode should be omitted entirely by Mademoiselle from her memoirs, otherwise so detailed about her marriage projects? Could it be that she failed to set it down because she came to believe that it *was* what it had pretended to be, that it was so very definitely the beginning of her big mistake? No one, certainly, can blame Mademoiselle for having been skeptical. But, equally certain, the cardinal had indeed considered making her queen. He would have had to persuade the king and his mother to accept Mademoiselle, older than the one, in disfavor with the other. But Mazarin had persuaded Anne of Austria to accept many things, and this would have been just one more—a device to unite the two factions of France. The country was being devastated by the Fronde: Mademoiselle as queen would be better than Condé or Monsieur as king or co-king.

That evening, at a party of Frondeurs in the Luxembourg, weary after her strenuous day, Mademoiselle knew nothing of the cardinal's words on the heights of Charonne. She was listening to other words. "The prince paid me a thousand compliments, and told Monsieur that I had done so well that I deserved his praise. Monsieur thereupon said that he was satisfied with me, but his words lacked the affection I felt they should have. I attributed it to the remorse he must be feeling that I had done what *he* should have done. So on that occasion his indifference, which I always find so hard to endure, was actually a consolation: I wished that his feelings might always be as proper as they were then.

"When I reflected, that evening, and whenever it has occurred to me since, that I had saved the army, I confess that I felt and feel great satisfaction; yet at the same time it amazed me to think that I had been instrumental in bringing Spanish cannon and Spanish flags into Paris. The joy that I felt at having acted on this occasion in a manner so out of the ordinary—the whole adventure was something that had perhaps never before befallen a woman of my rank—kept me, that evening, from having the thoughts I might have had. But that night I slept not at all: all those poor dead men were too present in my mind."

9

I T TOOK MADEMOISELLE a few months to discover how very dead she had killed *mon petit mari*.

But almost from the very moment of the retreat from the Faubourg Saint-Antoine it was clear that the Fronde was doomed. Only two days later, in a ceremony at the Hôtel de Ville, designed to proclaim Mazarin an enemy of the state and Monsieur once again lieutenant-general of the realm and sole spokesman for the king, the noble Frondeurs were so arrogant that Parlement and the municipal councilors demurred; the nobles were exasperated; their troops began to fire; councilors and other citizens were massacred and part of the Hôtel de Ville went up in flames. Indeed, the entire tragedy may have been planned from the beginning; people whispered that it had been, that it was Condé's gesture of disdain for Parlement. In any case, the massacre at the Hôtel de Ville was, as Mademoiselle puts it, "the knockout blow to the Fronde." The party fell rapidly to pieces. The leading Frondeurs began challenging each other to duels; Monsieur began sending people to the Bastille; the troops admitted into the city abused the populace. Paris was sick of the Fronde. Much of France was literally sick of it: all over the country fields, forests, and villages lay waste; hosts of unburied corpses befouled the air.

Two years before, a son had been born to Monsieur and Madame. His arrival had been the cause of family rejoicing, for he would inherit Monsieur's *apanage*—a great benefit to his mother and sisters, who would otherwise have to see everything—the pension, the duchies of Chartres and Orléans, the county of Blois, the governorship of Languedoc that had been a present from the regent —all revert to the crown. Now, as the Fronde ended, the boy died: it was God's punishment on Monsieur, people murmured, for the treasonable war he had been waging. The court sent a cold message saying that the infant must not be buried in the royal vault at Saint-Denis.

Citizens began to wear bits of paper in their hats—a sign that they were for the court—instead of wisps of straw, the emblem of the Fronde.

Now, with everything falling apart, the duc de Lorraine—he was Madame's brother from Nancy, come to Paris with his troops to help the Frondeurs—tried to revive Mademoiselle's interest in an old marriage project, the one with the emperor's brother, the archduke, who still stood a chance of becoming ruler of Flanders. "You'd be the happiest person in the world," he said. "He'd take no part in anything. He'd spend all day long with the Jesuits, or writing poetry and setting it to music; you'd have full charge of everything. I know the Spaniards would trust you completely, and the only trouble you'd have with the archduke is that he'd make you listen to operas. Operas bore you, I know; actually, they're quite pleasant. The archduke's the nicest man in the world: seriously, wouldn't you care for him?"

Mademoiselle sighed. "It's just that getting married is such a tremendous business; it's impossible to hear it talked about so often without feeling badly."

Then, in October, came the news: Mazarin, "for the good of France," was voluntarily exiling himself, going once again to Cologne, so that it could no longer be said that his presence was the cause of dissension between the French king and his subjects.

Parlement lost no time in inviting the king to return to Paris. Condé and the duc de Lorraine left the city. They took their troops with them; they hoped to return when the men had been put in winter quarters, they told Mademoiselle, and then there would be "dances and plays and all kinds of pleasures to reward us after everything we've been through." But it was a hollow hope. "I have never seen anything more beautiful than the *grande allée* of the Tuileries that day, full of finely dressed people," Mademoiselle says. "Everyone was wearing new clothes, because that day marked the end of mourning for my half brother; besides, it was the season for new winter costumes. The prince's was charming, black on gray, with accessories of flame-color, gold, and silver, and a blue scarf *à l'allemande,* under an unbuttoned jacket. I hated to see them go: I confess I wept when I said good-by. After their departure, it was as though there were no one left around us, and everything was gloomy, especially since the rumor was that the king would soon be back and we'd all be sent away."

It was indeed the end.

One morning while Mademoiselle's hair was being done, she received a visit from Sanguin, the king's maître d'hôtel. "Here is a letter," he said, "that the king has ordered me to give you." And in the letter *mon petit mari* said that he was returning to Paris; and that since he had no other lodging to offer his brother, the duc d'Anjou, except the Tuileries, Mademoiselle would kindly move out not later than the following afternoon. Until she found another home, she could stay "with the duc de Damville, in the rue de Tournon"—Damville was Monsieur's first equerry.

The reason for the order was clear enough. The king was returning not to the Palais-Royal, which Richelieu had built for himself and bequeathed to the crown, in which Anne of Austria, her two sons and Mazarin had lived during the regency, and through which the Paris *canaille* had trooped one night to see the sleeping royal child; the king was returning to the Louvre, ancient palace of the kings of France. It was unthinkable that Mademoiselle, *grande Frondeuse,* should continue to live in the Tuileries, connected with the Louvre by a corridor. The house of the duc de Damville was only a step from the Luxembourg; apparently, for some reason of his own, disquieting to speculate about, the king wanted rebel father and rebel daughter close together. Perhaps they would be easier to arrest that way.

Mademoiselle went to Monsieur in the Luxembourg. "What shall I do?"

"Obey."

She said she hoped he would remain true to Condé, who had risked so much, and who was still defiant. But Monsieur refused to discuss anything with her. She had hopelessly compromised herself with the court, he said bitterly, by her crazy escapades at Orléans and at the Porte Saint-Antoine, and he wanted nothing more to do with her. "You were only too delighted to be a heroine," he said sarcastically. "Whatever happens, you can always console yourself by thinking of the praise you got."

Even from Monsieur, this was too much. She reminded him passionately that she had gone to Orléans and to the Porte Saint-Antoine at his order—not his *written* order, it was true, though to Orléans, at least, he had written her his praise. Nor would she refuse to do as much for him again: she would consider it her duty. "I should never forgive myself if I failed to obey you and serve you. If you are in disfavor it's right for me to share your misfortune. It is better to have done what I have done than to suffer for having done nothing. I don't know what it is to be a 'heroine': my birth made me incapable of doing anything that isn't grand and exalted. You can call it what you like; I call it pursuing my own bent, traveling my own path: I wasn't born to follow others." And she asked her father to let her move into the Luxembourg until they both learned what the future would bring.

"I have no room for you."

"But there isn't a soul here who wouldn't give up his room for me. No one has a better right to live here than I, I think."

"I need everybody who is here. Nobody is to move out."

"Then I'll move into Condé's house—it's empty." (It was also next door.)

"I forbid you to."

"Then where do you want me to go?"

"Wherever you like."

And Monsieur left her.

Out of the Tuileries, therefore, "the most agreeable dwelling in the world, and one I love," the palace that had always been her home, Mademoiselle moved immediately. Not to the house of the duc de Damville—if she couldn't be in the Luxembourg or at Condé's, she refused to come near—but to the house of *la comtesse de Fiesque la jeune*—daughter-in-law of her governess. Every day at dinner the king's twenty-four violins came and played for her in her refuge. With a group of her friends she watched from Madame de Choisy's window the king's triumphant re-entry into his capital on October 21. The city was illuminated; a peddler was selling festive lanterns to be hung in windows. "*Lanternes à la royale!*" he called.

"Haven't you any *à la Fronde?*" cried Mademoiselle.

Some people were saying that Mademoiselle would be exiled, others that she would be imprisoned. Under the circumstances her hostess's mother didn't like having her in the house. "You'll have to make up your mind what to do with yourself," she said. "I'm old and unwell. I don't want any trouble with the court. Good-by. I'm going to stay in my room till you leave. Then if anybody asks me about you, I can truthfully say I don't know a thing."

The day after his return, the king proclaimed from the Louvre that in the future Parlement was to have nothing to say in affairs of state, and that various individuals were to leave Paris immediately; among them were the duc de Beaufort, the fishwives' darling, who had recently killed his brother-in-law (a fellow Frondeur) in a duel, and Broussel, whose crime consisted of being one of the original parliamentarians arrested by Mazarin. The wind was blowing not from Bordeaux, but from Cologne. The cannon atop the Bastille had been turned around again. For the next hundred years even the fishwives would do less shouting.

The absence of Monsieur's and Mademoiselle's names from that first list of exiles, the failure of the court to send them any message, could mean anything—possibly arrest; at the very least it was an invitation to self-banishment. Monsieur, hearing that the king was about to "request" him to leave Paris, lost no time. He set out for his château at nearby Limours; his wife, expecting another child, he left behind, and their daughters with her. He sent no farewell to Mademoiselle—only the order that she not follow him to Limours. (It was where she had had her first happy reunion with him, when she was five and a half.) If she did, he would send her away. She should go to one of her own estates.

Mademoiselle, although she found it hard "to be abandoned in misfortune by the person in whose cause she had suffered it," and although she "couldn't put the refusal of a shelter in the Luxembourg out of her mind," was obedient as always. Besides, her friends at court were sending her notes warning her of arrest. With Madame de Frontenac, with Préfontaine the faithful secretary, with her maître d'hôtel Guérinière, she climbed into a plain borrowed coach; and followed by footmen, maids, and two ladies in waiting, they rolled out of Paris. Mademoiselle's house in suburban Bois-le-Vicomte, once so gaily promised by Madame de Choisy to Bartet in exchange for the queenship, was now uninhabitable, for Mademoiselle had turned it into a hospital for the soldiers wounded at the Porte Saint-Antoine; besides, she sensed that the court would want her farther away. The best refuge would be her duchy of Saint-Fargeau, where she had never been, a hundred miles from Paris in the direction of Burgundy. It was a three-day coach trip at the quickest, and household goods would have to follow heaven knew how much later on muleback. "Saint-Fargeau is a place so little known," says Mademoiselle, "that everyone would think me in another world."

So that was why Mademoiselle, handsome, royal, and rich, found herself at twenty-five unmarried, living in exile, her only establishment a remote château—"everything around it so wild that there weren't even any greens to put in the soup"—where she had nothing better to do, at first, than repair the buildings, land-scape-garden, do needlework, read, and write her memoirs. She was about equidistant from Paris and from Monsieur: the king had "permitted" him to move to Blois—farther from the capital than Limours.

Mon petit mari, when he learned where Mademoiselle was be-taking herself, wrote her a letter, which she received en route. He was happy to tell his first cousin, he said, that her choice of resi-dence was completely agreeable to him; and he assured her that she could *remain* there in perfect safety. The italics are ours: Made-moiselle had no need of them. "I replied," she says, "thanking him for the honor he paid me in thinking of me. I was happy that my stay at Saint-Fargeau was agreeable to him; that as for my per-sonal safety I had never any doubt of it—I had nothing on my conscience to cause me any worry in that regard; that my conduct and my intentions had always testified to my fidelity in His Maj-esty's service; that I feared nothing, that I was incapable of per-forming any action unworthy of the rank to which God had willed me to be born, and of a good Frenchwoman."

To such an extent was Mademoiselle herself one of those of whom she writes in her memoirs: "In my experience in the Fronde I met plenty of people who admitted to being against other peo-ple, but I never met anyone who admitted to being against the king."

Condé, his cause hopelessly lost, but disdainful of repentance or exile at the king's pleasure, accepted Philip IV's offer that he become generalissimo of the Spanish armies—France's arch-enemy in the field. Mademoiselle refused to hear him called a traitor. "The designs of great princes are like the mysteries of the Holy Faith," she writes. "It is not up to us to probe into them: they must be revered, on the assumption that they always advance the welfare and safety of the country."

Mazarin's "exile" was brief: in February thousands of cheering Parisians—the same Parisians who had cheered Mademoiselle—welcomed him back to the Palais-Royal.

Part Two

INTERLUDE:

MADEMOISELLE FINDS HER KING

1652–1660

D ESPITE EVERYTHING, the flight from Paris had been something of a lark.

Under the circumstances, there was relief in departure. "As soon as I had crossed the Marne I forgot Paris; I felt myself ready for anything fate had in store." The ladies wore traveling masks, Mademoiselle baptized herself Madame Dupré, and her companions pretended to be her bourgeois brothers, sisters and cousins; for until the trip received court approval, there was still danger of arrest.

In a village inn near Provins Mademoiselle had an amusing conversation with an itinerant Dominican. Where was she coming from, he wanted to know; and when she said Paris, he asked for the latest news. Mademoiselle and Monsieur had both gone into exile, she said. "I'm sorry to hear it," said the friar. "Monsieur is a good man, and Mademoiselle's a fine girl. She carries a lance as easily as you wear a mask. She has guts. Don't you know her at all?"

"No."

"What, you don't know that she climbed the walls of Orléans and saved Condé's life at the Porte Saint-Antoine?"

"I told him I'd heard about her. He asked if I had ever seen her, and I said No. He began to describe her:

" 'She's a tall, well-built girl—as tall as you, quite good-looking; she has a rather long face and a big nose; I don't know whether

[101]

your face is as much like hers as your figure; if you'd take off your mask, I could see.'

"I told him that I couldn't take it off, that I'd recently had smallpox and was still red. I asked him if he'd ever spoken to Mademoiselle.

" 'A thousand times. I could pick her out of a hundred. I've often been to the Tuileries, where she lived, and I knew her almoner. Besides, she came to Mass with the queen almost every first Sunday of the month at our house in the rue Saint-Honoré.'

"I asked him if she was devout. He said no, that she had once had an urge to be, but had got bored and stopped: she'd gone at it too violently to be able to keep it up. I asked him if he knew her stepmother. He said yes, that she was 'one of those saints one doesn't have any desire to pray to.'

" 'Mademoiselle's stepmother,' he said, 'is a woman who is always in a chair. She never walks a step. She's a sluggard. Mademoiselle herself has spirit. She's a quick mover. There's an enormous difference between them. And you, Madame, who ask me so many questions—who are you?'

"I told him that I was the widow of a gentleman from Sologne, that my house had been looted by the army and that I'd gone to Orléans. I'd had bad luck, I said: I'd left Orléans early the very day Mademoiselle had arrived, and so I'd missed her. I was on my way to Champagne, to stay with my brother and sister-in-law.

" 'If you ever get to Paris,' he said, 'come to see us in our house in the rue Saint-Honoré.'

"I told him I was a Protestant. He wanted to convert me then and there; I told him that it was too serious a matter to treat casually. I hoped to be in Paris during the winter, I said; we'd discuss it then. He told me his name—I've forgotten what it was—and we said good-by. The encounter amused me a good deal. It made me feel optimistic about the rest of my trip."

But Mademoiselle's optimism collapsed when she saw Saint-Fargeau. They arrived at two in the morning, and the desolate

dilapidation of the place where the king had told her she was "free
to remain" brought home to her for the first time everything she
had lost. "The drawbridge was broken, the house was an old place
with doors and windows missing, and weeds were growing knee-
high in the courtyard. It all filled me with aversion and horror.
The wretched bedroom I was taken to had a pole standing in the
middle to prop up the ceiling. I was so frightened and depressed
that I burst into tears. I was grief-stricken to be away from the
court and to have no better place to live in than this." Her hysterical weeping didn't last long, but to spend the rest of the night
at Saint-Fargeau was something she couldn't face. Préfontaine
learned that two leagues further on there was a comfortable house
belonging to one of the estate superintendents; there five of the
party went by horseback, awaking the superintendent at three in
the morning; and there Mademoiselle stayed two days.

"I had a great scare while I was there. During the night I awoke,
and I heard Madame de Frontenac's bed-curtain open—she was
sleeping in a bed close to mine—and a moment later I heard it
close again. 'Are you out of your mind,' I asked her, 'to open your
curtain at this time of night?' 'It's the wind,' she said.

"The room we were in had a low ceiling, there were windows
only on one side, and that night there was no wind whatever. I
was frightened, and said, 'Come into bed with me.' She didn't
have to be asked twice, and as she came I heard her bed-curtain
open again. Neither of us said a word till daybreak. Then she
confessed that she had *seen* her curtain open (I always have a
night light in my bedroom). Her first thought had been to rush
into my bed, but she had controlled herself out of respect and
fear of frightening me. Twice she had seen her curtain open and
close. We discussed what it might mean, but found no answer. A
few days later I learned that the son of my wet nurse, a boy who
had been in my service, had been killed that night with my company of infantry; I knew then that it was he who had come to bid
me farewell. I had Masses said for his soul. . . ."

But Saint-Fargeau had to be faced again sooner or later, and on second view, by daylight, it seemed less grim. "They showed me an apartment that I hadn't seen that first night, one that seemed more comfortable. It was the duc de Bellegarde who had had it made so; Monsieur had allowed him to live at Saint-Fargeau during my minority, in return for losses he had suffered in Monsieur's service. This apartment had been made out of part of a long gallery which went the length of one of the walls of the house. That very day I decided to change the fireplaces and the doors, and asked if there wasn't an architect in the neighborhood. I had the work started right away, and for the time being had to sleep in the attic." Her furniture hadn't arrived yet from Paris, but: "Fortunately for me the bailiff of Saint-Fargeau was recently married, and had a new bed."

Still, Saint-Fargeau struck Mademoiselle as really ugly. It was a forbidding, feudal place with thick walls and heavy towers; perhaps the king would allow her to live somewhere else. In December Monsieur allowed her to call on him at Blois. "He was quite pleasant with me during that visit—it's true it didn't last long: I was at Blois only two days"—and while there she inspected the nearby château of Chateauneuf-sur-Loire, which was for sale. But there, despite the beauty of the house and gardens and canal, and the view of the Loire itself at the end of the park, Mademoiselle disliked the absence of trees. Besides, the king might not care to have two such prominent Frondeurs as the father and daughter so close together in exile; he might fear they'd begin to *fronder* again.

"As soon as I was back, I changed bedrooms. Chimneys had to be built through the rooms I'd been using, so I fixed up another that had a beautiful view—scarcely surprising, since it's in an attic. From morning to night I was busy with my needlework, and I left my room only to take dinner downstairs or to go to Mass. That winter it was too nasty to go out much. Whenever there was a moment of good weather I got on a horse, and when it was too cold for that I walked and supervised my workmen. First I made a mall, cutting it through woods that were choked with brambles; when it was done, it seemed too short, so I added a hundred-foot terrace. That made a fine effect: from the terrace you see the châ-teau, a part of the town, woods, vineyards, a meadow with a brook that's a pond in winter—the landscape is quite charming. While I did my needlework I had someone read aloud; and it was at this time that I began to enjoy books. . . ."

Mademoiselle began to write as well. She sent for a printer from Auxerre; he set up his press in an unused room and printed her first production, a fictitious life of a court lady. Then, since she greatly relished the memoirs of Marguerite de Valois, first, divorced wife of her grandfather Henri IV, she decided to write her own, encouraged by Préfontaine and the others.

"In the past I found it very hard to conceive," she began, "what kind of mental exercise anyone accustomed to life at court, and born to the rank that I occupy, could possibly engage in when obliged to live in the country: for it always seemed to me that nothing could sweeten exile, and that for persons of high birth banishment from court could be nothing but solitary confinement however numerous one's servants and visitors. However, since my retirement, I discover with pleasure that the recollection of things past is sufficient to keep such a retreat from being too disagree-able. One has the leisure to recapture one's experiences in proper order, to write them down. . . ."

All her recollections of events up to the collapse of the *Fronde* —about six hundred pages in a modern printed volume—were written down at great speed, and with great illegibility, at Saint-Fargeau that first winter. One pities Préfontaine, who transcribed them. The illegibility of Mademoiselle's still-surviving manuscript is spectacular, unique; her handwriting is cryptological. "Even when I write carefully," she says complacently, "no one can read me." Nor is Mademoiselle's spelling at all orthodox: Madame de Saint-Georges had known better than to ask a *fille de France* to follow orthographical rules. And there was another literary distraction at Saint-Fargeau: Mademoiselle wrote to Condé "by every mail." He answered her faithfully, in spelling as aristocratic as hers.

So the first months of exile were passed, while in Paris "the court didn't have ears enough to listen to all the people who were suing for pardon."

Out of favor with the court though she was, Mademoiselle received two marriage proposals that winter. Neither could be considered for an instant.

The first was from Ferdinand-Maria, elector of Bavaria. "He didn't seem very eligible to me; his father and mother were still living and he was only fifteen years old; besides, life in their house"—she refers, one assumes, to the Wittelsbach palace in Munich—"was lonelier than in a convent."

And the second proposal was even less suitable, coming as it did from "a mere princeling"—the count Palatine, Philip-William, duke of Neuburg. It was Monsieur himself who told Mademoiselle of this proposal—it had been tendered him at Orléans by a Jesuit priest, Père Jean-Antoine, who had brought it direct from Düsseldorf, the duke of Neuburg's capital. "I told Monsieur that I thought he must have forgotten who he was, to want me to marry a German princeling. Madame said that members of the duke's family had married princesses of Austria and Lorraine. I replied that others might marry as they wished; as for me, I would by no means consent to such a match; and no more was said about it."

But the duke's priestly love messenger was persistent; he came to Saint-Fargeau, where he took lodgings in the Augustinian monastery and sent to the chateau a flowery letter to Mademoiselle in his patron's handwriting together with word of his own arrival. Mademoiselle refused to "receive" the princeling's letter: she merely read it, copied it, and had it returned to the Jesuit. "Mademoiselle:" it began, "Since the rare virtues and perfections that heaven has joined to Your Royal Highness's exalted birth have caused your praises to be sung everywhere, I hope that you will forgive me if I find myself among the number of those who seek the honor to serve you. Such would be the true good fortune I passionately long for. . . ." Nor could she resist seeing the messenger himself; and since to receive him openly would inevitably give rise to gossip that she was considering the princeling's offer, she had Préfontaine smuggle Père Jean-Antoine one evening through the dark attic, "where he was sure he'd break his neck," into her room, where she had hidden Madame de Frontenac under a table.

"His entrance was comical: a grotesque-looking Jesuit wearing traveling boots and country clothes! He was holding up his coat with both hands and had an expression on his face that was absolutely mirth-provoking; when he came close to me he screwed up one of his eyes in order to see me better; I was dying from wanting to laugh. Préfontaine couldn't control himself, and took his leave respectfully, but I had told him to listen at the door to everything that was said." The Jesuit extended to Mademoiselle the duke of Neuburg's compliments, and Mademoiselle returned them. She would always be obliged to the duke for showing her such marks of his esteem, she said, but "in the state in which we were it didn't look as though I were ever going to marry. My whole family was dispersed: my father was in disfavor with the court, my cousin the prince de Condé was abroad; and I didn't want to marry if they couldn't all be at my wedding."

The Jesuit drew two portraits of the duke, of two different sizes, out of his pocket, and said: "He is the finest man in the world. You'll be only too happy with him. His first wife, the king of Poland's sister, died with joy every time he returned from a trip."

"You frighten me," said Mademoiselle. "I'd be afraid of loving him too much and dying of it. That's why I won't marry him."

The Jesuit scolded her. "Do you think you're too *young* to marry?" he impertinently asked.

"Not too young, but young enough so that I don't have to hurry," retorted Mademoiselle; and she called Préfontaine, who led the ridiculous priest away.

To Mademoiselle, both those proposals were presumptuous if not downright insulting: "There has never been a *fille de France* who married a *petit souverain.*"

Her double failure, several years before, to achieve marriage with the emperor she continued to lament. She called that repeated fiasco the "bad spot" of her life—and indeed Ferdinand III seems to have been an amiable and generous man, personally perhaps the best of her many possibilities. Now this new flurry of marriage talk at Saint-Fargeau made her come out strongly against *galanterie.* Monsieur was displeased and worried by her loyal correspondence with the rebel Condé—less because of what it might do to impede Mademoiselle's eventual reconciliation with the court than because of the delaying effect it might have on his own; and he believed or pretended to believe that her refusal of the German proposals was due to an agreement she had with Condé—an agreement to keep herself unattached so that she could marry Condé if and when his wife died. Mademoiselle burst out indignantly when she learned that her father was talking about her in that way. She might very well marry Condé someday, she said, if his wife did happen to die, if the court forgave them both their past behavior and approved the match, and if, of course, Monsieur approved it also. Condé was "her kind of man" —she said it in almost those words. He was grand, heroic, warlike, worthy of the name Bourbon; he had been—though she didn't think it necessary to remind Monsieur of this—Monsieur's ally. But to think that she had any agreement with him, especially one dependent on the death of a woman who was, after all, no older than herself—*that* was preposterous. It smacked of the romanesque. "Do you think I'm one to get married like damsels in

novels? Do you think I'm waiting for some Amadis to come quest-
ing for me on a palfrey, cleaving in twain everyone who crosses
his path? Do you expect me to mount another palfrey and go off
with him, like Oriane?"

One night that winter they had as an unexpected visitor at
Saint-Fargeau, the comte de Frontenac (the future governor of
Canada); and when his wife, Mademoiselle's companion, who
had eloped with him as a young girl but who had been avoiding
him for years, greeted his arrival and his conjugal demands with
screams of terror and revulsion, Mademoiselle, who had "never
noticed" the wife's aversion for the husband, was confirmed in
many of her feelings: "Madame de Fiesque scolded Madame de
Frontenac, and told her that she was bound in conscience to go to
bed with her husband if he wanted her to. That only redoubled
her tears. Madame de Fiesque brought out books to show her the
truth of what she said; things became so violent that I began to
think we'd have to send for Monsieur le curé and his holy water
to exorcise Madame de Frontenac. As for me, I was greatly astonished to see all this. I have always had a great aversion for love,
even for legitimate love, so unworthy of a noble soul has this
passion always seemed to me. This scene confirmed me in my feelings, and I saw clearly that deeds done out of passion seldom
breed rational consequences. I saw that passion dies quickly, that
one is wretched for the rest of one's days if one's marriage is
based on anything so short-lived, that one is better off to marry
rationally: there may be aversion at first, but there will be all the
more love later. These opinions are based on what I saw of Madame de Frontenac; everything I say is based on her example. Poor
Monsieur de Frontenac had no idea of what was going on. That
night, when I retired, he went off to his room very cockily, in
every expectation of being joined by his wife; and indeed after he
had waited for her a little while she did go to him. The next
morning when I awoke I was astonished to see her enter my room
fully dressed: it was still quite early."

No, less than ever were such things for Mademoiselle. She preferred to sit in the theater she had arranged in one of the big rooms at Saint-Fargeau and enjoy the troupe of actors she had found playing at Sully-sur-Loire and brought back with her for the rest of the winter. "The theater was well lighted and decorated; the audience certainly wasn't very big, but some of the ladies weren't bad-looking. We wore hats trimmed with fur and feathers; I'd had them copied from one that I'd seen the duchesse de Sully wearing out hunting; we made them larger or smaller according to taste, and they were very pretty. When Lent put an end to the plays, battledore and shuttlecock began; I like active games, and played two hours in the morning and two hours in the afternoon. My new mall was finished, and I played there with Madame de Frontenac. She always won: I was more dexterous, but her strength was too much for me." When company came, there was dancing. "We led a pleasant enough life, quite free of boredom. But then I'm the least bored person in the world. I'm always busy, and even when I daydream my reveries keep me entertained."

But alas! The other ladies in the house had a much lower boring point than Mademoiselle. And though it wasn't necessary to pay too much attention to the boredom of the waiting women and the other upper and lower servants (quite a large staff had gradually joined Mademoiselle at Saint-Fargeau, coming to her from Paris and Bois-le-Vicomte), the boredom of the countesses was dangerous.

"The countesses" was the collective name that Mademoiselle gave the three principal female sharers of her exile: the two comtesses de Fiesque (the old governess and her daughter-in-law, both in disgrace because the young comte de Fiesque, son of the one and husband of the other, had followed Condé) and the comtesse de Frontenac (in disgrace because she had preferred to remain with the disgraced Mademoiselle rather than rejoin her husband).

The Fiesque ladies had arrived in Saint-Fargeau after staying long enough in Paris (where they were placed under guard) to supervise the expedition of Mademoiselle's household staff and household possessions; and whereas in Paris Mademoiselle had been able to control her governess's tendency to intrigue, in the country it got out of hand. Even in Paris, the old lady, keeping Mademoiselle's true destination a secret for the time being lest guards be sent to arrest her, had spread the rumor that she had fled to Flanders—fled, in other words, to the enemy: a scarcely discreet choice of *canard*. So greatly did this displease Mademoiselle that when the governess finally turned up at Saint-Fargeau "in a litter, one morning when no one was expecting her," Mademoiselle greeted her sarcastically: "Ah, Madame. How do you happen to come here, you who thought I was in Flanders?" But the old lady wasn't very well, and spoke penitently, and Mademoiselle forgave her. Before her arrival, Mademoiselle had warned Madame de Frontenac against her; but the older woman very soon charmed the younger and filled her with dislike for the person Mademoiselle depended on most: the faithful and hard-working Préfontaine, who well knew the old lady's character and constantly offended her by refusing to gossip about Mademoiselle's affairs. As for the younger comtesse de Fiesque, she was later ruefully described by Mademoiselle as "a lady very good at getting up assemblies, and whom it's a pleasure to call on in her own home; delightful in a social group, but—not to live with."

All this might have remained in the realm of what Mademoiselle calls *"les micmacs de petits ménages"*—intra-household intrigues—if the countesses hadn't been bored and if another household hadn't become involved.

It was Monsieur who had appointed Madame de Fiesque his daughter's governess ten years before, eager to keep the intriguer out of his own household; and now came the time for him to profit from his choice. For Monsieur, in his exile at Blois, was soon up to something.

The fact is scarcely surprising—Monsieur's weakness for *mic-macs* had always been pronounced; and besides, Mademoiselle's outburst against love and passion is a veritable announcement, her way of telling us, that Monsieur was disturbing her. Just as her first outcry against *galanterie* had come when she had first been troubled and depressed by her discovery of his nature as revealed by his betrayal of Cinq-Mars, so now her new denunciation of the affections coincides with her discovery that he was involved in a new betrayal—a betrayal, this time, of her.

The discovery began quietly enough. "The matter of the accounting of my guardianship during your minority isn't settled yet," he told her when they met at Orléans that winter. "I'd like to get it over with. Tell your people in Paris so, will you?"

Innocuous-sounding words: but quite sufficient to herald a great change in the life of Mademoiselle.

During her first twenty-five years she had had little to do with her money except spend it. On her mother's death her father had been made her guardian; but because of his prolonged absences "with the army" and elsewhere, her affairs had been managed by administrators appointed by Richelieu. When Monsieur was allowed back to Paris by Mazarin and the queen-regent, the administrators handed him their accountings; and from then on Monsieur and his officers and lawyers were in charge. Then, when Mademoiselle came of age, control passed into her own hands; and Monsieur "gave" her Préfontaine as secretary and business manager. Préfontaine—his first name isn't a single time mentioned by Mademoiselle—was a gentleman who had done good work as secretary of the French envoys to Münster during the negotiation of the peace of Westphalia: some of his dealings had been with Mazarin himself. Préfontaine had been presented to Monsieur by Monsieur's own chancellor, Monsieur de Choisy, whose relative he was: this was a recommendation indeed, for it was desirable that at the time when Monsieur's account of his guardianship was being prepared and presented, the person in

charge of Mademoiselle's affairs should be someone with whom
Monsieur's officers and lawyers could work in harmony. But the
agitations of the Fronde had set in; access to many of Mademoiselle's properties had been cut off; the guardianship accounting
remained in abeyance. Whenever Mademoiselle needed money,
she simply asked Préfontaine for some. The very morning of the
flight from Paris, for example, "Préfontaine didn't appear until
nine o'clock, and I scolded him horribly. When I had said everything I had to say, he replied: 'But you can't and you musn't leave
Paris without a sou. I've been getting money, as you told me to.
So I don't think, Mademoiselle, that I deserve to be scolded for
coming a quarter of an hour late.' " For purely legal matters Préfontaine had hired an assistant, a lawyer named Nau. When
Mademoiselle took Préfontaine with her into exile, Nau remained
in Paris, constantly occupied with her affairs in and around the
Palais de Justice.

So now Mademoiselle wrote to Paris, on her father's order, to
say that the guardianship accounting was to be expedited. She
wrote to her father and told him that she had done so. The correspondence about the accounting was soon voluminous; some of
the letters began to be "quite sharp"; and in Saint-Fargeau Mademoiselle found herself becoming a businesswoman. "I began to
hear more about business matters than I had ever heard in Paris,
where I had always refused to listen to them. I began to pay attention, and to enjoy it. Préfontaine showed me the letters he received in every mail, and the answers he wrote, sometimes I wrote
answers myself. One day I told him: 'It isn't enough to keep an
eye on my legal affairs and help increase my income: we must pay
attention to my household expenses as well. I'm convinced I'm
being cheated.' " The Infanta Isabel of Spain and the Grand
Duchess Christina of Tuscany, two illustrious royal ladies whom
Mademoiselle much admired, had been famous for the supervision they gave their household accounts: why shouldn't Mademoiselle emulate them? All work, all services, all purchases,

Mademoiselle now closely observed; and what discoveries she made! Padded bills, false accounts, fictitious services: "There was even one man who admitted to me that his confessor had refused him absolution unless he made restitution to me"—but this man had preferred to go without the absolution until Mademoiselle challenged him.

The discovery of cheating by tradesmen, workmen, and servants was only a curtain-raiser. From Monsieur at Blois came a footman, one day, bearing a document concerning the guardianship accounting that needed Mademoiselle's signature. She and Préfontaine looked at it, then looked at each other. The "sharp" letters that had been passing back and forth had been one thing; this was another: "One had only to know how to read, to see how totally it was against my interests." When Mademoiselle, shaken, wrote to Monsieur's secretary, Goulas, proposing that she and Monsieur put the matter mentioned in the document in the hands of arbitrators, Monsieur replied that "it was beneath the dignity of a *fille de France* to submit her affairs to arbitration." Correspondence now redoubled; and correspondence with Monsieur became impossible. "Everything I wrote him he now put a false construction on; and whenever he wrote me something that was proper, and I agreed to it, he immediately wrote again retracting it."

But from the very confusion came an ugly light that glaringly illuminated the affair: unquestionably, during Mademoiselle's minority, Monsieur had appropriated large sums of her money; and unquestionably he was now doing his best to keep some of it. When Blois learned that Saint-Fargeau was alerted, there was fury: fury not only against Mademoiselle herself, but against Préfontaine. Old Madame de Fiesque sent Monsieur regular reports of the long hours Préfontaine spent with Mademoiselle over account books and letters: it was Préfontaine who had spoiled the game by encouraging his employer to pay attention to her affairs. How clear it was that Monsieur, in giving Préfontaine to Made-

moiselle, had counted on Préfontaine to be faithful to *him*, since
Préfontaine owed his position to Monsieur and to Monsieur's
chancellor Monsieur de Choisy his relative!

Préfontaine was almost painfully fair-minded. He was fully
loyal to Mademoiselle, but he lost no chance of speaking well to
Mademoiselle of Monsieur: it was not Monsieur, he kept assuring
her, but "the men around Monsieur" who were responsible. Mademoiselle took this to be a veiled reference to his own relative,
Monsieur de Choisy; and once, on a day when she was particularly
upset, she so lost her temper with Préfontaine, jeering at him for
being related to such a crook, that he quietly got on a horse, rode
away from Saint-Fargeau, and took refuge in the home of a
friend. But that same night Mademoiselle penitently sent after
him; he returned, and he patiently convinced her that despite ap-
pearances, Monsieur de Choisy was innocent. Reluctantly he indicated that the chief instigator of Monsieur seemed to be the secretary, Goulas, who was at Blois and with whom they had to be
in constant correspondence.

Mademoiselle tried to adopt Préfontaine's phrase "the men
around Monsieur." She used it whenever she remembered to. But
it was just a phrase. Monsieur was heavily in debt from years of
gambling; and Monsieur was worried about the future of Mademoiselle's three half sisters—the fourth, born after Monsieur had
left Paris, was already dead, like his only son. The entire dowry
of Mademoiselle's mother had been inherited by Mademoiselle;
Monsieur's second wife had brought almost no dowry except
"enough muskets and pikes to arm two regiments"; and as for
Monsieur's great *apanage,* since he had no male heir, every bit of
it would revert to the crown the moment he died. Monsieur was
very uxorious with the second Madame; he loved his three new
daughters: to safeguard their future he was mulcting Mademoiselle.

By the time the full ugliness of the situation became apparent
it was early summer, good traveling weather, and Monsieur or-

dered Mademoiselle to come to Blois and discuss everything. But Mademoiselle, heartsick, couldn't face the scenes she knew would take place; besides, she heard that Monsieur was "promising that once in Blois he'd make me prisoner, and I'd never get away." Préfontaine ridiculed this gossip and urged her to obey, but she pretended to be ill. "See how yellow I am!" she kept exclaiming, though she had "a wonderfully healthy look." Once again Monsieur ordered her to come, and she put her horses out to grass and said she had no transportation. He ordered her a third time; this time she felt she had to go. "I wept and wept, to such a point that during the night before my departure I developed a horribly sore throat. Still, my doctor thought I could go. I spent the night at Sully; my throat grew worse; they bled my foot; that helped. The next day I wept all the way in the coach. . . ."

But at Blois, where she arrived so weak that she had to be carried to her room in Madame's sedan chair, Monsieur executed one of his celebrated somersaults. He was willing to cheat Mademoiselle, he was willing to quarrel with her—but not, just now, in her presence. "He told me that I had been very wrong to make difficulties about coming, in the thought that he would put pressure on me about our business affairs; he had never used his authority to do violence to anyone, and he wouldn't begin with me. He spoke to me most kindly; he professed the most affectionate feelings for Préfontaine and myself. One day I *wanted* to talk about our affairs, but he ran away—he refused to hear them mentioned."

It was only a lull, of course, Mademoiselle knew that—investigation had uncovered so many irregularities that it would be a miracle if a lawsuit were avoided; but she was glad not to press matters at present, glad to travel a little up and down the Loire. "I went from Blois to Amboise, where the marquis de Sourdis, who had been made governor there, treated me magnificently and received me with a cannon salute, the loudest I ever heard. I told everyone it was to make up for the shabby welcome he'd shown me

at Orléans." At Chenonceaux the exiled duc de Beaufort gave her
a splendid dinner; she visited other exiled Frondeurs; she visited
her aunt the abbess of the convent-monastery of Fontevrault; at
Tours she found the troupe of actors who had spent the winter
with her at Saint-Fargeau, and she went to the theater every day.
It was quite like the tour she had made fifteen years before, when
as an eleven-year-old girl she had played with Monsieur's sixteen-
year-old favorite, Louison Roger.

This time she found Louison Roger again. Or, more precisely,
she found and visited, in the convent of the Visitation in Tours,
a nun named Mère Louise: such was the penitent Louison's new
name and new quality. And also in Tours she found the young
son of Louison and Monsieur, now an adolescent. "I thought he
was a nice-looking boy, and it seemed to me too bad that he
should waste his time—I mean waste what remained of his stu-
dent years; he was attending a Jesuit school, and among bourgeois
in Tours he certainly wouldn't perfect himself. So I took him with
me. I thought that if I asked Monsieur's permission, he might
well refuse me; he might not like the boy to be with me, and
would make me send him back. Whereas if by good luck Monsieur didn't say anything, I might try to make a gentleman of him.
He had no name; he was called simply *le mignon*—he was too
big to be called that. I was hard put to it to find a name for him.
My only properties were large, important places, whose names have
been borne by princes of the blood; I didn't think the boy merited
a name like that. I gave it a good deal of thought; then I remembered that I had a property near Saint-Fargeau called Charny; it's
a nice name, and I called the boy the chevalier de Charny."

Mademoiselle's "nice-looking" half brother had been christened Louis—the closest his mother could come to giving him her
name. He wasn't penniless: when Louison entered the convent,
she left him a modest income. But for an unrecognized illegitimate youngster among the bourgeois, elevation by Mademoiselle
amounted to rescue. Monsieur reacted to the news as he always

reacted when he heard that someone else had done something which it would have been decent of *him* to do. "When Monsieur learned that I had taken the chevalier de Charny with me, he said to people around him: 'It's a friendship that won't last long. My daughter will soon send him back to his relations.' He let me know that I wasn't to bring the boy to Blois or Orléans, so I sent him ahead to wait for me on the road to Saint-Fargeau. When I rejoined Monsieur at Blois he asked me about everything I'd been doing, and about Mère Louise's relations. But not about her or her son." Never, to the end of his days, did Monsieur mention the boy to Mademoiselle.

Many of Monsieur's contemporaries lavished as much affection on their bastards as on their children born in wedlock; they often legitimized them or recognized them and missed no chance to help them make their way in the world. But Monsieur had lost his only legitimate heir, and along with him all chance of passing on his *apanage* to his family: perhaps the bitterness of that disappointment made him the more adamant in insisting that his living son Louis, chevalier de Charny, be kept out of his sight. And Monsieur certainly woefully misunderstood his oldest daughter: there was never anything faint-hearted or fickle about Mademoiselle's loyalties. He was adept at abandoning people, but she was not. She never sent the chevalier back to his relations. And her loyalty to Monsieur himself was so strong that Monsieur had a hard time killing it.

2

D URING THE FOUR and a half years of this first exile of
Mademoiselle at Saint-Fargeau, most of the threads and
patterns that had formed the design of her life in Paris
were missing. After the two proposals from Germany the question
of establishment lapsed—"My rank is such that I can't marry
without the court taking a hand in it, and for the court to be interested, Monsieur would have to be on better terms with it than
he is." There was no long-drawn-out wooing; there was no Fronde
with ever-changing events—nothing epic or dramatic like the
entry into Orléans or the turning-round of the cannon of the Bastille.

Such stirring adventures were replaced by the slower rhythms,
the quieter happenings, of country life. "On my return to Saint-
Fargeau"—she refers to her return with the chevalier de Charny,
after the inconclusive visit to Monsieur at Blois—"I had one of
those joys that one has in the country: I found my new apartment finished, and I furnished it and moved into it. There was an
antechamber where I always took my meals, and outside my bedroom a gallery where I hung the portraits of those nearest me:
my grandfather King Henry IV, my grandmother Marie de Médicis,
the king of Spain and his late queen my aunt Elizabeth, the late
king of England and his queen my aunt Henrietta-Maria, my
father, my mother and my stepmother, my uncle the late king of
France and his wife Anne of Austria, my first cousins the present

king and his brother, the duke of York, the prince de Condé
and his wife, and my grandfather the duc de Montpensier. The
portrait of the last-named hung in the most prominent place, even
though he was less of a *grand seigneur* than the rest: he was the
head of the house—if I hadn't inherited his possessions, I wouldn't
have any."

Mademoiselle was quite aware of the nature of her taste in pictures. During her recent travels she had seen the treasures of the
comte de Béthune—a famous collection of pictures and manuscripts which the count was to bequeath to the king and which has
since entered the national museums and libraries of France. "Since
I don't know much about pictures, it wasn't the most beautiful
that I looked at the longest," she says frankly. "What interested
me most were the portraits of famous men of Europe, especially
members of the courts of my grandfather and my uncle and the
present king, with inscriptions recounting their greatest achieve-
ments." In the gallery at Saint-Fargeau there were still other portraits, including one of another of Mademoiselle's aunts, Christine, duchess of Savoy, known as Madame Royale, who sent her
likeness from her court in Turin. "There are still some empty
places," Mademoiselle records, "and I have enough first cousins to
fill them."

In the portrait gallery Mademoiselle installed a billiard table.
"I love active games. My bedroom is quite pretty, with a *cabinet*
and dressing room at one end and a little study where there is
room only for me. After my eight months in the attic, I felt as
though I had moved into a fairy palace. In my study I hung a
quantity of pictures and mirrors, and I felt that I'd created the
greatest masterpiece in the world. I showed off my apartment to
all who came to see me with as much satisfaction as my grandmother must have felt when she showed people through the Luxembourg."

With her own apartment finished, Mademoiselle set to work on
the rest of the house. "I had an architect named Le Vau," she tells

us, "come down from Paris." Such a serenely casual reference to
a great artist is characteristic of Mademoiselle: Louis Le Vau is
one of the grand figures in French architectural annals, designer
of portions of Versailles, the Louvre, the Tuileries, and the Insti-
tut de France. Elsewhere Mademoiselle speaks of asking her
uncle, the chevalier de Guise, to bring back from Italy somebody
entertaining with whom she could talk Italian; he brought her a
young Florentine "named Baptiste," who stayed with her a few
years and later "became famous as a song writer." This, we discover, was none other than Jean-Baptiste Lully, born Giovanni
Battista Lulli. "When I was exiled, Baptiste didn't want to live
in the country," Mademoiselle says, "and asked me to let him go,
which I did." But other stories have it that Mademoiselle dismissed Baptiste, when she learned that one of the songs he was
constantly writing was too sarcastic at her expense to be respectful. And for a time Mademoiselle's secretary in charge of philan-
thropies was Jean Segrais, whom she calls "a kind of scholar with
a pretty wit"; Segrais is forgotten today, but he was made a member of the French Academy for his poetry, which included translations of Virgil.

As she rebuilt her old château, Mademoiselle began to like it.
"The time I spent on it certainly wasn't wasted. The remodeling
gave me much pleasure, and those who see it in the future will
find it quite magnificent, well worthy of me. I did the best I could
with it; all I did was to repair an old house, which nevertheless
had something grand about it, even though it was built by a private citizen—a minister of finance under Charles VII. It's worth
telling," she goes on, "how the house came to me, since there's
quite a distance between myself and Jacques Coeur"—thus casually
Mademoiselle lets drop the famous name of the "private citizen."
"When Jacques Coeur fell into disgrace, his property was ordered
to be sold, and the duchy of Saint-Fargeau was bought by my an-
cestor Antoine de Chabannes, *grand maître de France.* Then, during the reign of Louis XI, when Chabannes himself fell into dis-

grace, he was accused of having taken advantage of his former favor and of the disgrace of Jacques Coeur to buy Saint-Fargeau for a song. So he bought it again: he wanted to avoid any imputation of such a vile transaction. I'm well informed about what I say, for much to my pleasure I found the documents here at Saint-Fargeau. I myself should be very troubled by the thought that any of my property really belonged to someone else: I should even dislike it extremely if any of it had come to me through confiscation. Such is not the case, thank God; everything I own came to me quite properly."

Mademoiselle adopted what country pleasures she could. She imported some horses from England—"It's a distraction, in the country, to like horses: to see them, put them through their paces, ride them, lend them to your visitors. . . . I hunted hares with greyhounds belonging to some of the gentlemen living near by; this gave me the desire to have dogs of my own, and I sent to England for a pack. When they came I hunted three times a week and took great pleasure in it. The country around Saint-Fargeau is excellent for hunting, and especially good for English dogs. They're too fast for most women, but I followed them everywhere." In addition to her English horses and English hounds, Mademoiselle acquired from Germany a team of *chevaux isabelles* —yellowish horses with black manes and markings, whose French name was inspired by the Infanta Isabel of Spain, archduchess of Flanders, one of the great ladies of the last generation whose attentiveness to their household accounts Mademoiselle had begun, at Saint-Fargeau, to copy. More precisely, the horses' name was inspired by the color of Isabel's famous undershirt. She swore, the day her husband laid siege to Ostend, that she wouldn't change it until the city capitulated. Ostend held out for three years. . . .

Every winter there was a troupe of actors at Saint-Fargeau, and there were dances when the group was large enough—one dance, a masquerade, happened to coincide with news of a victory that Condé won for the Spanish, an unfortunate circumstance that didn't fail to get talked of at court. In the summer there were house parties and excursions and evening picnics in the woods with colored lights and music, "to show that we weren't bored even though we weren't in Paris." Madame de Sévigné was present at one festivity: she was just beginning to write her famous letters, and her bread-and-butter letter to Mademoiselle is partly in verse, a salute to a *"belle et charmante princesse. . . ."* Mademoiselle was free to make visits—she had only to stay away from Paris and from wherever the court happened to be; she visited watering places, the châteaux of friends, and, on two occasions, a foreign royal celebrity who interested her—the notorious Christina, who two years before had abdicated the Swedish throne and was now touring France without ladies in waiting or maids of honor. Her attendants were all men, and she herself often wore men's clothes.

"I learned that the queen of Sweden was at Fontainebleau, and since our paths were almost bound to cross, I sent to the court, which was at La Fère, to ask if the king approved my seeing her: even though I was in exile, it would have been unfitting for me to see a foreign princess without the king's permission. When he replied that I might go, I immediately sent a gentleman to Fontainebleau with my compliments, to ask where I might see her and on what basis she would receive me. She made no objection to giving me an armchair"—this meant that Christina recognized Mademoiselle as fellow royalty—"and when I arrived I found her in a beautiful room decorated in the Italian style where she was about to watch a ballet. I had heard so much about her strange way of dressing that I was dying of fear lest I laugh when I see her. As my name was called out and everyone made place for me, I caught sight of her: she surprised me, and there was nothing about her that made me want to laugh. She was wearing a gray skirt with gold and silver lace, a tight-fitting angora jacket of flame-color with the same lace as the skirt, at her throat a handkerchief of Genoa lace tied with a flame-colored ribbon; she had a blonde wig with a bun behind and carried a hat trimmed with black feathers. She has very white skin, and blue eyes that are by turns very gentle and very bold; her mouth is large but pleasing, she has beautiful teeth and a big aquiline nose; she is very short —her jacket hid her bad figure. By and large she looked to me like a pretty little boy.

"She embraced me and welcomed me; she gave me her hand to help me climb over a bench, and said, 'It would be more in your temperament to jump over it.' When I presented the comte de Béthune to her, she talked to him about his manuscripts: she was happy to let him see that she was well acquainted with everyone and everything. After the ballet we went to see a play; there she surprised me by praising the parts that pleased her. She swore to God, slouched in her chair, stretched her legs this way and that, hung them over the arms of her chair; I've never seen such postures taken by anyone except Trivelin and Jodelet, the Italian and French clowns. She repeated lines that she liked; she spoke on all kinds of subjects; and what she said she said pleasantly enough. She fell into deep reveries, let out deep sighs, then all of a sudden collected herself like someone who wakes up with a jerk: she's completely extraordinary. After the play there were refreshments, and then we went to see fireworks over the canal. Here she held my hand, and when I shrank from some rockets that fell close to us, she made fun of me: 'What? A woman who's seen and done the things that you've seen and done—afraid?' I replied that I was brave only when the occasion demanded it, and that that was enough for me. She said that her dearest wish was to take part in a battle, and that she would never be content until she did; she envied the prince de Condé all his glorious feats of arms. 'He's a good friend of yours?' she asked.

"I answered 'Yes, and my very near relation.'

" 'He's the greatest man in the world,' she said. 'No one can take that distinction from him.' "

Mademoiselle saw Christina again a few weeks later, at Montargis, when she was on her way to Rome after having spent some time with the French court at Compiègne. "I found her in bed, a candle on the table beside her. She had a towel wrapped around her head as a nightcap, and there wasn't a sign of a hair—she'd recently had her head shaved. Her nightshirt was buttoned up to her neck and had no collar, just a big knot of flame-colored ribbon. Her sheets came up only halfway, and the coverlet was an ugly green. She didn't look pretty like that. But the next morning I got up early to bid her good-by and she did look well, properly powdered and wearing a new jacket. She urged my friend Madame de Thianges to go to Rome with her, and told her it was stupid to stay with her husband; the best of husbands was worth nothing, she said, and the best thing to do to one was to leave him. She railed against marriage, and advised me never to marry; she said she thought it was abominable to have children."

But interesting though it doubtless was to catch those glimpses of "the queen of the Goths," as Mademoiselle called Christina, pleasant though it was to visit more conventional acquaintances or be visited by them, to rebuild, and to hunt, it is difficult to believe—Mademoiselle being Mademoiselle—that such diversions as those, even when supplemented by needlework, playgoing in her own theater, reading and writing—were enough to keep her from being bored.

And yet Mademoiselle insists that during her exile she was not bored. The contrast she draws between her own lack of boredom and the boredom of the countesses, the night picnics undertaken to show that life wasn't boring even away from Paris—those are only two of her many references to the subject; and later, when she is forgiven and restored to favor, there will be amid her carefully respectful remarks to Anne of Austria a stubborn denial which she must have known the queen could find only displeasing: denial that she had ever been bored in exile.

Were the facts a little different, we should be tempted to see in

Mademoiselle's insistence a case of protesting too much—tempted
to say that Mademoiselle was whistling to keep up her courage,
lying to cheat Anne of Austria of satisfaction. Actually, it seems
quite possible that Mademoiselle was telling the truth. She never
said that she *enjoyed* her exile. She never said that she wasn't unhappy during it, or desperate, or frantic, or enraged, or heart-
broken—all she said was that she wasn't bored. Reading Mademoiselle's memoirs with reasonable care, we see that all those
occupations—the building, the hunting, the visiting and all the
rest—were only the veneer of her life during those years, that
they were like a pleasant-tasting icing, painstakingly and gallantly
concocted by herself to hide a revolting, loathesome core that was
half poison, half emetic—and, seeing that, we see the true meaning, the true reticence and understatement, of Mademoiselle's
insistence that she was not bored. There may have been occasions,
one suspects, when Mademoiselle longed for boredom. But she
had no time for it. It was Monsieur who saw to that. It seems to
have been Monsieur's goal, during those four and a half years of
Mademoiselle's exile—a goal that he brilliantly achieved—to
keep his daughter from boredom by keeping her in anguish.

Monsieur's behavior sprang from Monsieur's character, of
course—a character that the reader has had glimpses of already;
and it sprang from Monsieur's straitened circumstances—or rather
the straitened circumstances in which he feared to leave the
second Madame and their children. And it sprang from a host
of other considerations and concepts, among them one that we
find difficult, in our very different day and age, to measure or even
clearly to conceive: the concept of authority. The entire trend of
Mademoiselle's times in France was toward the lodging of increased—indeed, absolute—authority in the person of the king.
Mademoiselle's grandfather Henri IV had been among his nobles
like a strong, respected father among a group of hot-blooded sons.
The weakness of Louis XIII and the harshness of Richelieu on
whom he called for help had encouraged *his* nobles in rebellion;

now, defeated in the Fronde by their own cross-purposes and by Mazarin, they were obsequious before Louis XIV. If, after Mazarin's death, Louis XIV had really uttered the fictitious words *"L'État c'est moi,"* he would have done so as a simple statement of fact. The Fronde, for all its absurdities, was the last attempt before the French Revolution by members of another class, in this case, chiefly the nobility—the bourgeois in Parlement had been the first to give up—to say *"L'État c'est nous."* And the palace of Versailles, which Louis XIV was now about to begin—that new palace, distant from all memories of the Fronde, in which the king was about to install himself like a God and in and around which the nobles, self-exiled from their estates to bask in the royal favor, would cluster like servants—Versailles was the symbolic apogee of tyrannic authority. In Versailles the officers of the king's bedroom would genuflect as they passed his bed, even when it was empty.

One of the fatal futilities of the Fronde had been the exaggerated individual authority claimed for himself by each of the noble Frondeurs. Rebels against the king as they were—or, to respect their own distinction, rebels against the king's prime minister—they were all imbued with the same maniacal self-glory as the monarchy itself. The nobler the Frondeur, the more overweening his pride; indeed, so galloping were the cases of self-importance suffered by such near-monarchs, such princes of the royal blood as Condé and Monsieur, that it was their very closeness to the throne that made them the leading Frondeurs. Condé was so wildly glorious—glorious beyond most—that rather than surrender he entered the service of Spain; Monsieur displayed the reverse of the same medal in the obsequiousness with which he crept into obscurity.

But in his retreat Monsieur remained Monsieur—son, brother, and uncle of kings of France, for years heir apparent himself to the throne; and in his retreat Monsieur retained the authority that birth brought him. The court despised him personally, politically it was determined to keep him impotent; but the court was obliged, by the respect due its own royal fetishes, to consider him as one of themselves. He was recognized as *seigneur* of all his *apanage*—the very fact that he had it was a reminder of who and what he was; and, more privately, he was recognized as head of his immediate family, with all the authority over wife and unmarried daughters lodged, in those days, in husband and father. Mademoiselle, herself so great an admirer of privilege and authority in herself and her few peers, bore Monsieur, in addition to her wistful, her all but unquenchable, affection, the immense respect due a father who was also a prince of the blood. And over Mademoiselle Monsieur, or the men around Monsieur, well knew how to exploit the considerable authority that he possessed.

"There is nothing so tiresome as other people's business," says Mademoiselle, "especially when there's wrangling involved"; and "as for *my* business, you'd need a set of lawbooks to understand it." Furthermore, she says, "continual misfortunes, and the griefs they cause, are capable of blunting even the best of memories." However much Mademoiselle may have forgotten of the complications of her business with Monsieur, the grief and confusion it caused her are betrayed in the way she writes about what she remembers: the pages of her memoirs devoted to these troubles lack some of the vivacity, the clarity, of the rest.

Without a set of seventeenth-century French lawbooks, the affair of Mademoiselle-Monsieur can be summarized approximately and fairly briefly.

Just as Monsieur had baffled his daughter by refusing, at Blois, to discuss business matters after furiously ordering her to come for just that purpose, so, after seeing her again a few months later and being equally silent about business while they were together, he startled her by sending after her, almost the moment her back was turned, a process-server who handed her a summons. Thus

Monsieur opened legal hostilities: *she* owed *him* money, he claimed, and he demanded it.

With the aid of Préfontaine and Nau, Mademoiselle began reluctantly to draw up her reply—it wasn't easy, since Monsieur had many of her documents and refused to let her see them. But before the reply was ready, he changed his tune again. "This time he sent me a message by the comte de Bury, saying that he didn't want to play around with the formalities of the law, and that if I didn't give him of my own free will what he asked for, he would appropriate all my possessions and let me have only what he chose."

In the solitude of her study Mademoiselle wept: never before had Monsieur's hostility, and his peculiar craziness, been so savagely fused. Once again she begged him to let his claim be arbitrated; and this time she suggested, on Préfontaine's advice, that the arbitrators be chosen by her grandmother, the duchesse de Guise. The old lady seemed like a good choice: she would probably be fair to Mademoiselle because of the relationship, and yet by her second marriage she was related also to the house of Lorraine—the house of the second Madame; and besides, Monsieur knew that Mademoiselle and her grandmother had never seen much of each other or got on very well. To her relief Monsieur accepted; Madame de Guise accepted also; but throughout the year of arbitration Monsieur behaved abominably very often. Mademoiselle was constantly ordered to Blois, where "the air absolutely disagrees with me; I'm never there without getting severe headaches and heavy colds, though I'm perfectly well everywhere else." Sometimes, at Blois, Monsieur "wasn't niggardly with *external* marks of affection"; but whenever Mademoiselle saw him she wept. He adopted the habit of remarking to her and to others: "My own daughter's trying to trap me; she needn't think she'll get away with it." Monsieur never allowed her to see a single original document; she was always shown copies, even though, at Blois, the originals might be "in the next room."

Still, when Madame de Guise's arbitrators had finished their work and issued their opinion, Mademoiselle was content: "It was not at all to my disadvantage; they did right by me. They obliged my father to pay all the family debts because during my minority he had used money belonging to me; in addition, he was obliged to give me considerable sums. Certain parts of his indebtedness to me they forgave."

On the basis of those findings Madame de Guise had a document prepared for the signatures of Monsieur and Mademoiselle; they had agreed to sign it without reading; and when Madame de Guise presented it to them at a ceremony at Orléans attended by many dignitaries, they did so. After signing, Monsieur and Mademoiselle embraced. They were formally reconciled.

But the next day Mademoiselle and Préfontaine read the document. Its role was to put into practical effect the findings of the arbitrators; for this it listed in detail the revenue accruing from each of Mademoiselle's various properties, which came under the widely differing jurisdictions of innumerable sets of intricate local customary laws. By now Préfontaine and Mademoiselle together had familiarized themselves with much of the financial detail; as they read, they came upon error after error of computation; each error could have been made only by someone at least as familiar with the properties as they—in other words, by the men around Monsieur. The dozens of small errors made up into an error that was immense—so immense that it had the effect of reversing the arbitrators' very intention. Mademoiselle found herself bound to pay half the debts that the arbitrators had intended Monsieur to pay! Madame de Guise, it was clear, had favored her relations of the house of Lorraine.

For three days Mademoiselle said nothing. She sent quietly to Paris, asking Nau to talk privately with the arbitrators about her discovery. And then, armed with their indignant replies, she requested another meeting with Monsieur, Madame de Guise, and the same dignitaries who had been present at the signing, and told *them* what she had discovered. And she said graciously that she would be glad to sign a certain other document they were now presenting to her—a second document confirming the validity of the first—if they would allow her to add the words "except for errors in computation."

It was amazing how rapidly the meeting broke up, how rapidly Monsieur left Orléans for Blois.

And it was amazing how rapidly Monsieur struck back. "Certain people have advised me to use violence with my daughter," Monsieur told the comte de Béthune, knowing that the count would repeat his words to Mademoiselle at Saint-Fargeau. "They advise me to shut her up in my château of Amboise; there I could do anything with her I liked, and in my own way. But I don't have a violent spirit; I don't want to treat her like that." He treated her differently. He struck at her through others.

"On September 9," Mademoiselle records, "I was wakened and told that a messenger had arrived from Monsieur. I told them to send him in, and he handed me a harshly worded letter in which my father ordered me to dismiss Nau from my service."

Mademoiselle wept. "It's unheard-of that someone over twenty-five should have her servants dismissed, that she not be allowed to employ whom she wants. Nau is a man who doesn't know what the Louvre or society is; he knows only the Palais de Justice; he is in no sense an intriguer. The men around Monsieur had him sent away just to complicate my affairs."

That was Thursday. Amid her tears, Mademoiselle thought she knew what was coming next. Préfontaine didn't believe her. "Mademoiselle, haven't you noticed that Monsieur always does me the honor to talk to me when I'm at Blois? Haven't you noticed how well he treats me?"

On Sunday came letters from Paris. "I opened a packet from Monsieur LeRoi, Préfontaine's brother. In it was a letter he had received from Monsieur. Before opening it, I said to Préfontaine, 'This is it.' For a little time neither of us could bear to open it;

finally I did. In it Monsieur wrote to Monsieur LeRoi that the high opinion he had of him and his brother made him want to treat Préfontaine differently from Nau; he begged Monsieur LeRoi to request his brother to resign from my service. My tears redoubled; I had a double reason for shedding them, and I did so with such vehemence that the comtesses de Fiesque and de Frontenac came into my study. They well knew what had happened, but they pretended not to, and began to weep with me."

Mademoiselle's old governess had died after a year at Saint-Fargeau, and more and more openly her daughter-in-law and Madame de Frontenac had practiced the ways of intrigue they had learned from her. In vain had Mademoiselle implored Monsieur to relieve her of them; the more she implored, the more he valued them as spies.

"I thought of writing to the queen, and even to Cardinal Mazarin, and telling them that in my fear that the men around Monsieur would prevail on him to resort to violence against my person, I was going to take shelter in the convent of the Val-de-Grace until my business with him was at an end, since this was the cause of my persecution. The countesses thought this an excellent idea, and said it was the best thing I could do. Préfontaine didn't think so at all; he said that to take refuge in a convent might have grave consequences; once there, certain people might be glad to see that I remained. Besides, such a step would enrage Monsieur still further. My only course was complete obedience, with the hope that in this way Monsieur might be mollified. I felt that he was right, and agreed with him."

Préfontaine stayed on at Saint-Fargeau for ten days, putting Mademoiselle's papers in order and giving instructions to her and to his clerk, who would be the only person left to help her with business. Then he went to the abbey of Gramont in the Limousin, where the abbot was one of his friends. "He chose the most isolated spot he could find, to show everyone that he had no intention of interfering in anybody's affairs. It is easy to imagine his regret in leaving me, and the regret with which I saw him go. Everyone at Saint-Fargeau was distressed, except the countesses and a few of my servants who were in their cabal."

Then came another message from Blois. "The comte de Béthune wrote that Monsieur considered it wrong of me to keep Préfontaine's clerk."

"So there I was," says Mademoiselle, "at odds with the court and with my father, and without anyone to give me any help with paperwork. I read and answered all the letters from my tenants; I corresponded with lawyers in Paris about my affairs: the men around Monsieur had put me into such a corner that I *had* to be clever. I recognized then how right Préfontaine had been to want me to know about my affairs, to insist that I pay attention to them when I had no desire to do so: if I'd remained ignorant about them, they'd be in worse state than they are now. If anyone had ever told me while I was living at court that someday I'd be familiar with the price of bricks, chalk, sand, plaster, and wagons, and with workmen's wages and all the minutiae of building, and that every Saturday I'd draw up my own accounts, I'd have been very surprised. Nevertheless I did just that for a year and more, because I had no one around me in whom I had any confidence."

And it was now, when Monsieur refused to communicate with Mademoiselle except to return a flat No whenever she suggested the name of someone who might take Préfontaine's place, when his behavior toward her made her feel "battered" and caused her to burst into uncontrollable tears during meals—a weakness the countesses found comical—it was now that Monsieur received the king's absolution. Three and a half years after the end of the Fronde his exile was declared ended, and he was invited to return to Paris.

Even earlier there had been a rumor that the court, suspecting that Mademoiselle was secretly sending money to Condé, planned to deprive her of control of her fortune and give it to Monsieur, disgraced though he was. That was done only in the case of insane persons and criminals: Mademoiselle knew that she was neither, and she dismissed the rumor as foolish. But now, with Monsieur back in favor, she did feel herself in danger. "Surely, a person under the authority of a father who is a *fils de France* and reconciled with the court has everything to fear." How right Préfontain had been, to tell her to keep out of convents! How helpless she would be, trapped in the Val-de-Grace, the favorite convent of Anne of Austria!

Now Monsieur's hostility became ever wilder. "When Monsieur arrived in Orléans on the eve of Holy Thursday, he was told that my major-domo was in the city. He had gone there on private business of his own, but Monsieur assumed that he was there to arrange for lodgings for me. Monsieur fell into a fury, into such a transport of rage that he didn't know what he was saying. He ordered a lieutenant of his guards to find me at once, and to tell me that if I had any idea of coming to Orléans, I'd find the gates shut in my face. This lieutenant arrived as I was having supper, so frantic, poor boy, because of the state in which he had seen his master, that he could scarcely speak. I told him that Monsieur could rest assured that I wouldn't dream of going to Orléans if he didn't wish me to."

That tantrum caused her bitter reflections: "If anyone had told me, when I was at Orléans in 1652 and kept the king out of the city on Monsieur's orders, that my reward would be that in four years Monsieur would be there and would shut the gates in my face and treat me as harshly as he could—that person would have given me valuable information. By acting on it I could have made peace with the court in such a way as to forever avoid being mistreated by my father or anyone else; indeed I might have been in a position to be of use and protection to him. Recollections like these are murderous: I'd be happy to have no memory."

Monsieur, going on from Orléans to take the waters at Bourbon, passed within a quarter of a league of Saint-Fargeau but refused to see his daughter; and when, a little later, Mademoiselle sent one of her footmen to Blois to let Monsieur know, as a dutiful daughter should, that she was briefly leaving Saint-Fargeau to take the waters at Forges, "Monsieur saw my footman, flew into a rage against him, and screamed abuse. The boy was so frightened that he came racing back to me. He was a Basque who spoke French none too well, and he said to me, "Monsieur say something about business. You break your word. He throw me out window." And Monsieur threatened also to secure from the court *lettres de cachet* that would cause Nau and Préfontaine to be imprisoned respectively in Pau and Perpignan.

So fearful was Mademoiselle of anything coming from Blois that she "passed a letter from Goulas over a flame, fearing that it might carry some subtle poison." She knew that Goulas had said to Monsieur: "The Romans had the power of life and death over their children: aren't you a great enough prince to act toward Mademoiselle as you wish?" When she reflected that instead of "throwing Goulas out the window" for saying that, Monsieur had "contented himself with saying nothing," and when she thought of how often he had threatened her with "perpetual imprisonments, convents, and starvation"—at such moments she sank into "melancholy reverie" and had a recurrent sinister thought: "I remembered that Monsieur was the son of a Médicis. . . . The queen my grandmother was a good woman, without any of the faults of her race and nation; but sometimes such blemishes skip one generation. . . ." Or was it in herself, perhaps, Mademoiselle wondered, that the "venom of the Médicis" was showing itself, that she should have so dreadful a thought about her father?

But now Monsieur's inhuman treatment of his daughter was common knowledge, but Mademoiselle did not always welcome sympathy. During one of her rounds of visits she met, for the first time since her exile, Henrietta-Maria. "Think," said Charles's mother, "if you had married my son, you wouldn't be in the straits you're in with your father. You'd be your own mistress and could choose your own servants. You might even be on the English throne. I'm persuaded my poor son could be happy only with you. If you had married him, he and I would be on better terms than we are; you would have helped us get along better."

Henrietta-Maria didn't seem to feel the scratch buried in the velvety reply of Mademoiselle, who had indeed heard that Charles, still in exile, was tiring of his mother's continued bossiness. "Since he doesn't get on well with Your Majesty, is it conceivable that he would with any other woman?"

It seems to have been the countesses who first opened Mademoiselle's eyes to the full meaning of Monsieur's merciless behavior. They opened her eyes by disappearing. Quite abruptly, the countesses left Saint-Fargeau. With Préfontaine and his clerk gone, their usefulness as spies was apparently at an end; Monsieur told them they might go, and they didn't conceal their delight at departure. What interested Mademoiselle, amid her relief at seeing them go, was where they went. They went to Paris. The countesses, like Monsieur, were forgiven their sins, permitted to return to court! The king was clearly disposed toward amnesty. But Mademoiselle remained unamnestied. Why was this?

If there remained, at this point, any lingering doubt in Mademoiselle's mind as to the answer, it was quickly dissipated by a new overtness, a new shamelessness, in Monsieur's tactics. Mademoiselle's stinginess and callousness, he was telling everybody, were unbelievable. Her unfortunate half sisters, poor penniless waifs, she despised; nothing would please her more than to see them begging in the streets or languishing in foundling hospitals. Her stepmother she likewise jeered at because Madame was no heiress. A fine thing, for an immensely rich young woman to sneer at members of her immediate family in their poverty, to allow them to perish from want! Such was Monsieur's new line. It wasn't intended to be believed, of course—everyone knew that Monsieur still drew a large pension from the court, still enjoyed the revenues of his duchies and his county and his governorship; it was meant merely as a message to Mademoiselle. Blackmail!

Mademoiselle's exile could last indefinitely, the message meant; or, she could shorten it by buying off this *fils de France* who was reconciled with the court.

Mademoiselle resigned herself to the inevitable—especially when the king's chancellor, in ways truly difficult to understand without a set of lawbooks, let her know that the king would be pleased—this was an order—to see father and daughter reconciled. She knew the sum Monsieur wanted—it had been clearly stated in the amount of the "error in reckoning" in the arbitration document—and now the comte de Béthune drew up a letter that seems to have been little more than a deed of transfer. "I'll not copy the letter here," she says bitterly in her memoirs. "It was the comte de Béthune's, not mine." It stated that she was acting of her own free will, uncoerced. As she signed, her bitterness overflowed against the father who was forcing her to "buy his friendship." "We forgot to state," she bitingly remarked to the comte de Béthune, "that I'm the one who's using coercion: I'm forcing my father to accept my money."

The letter was sent to Blois. "I'll be welcomed there like the Messiah," Mademoiselle prophesied. By return of messenger she received letters from Monsieur and Madame. "Let me prepare myself," she said sardonically before opening them, "lest I die of joy." The letters were, of course, "the most affectionate in the world."

She went to Blois. "I went straight to Monsieur's room. He greeted me, and told me he was happy to see me. I replied that I was enchanted by the honor. He was exceedingly ill at ease, and didn't know what to say; if it hadn't been for my dogs, one of them called Queen, the other Madame Mouse, both of them *levrettes,* no one would have said anything. Monsieur began to pet them. Everything he did with the intention of pleasing me made me feel wretched; I felt like weeping. Nothing remarkable happened at Blois while I was there except that Madame Mouse fell into the moat and dislocated her leg. As I was returning from a walk I heard her yelping, and ran to her; the doctor tried his best to set her leg, but couldn't, and to help things along they put her in a manure pile in one of the courtyards. Monsieur went out at midnight to see how she was. This was considered by the *hoi polloi* a wonderful proof of my father's tenderness; as for myself, I should have preferred marks of affection and kindness that were more essential."

And from Blois "Monsieur wrote to Cardinal Mazarin to tell him that I was reconciled with him, and to beg him to tell Their Majesties that I should be glad to come and pay them my very humble respects." Mademoiselle had written to Condé shortly before to say that they must stop corresponding. "I have to surrender," she told him. "If I find myself able, with honor and without baseness, to come to an agreement with the cardinal, I shall do so, in order to escape my father's persecutions."

Mademoiselle's exile was over. She was without illusions. "If I had been on good terms with my father, I'd have been forgiven at the same time as he. When he was reconciled, he stipulated that I shouldn't be."

Less than ever now did Monsieur bring any possibility of joy to Mademoiselle. She had to keep looking a little further for his image.

"When the chevalier de Charny had finished his tutoring, I said to him: 'You're of an age to choose the profession that suits you best; I'm not going to force you into any. I hope that you'll succeed best in the one which you like the best, the one you're most inclined to follow. If you want to enter the church, you must study theology, and I'll send you to the Sorbonne. If you want to stay in the world, it's time to go to the academy.' [By *academy* Mademoiselle meant a fencing and riding-school attended by young aristocrats.] 'If fortune smiles on you, you can be happy whatever your situation; choose the one you like the best.' He told me that he had no inclination toward the church; he hoped to be a gentleman, and he wanted to distinguish himself in the army—that, he said, would force Monsieur to advance him. I sent for his uncle, his mother's brother, to come to Saint-Fargeau and take him to the academy, fearing lest Monsieur be displeased if I sent any of my own household with him. He was downcast at the thought of leaving me, but was easily consoled; he felt that he was going to a place where he could try to become a gentleman and worthy of serving me."

A year later, Monsieur interfered even in this. "The king had reactivated his company of musketeers, which had been dispersed during the first years of the regency: the king was very fond of musketeers. Mancini, nephew of Cardinal Mazarin, was captain; the musketeers were all the rage. The chevalier de Charny was on the point of finishing at the academy; I asked the comte d'Escars to ask Bas, a second-lieutenant in the company, to ask the king to give him a place in it. Monsieur learned of this through the countesses, and asked the king to refuse my request. So Bas told the comte d'Escars that the king had said he couldn't do it because of Monsieur; His Majesty was very sorry, he said, for the chevalier was a fine-looking young man. He had had the honor to be presented to the king while he was at the academy, and had made an excellent impression. When I saw how things stood, I sent the chevalier to carry his musket in the regiment of the guards, and I gave him two letters, one for the maréchal de Turenne, the other for the maréchal de La Ferté, so that he might enter whatever division would offer him the greatest opportunities. I recommended him to both generals."

In his exile at Blois, Monsieur had often been filled with fears. He had often said to Mademoiselle "that he'd never return to court; that if they tried to deprive him of his rights and starve him into submission, he'd camp at Chambord with all his staff; there was enough game there to keep him in food for a long time, and he'd eat the last deer before rejoining the court." And Monsieur made a gloomy prophecy: "He said one day that he thought the monarchy was approaching its end; that with things as they were, the kingdom couldn't continue to exist; that in all monarchies that had ever collapsed, their decadence had begun with changes like those that had been taking place in France. And he launched into a long series of comparisons to prove his point by past examples."

Monsieur's prophecy can either be laughed at because it was made just as the magnificence of Versailles was about to begin, or respected because it came true 130 years later. In any case, it's a pleasure to report that when Monsieur did revisit the court, he was treated with scant consideration. At La Fère, where he first paid his respects to the king and queen, "cardinal Mazarin pretended to have the gout in order not to have to come out to greet him, so that all France could see that it was Monsieur who had called on *him*. I think the cardinal was quite right," says Mademoiselle. "Had I been in his place I should have done the same. Monsieur had done him sufficient injury so that he ought to have been glad to make this kind of *amende honorable.*"

Monsieur's second court visit was at Fontainebleau. There the king and queen were playing cards when he was announced, and "they scarcely rose to greet him, and went on with their playing." The next evening he went walking with Their Majesties, and "as the king almost never wears a hat, that embarrassed my father, who wasn't as young as the king, and was in terror of the twilight dampness. The king and queen let him go a long time without telling him to put on his hat, even though he had put his gloves on his head to show them how apprehensive he was."

That spectacle of Monsieur, miserable in the dangerous dampness exhaled by the Fontainebleau forest at twilight, tortured by his disdainful sister-in-law and nephew, his hat in his hand and his gloves on his head, is a satisfying one, up to a point. And since Mademoiselle put it into her memoirs it seems possible that up to a point it satisfied *her*. At least one can hope so.

3

IT SURPRISED MADEMOISELLE that her feelings at the end of exile should be mixed.

"My joy wasn't as unalloyed as one would have expected. I kept seeking a thousand things to regret—among others, I was sorry not to have got back my Italian, which I had learned in earlier years, so that I could read Tasso. The truth is that the very day I wrote the comte de Béthune's letter I had taken down my Italian books, with that idea in mind. Still," she concludes, "beautiful though he is, few people would be sorry to go to Paris in order not to read Tasso." The words ring like a precious echo of her grandfather's famous "Paris is worth a Mass."

At the moment, however, the court was absent from Paris, close to a military operation in which the king was participating—the seige of Montmédy by the maréchal de la Ferté; and Mademoiselle, waiting at Saint-Cloud, was told that Sedan, close to the battle lines, had been chosen as the scene of her forgiveness. The court must be given credit for possessing a highly developed sense of the appropriate.

Northeastward, therefore, Mademoiselle sped in her coach early in August, 1657, accompanied by the comte and comtesse de Béthune. At Dammartin they were hailed by a throng of courtiers who had been waiting in order that all might travel to Sedan in the greater security of numbers, for the soldiers of Mademoiselle's friend Condé were making the countryside none too safe. At La

Fère they found Colbert—not yet minister of finance, but the
cardinal's personal steward—with two cartloads of the king's
money and an escort of musketeers. Then, at Rheims, they were
joined by part of the escort that the king had sent for Mademoiselle—120 gendarmes and light-horse under the orders of the
comte de La Salle; and the whole large party set out across the
plains of Champagne. They forded rivers, ate cold food in the
fields, ended each day's progress to the sound of trumpets: "it
was like a real military expedition."

At Vandy their escort was strengthened by a regiment of Ger-
mans, and as they approached the danger zone of Rocroi—scene
of a French victory won by Condé before the Fronde, but since
reconquered by Condé for the Spaniards—Mademoiselle told
Colbert she was sure there would be no trouble: "Condé is too
much of a gentleman not to respect whatever is under *my* protection." There was joking, then, as to what would happen if
Condé did attack: among his officers were some who owed their
lives to Mademoiselle's opening of the Porte Saint-Antoine—
what degree of gratitude would they display? The comtesse de
Béthune said that she was worried chiefly for the king's money:
in case of attack she would rush from her coach and go sit on it—
would the troops of Condé respect her person?

They reached the outskirts of Sedan on Saturday morning, August 1.

"Damville went ahead, to the meadow outside the walls where
we were told the queen was taking the air, to ask whether I might
approach her there. She replied that I might. I drove to the field,
my coach horses at full gallop, my gendarmes and light-horse beside me, their trumpets blaring triumphantly. As I approached the
queen's coach, they stopped and placed themselves in double file
between her coach and mine; I got out twenty paces from the
queen, walked up to her, and kissed her gown and her hands. She
did me the honor of kissing me and saying she was happy to see
me. She had always loved me, she said, though there had been

times when I angered her. She hadn't held my actions at Orléans against me; but as for the Porte Saint-Antoine. . . . If she could have laid hands on me then, she said, she would have strangled me. I told her that by displeasing her I had merited strangling; and my displeasing her, I said, had been the unfortunate consequence of my finding myself with people who had induced me to act contrary to my duty."

"I had intended to talk with you about that," the queen said. "I meant to tell you everything I had on my mind. But I've forgotten it all. We must talk no more about it. Believe me, I shall love you more than ever. It's six years since I've seen you, but I don't find you changed. You look better than you did: you're a little plumper; your complexion is better."

"Hasn't Your Majesty heard that I have some gray hairs?"

The queen said she had.

"I don't want to hide anything from anyone; I didn't powder my hair today, so that I could show you."

"She looked, and was surprised to see so many at my age. I told her that my grandmother Guise had been as gray at twenty as the day she died, and that on my father's side, too, gray hairs came early. She asked me if I hadn't been bored at Saint-Fargeau, and how I had kept myself entertained. I told her I hadn't been bored at all, and had kept myself entertained well enough."

"We have increased the guard at the gate in your honor," the queen said as they entered the city. "Ordinarily there aren't so many."

Mademoiselle enjoyed that. "So far, you've treated me like a foreign princess, come from abroad."

In Sedan the cardinal's nieces, Marie and Hortense Mancini, who had arrived from Italy since the Fronde, were presented to Mademoiselle; most of the queen's maids of honor were unknown to her too, and they also were presented; and gentlemen arrived from Stenay, near Montmédy, bearing messages of welcome from the king, from the king's brother the duc d'Anjou, and from the cardinal. All three of them said they were impatient for the seige to end so that they could come and see her.

The queen told Mademoiselle that she would find the king much changed, that he had "grown tall, broad, and sure of himself, and was looking well." He had been crowned at Rheims three years before, while Mademoiselle was at Saint-Fargeau; it had been hinted to her, in her exile, that no one would object if she attended the coronation *incognita,* but she had declined the indignity. Directly from the ceremony he had joined the army at Stenay for his first lesson of real warfare. Now, at nineteen, he was a veteran of several sieges. After Mademoiselle had been at Sedan only a few days came the news that Montmédy had fallen: the king had been allowed closer to the actual fighting than usual, and had signed the acceptance of capitulation himself.

He arrived at Sedan on Friday. "The queen was expecting him for dinner, and was watching for him from a window. He came at a gallop, and he was so wet and dirty that she told me that she'd rather I not have my first view of him until after he had changed. I told her his costume didn't matter to me. He came in, and disheveled though he was, I thought he looked very well. 'Here is a young lady whom I present to you,' the queen said. 'She's very sorry she was naughty. She'll be very good in the future.' "

The king laughed, and began immediately to tell them about the siege. The courtier-soldiers who were with him assured the queen that during a certain skirmish the king had been the first to enter a dangerous wood. "We did all we could to hold him back," they told her, "but there was no use." In their manner was apparent a great eagerness to please. Mademoiselle had long been familiar with this kind of eagerness—she knew it and usually valued it in persons close to herself and close to other grandees; but this was the first time in her life that she had seen, as its recipient, a maturing, promising young king of France.

Then a carriage was heard. "My brother," the king said.

The duc d'Anjou came in, "very trim in gray and flame-color.

After greeting the queen he came over to me, and drew me into a window alcove and kissed me. He seemed overjoyed to see me, and told me that I was much better-looking than I used to be. I told him that I found him grown; we found much to praise in each other."

"Go have your dinner now," the queen told Mademoiselle. "This evening you'll have supper with us *en famille*."

But before supper Mademoiselle went to the queen's apartments again, for during the afternoon she learned that the cardinal had arrived. She found him talking with Anne of Austria at a window. "The cardinal was just about to call on *you*," the queen told her as she appeared.

"I think, Madame," said Mademoiselle, "that it would be appropriate if you allowed the cardinal and me to embrace, after everything that has happened. On my side, it would come from the heart." And the next moment the queen had stepped aside and Mazarin was low before Mademoiselle, embracing her knees; she raised him up and kissed him, and they exchanged compliments. Soon they were joking about the past.

For the moment, banter was the tone the cardinal chose to use with her. He rode back from Mass the next day in her coach. "If anyone had told you in 1652," he said, "that in 1657 Mazarin would be riding beside you, you wouldn't have believed him. But here he is—the same Mazarin who did all those terrible things."

"I never thought he was so bad," Mademoiselle said. "I always thought things would turn out as they have."

He teased her about Condé, trying to trap her into praise or blame; but Mademoiselle side-stepped neatly: "When he's back at court, I'll scold him."

Had her father been willing, he said, she would now be queen of France; but Monsieur's bad conduct had rendered useless all his efforts on her behalf. "You mustn't stand on ceremony with me," he told her. "I am your servant. If you're formal with me I'll think you're treating me like one of those Mazarines."

With the king, things were different. Even from the beginning he was courteous, and not embarrassed or suspicious in her company as he might have been after what had gone before; but he was silent, reserved, cold—it was his way. With him there was no question of not being ceremonious: at nineteen, Louis XIV was well on his way to becoming the Grand Monarque. His young profile was like one on a Greek or Roman coin; he had immense stores of gravity at his command. But gradually he thawed with Mademoiselle. "After my dinner the second day the king came to see me; he spoke with me as civilly as one could imagine. I wanted to attend him back to his apartments, but he refused; I insisted, however, on seeing him as far as his coach. "Even if Your Majesty doesn't want me to, let me do it for the sake of people who would think me ignorant of my duty if I didn't.'

" 'I shouldn't allow it,' he said. And when we reached his coach he said, 'Since you order me to get in, I will: otherwise I shouldn't dream of doing it in front of you.' "

Every night Mademoiselle danced with him after supper. He had been very sorry, he said, to have had to refuse her request to make the chevalier de Charny a musketeer; but she was able to tell him that the young man was happy and popular in his guards regiment; on her way across Champagne she had news of him; he had been chosen to be one of Turenne's bodyguard. The king was very martial-minded, intoxicated by campaigns; his conversation was chiefly military. "Have you ever heard kettledrums?" he asked her enthusiastically after a long speech about his guards, his musketeers, his gendarmes, his light-horse, his cavalry, and his trumpeters.

Courtiers had advised Mademoiselle to flatter him as much as she could about such things, and this mention of kettledrums seemed to her an excellent occasion. But Mademoiselle's conception of flattery was her own. "Yes, Sire, I have heard them," she replied.

"Where?"

"I began to smile, and said to him very respectfully: 'In foreign regiments that were with us during the war.' "

The king was silent: he well knew what war she was referring to, and whom she meant by "us."

Mademoiselle went on smoothly. "I ought to be unhappy to remember it. It was at a time when I was displeasing Your Majesty. I beg your pardon: I should do so on my knees."

That was the kind of remark that Louis XIV was to answer to absolute perfection all his life. "It is I who should be on my knees," he told Mademoiselle, "to hear you talk so."

And when he resumed his description of his campaigns, she said, really flattering him this time, "The king your grandfather didn't go to war so young."

"But when he did go, he did more than I. Up to now they haven't let me go as close to the front as I'd like to. In the future I hope to get myself talked about."

Mademoiselle told him that he was quite right: "Kings should want to accomplish as much as other men."

She knew, of course, that he was in the midst of his first love affair. Not a carnal affair—earlier than this, everyone knew, when he had been fifteen, one of his mother's ladies in waiting, the one-eyed, forty-five-year-old Madame de Beauvais, had at the queen's request added his *dépucelage* to her other duties—but a real infatuation, tender and terrible, with Marie Mancini, the cardinal's seventeen-year-old niece. There was no possibility that Marie could ever be queen; the cardinal had stated that he "well knew the difference between his family and the house of Bourbon"; but no one was doing anything to halt the progress of the doomed attachment, and Mademoiselle knew better than to mention it. Christina of Sweden had done so, very brusquely—"If I were you, I'd marry somebody I loved," she had said to the king in Marie's presence—and no one had thanked her. Christina had also spoken crudely of the king's bashful manner: she said she "had the impression he'd never laid hands on Marie." It was almost true: the two young people whispered together, read poetry together, strolled together; they were living a wistful dream, whose duration depended on the demands of politics. Mademoiselle let the king choose his own topics of conversation: when she went out riding with him he showed her his horses, "one after the other."

She had decided it would be indiscreet of her to stay long at court this first time, and after twelve days she departed, giving as polite pretext her wish to take the waters at Forges. She was accompanied and escorted as when she had arrived.

She had reasons to feel that her reconciliation visit had been a success.

The king had been gracious to her; and she, for her part, had found him everything she thought a king should be: "His ideas seemed admirable to me. I was completely satisfied with him."

The queen had made her welcome, helped her change her outmoded way of doing her hair, complimented her on her dancing, and played cards with her until Mademoiselle's "lack of application" to the game made her nervous. The queen had become a gambler. "The greatest changes I know of in the world are that Your Majesty now plays and that my father has given it up," said Mademoiselle.

The queen sympathized with Mademoiselle over the conduct of the countesses at Saint-Fargeau—neither of them was a person she would have advised her taking in the first place, she said—and she deplored the behavior of Monsieur. Mademoiselle told her that the comte de Béthune and her other advisers had urged her not to set any conditions in her capitulation to Monsieur, not even the return of Préfontaine and Nau to her service: the slightest condition would have infuriated Monsieur and wrecked negotiations; it was better to hope that eventually he would soften and let her take back her faithful helpers. The queen was skeptical: "I hope it may turn out so. Those gentlemen probably had their reasons for giving you that advice. But I shouldn't have agreed to it. I'd have insisted on guarantees. Monsieur can be twisted in a different direction every moment: I know it from experience. How many promises he made me! How often he failed me! It would be very hard for me ever to trust him in the future."

Mademoiselle took comfort "in those marks of the queen's goodness and in the knowledge that I wasn't the only one toward whom Monsieur had acted badly."

As for the cardinal, the important thing was that he had intended—if he and the queen were telling the truth—to call on Mademoiselle before she met him at the queen's. And even if the words were insincere, their very utterance was a greater politeness than any he had shown Monsieur. He urged her to stay at court as long, and to return as often, as she liked.

And if Mademoiselle had played, perhaps overplayed, at Sedan, the role of erring, repentant daughter of the court—the naughty girl who is sorry and promises to be good, as the queen-mother had presented her to the king—who can blame her? Just as it was worth giving up Tasso to get back to Paris, so it was worth a little show of repentance to get back into the good graces of people from whom she *might* receive better treatment than from Monsieur. An indication of the true extent of Mademoiselle's repentance is shown, perhaps, in the portrait she had painted of herself, just about this time, by Pierre Mignard, the queen's painter-in-ordinary. Mademoiselle chose to go down to posterity holding lance and shield, against a background ruddy with a warlike glare—the glare, there can be little doubt, of the battle of the Faubourg Saint-Antoine.

But the most effusive welcome given Mademoiselle at Sedan we have barely mentioned. It came from Philippe, duc d'Anjou, the king's seventeen-year-old brother. It and he form a story in themselves.

4

WHEN MADEMOISELLE, speaking to Anne of Austria for the first time in six years in the meadow outside the walls of Sedan, had told her, ". . . on my father's side, too, gray hairs come early," she spoke of her father simply as *"mon père."*

The queen laughed at that. "I'm surprised to hear you say *'mon père,'*" she said. "Still, you're quite right: to say *'Monsieur mon père'* would be ridiculous."

To refer to one's father as *"monsieur mon père"* was normal respectful usage in polite society; but in the case of Mademoiselle's father the word *"monsieur"* was practically a title; for Mademoiselle to refer to him as *"Monsieur mon père"* would be the pretentious equivalent of saying *"le marquis mon père,"* or *"le duc mon père"*—that is what the queen had meant by saying it would be ridiculous.

Mademoiselle agreed with her, but went further. "That way of speaking is so common," she said, "that people like myself shouldn't use it. Besides, to call my father 'Monsieur' now that there is another 'Monsieur' wouldn't be right. It will take me a little time to remember to call my father 'Monsieur le duc d'Orléans' or 'His Royal Highness.'"

The name trouble reflected in Mademoiselle's words sprang from the fact that the next-younger brothers of two French kings were alive simultaneously. Each, because of his position, had the right to be called "Monsieur"; and the title, meant to be unique, became confusing. The younger brother of Louis XIV, the seventeen-year-old Philippe, duc d'Anjou, was now as much 'Monsieur' as was Mademoiselle's father, younger brother of the previous sovereign. It will be well for us, perhaps, to follow Mademoiselle's example: from now on Philippe will be "Monsieur" to us; Mademoiselle's father will be either "Mademoiselle's father" or "Gaston d'Orléans."

Mademoiselle's immediate reference to Monsieur, at the very instant of her reunion with the queen, was far from being an accident. The court had had something in mind, naturally, in forgiving Mademoiselle, in welcoming her back so warmly: nothing at court was done without reason. Indeed, it seems possible that the forgiveness of Mademoiselle's father, whom the court treated so carelessly after forgiving him, may have been a mere preliminary —a prerequisite, considering the respect due paternal authority— to the more important return of Mademoiselle.

Mademoiselle knew quite well what the court had in mind. The court was considering her as a wife for Monsieur.

"I'll marry you to our cousin Mademoiselle: she's very rich, she'll make your fortune"; those words, spoken by the king to Monsieur one day when Monsieur was asking to be given an *apanage,* had been repeated to Mademoiselle at Saint-Fargeau by a visitor from court. Even earlier than that: "One day when I was walking with Préfontaine at Saint-Fargeau and we were talking about a suitable establishment for me, he said 'I've thought of somebody who'll soon be suitable: Monsieur. He's growing up; before long he'll be a man. You're older than he is, but between people of your rank age has no importance.' " He was twelve years her junior: Mademoiselle didn't see why she should mind if Monsieur didn't, and according to the visitor from court, Monsieur had begun to count on the marriage from the moment his brother had mentioned it to him. "I was quite pleased to hear that he wanted it," Mademoiselle records.

At Sedan there were unmistakable signs of what was in the wind.

"You won't find that my son has grown very tall," the queen told Mademoiselle at their first lunch, "but you'll find him very nice-looking. He looks like you." (The queen always meant Monsieur when she said "my son": when she meant the king, she said "the king.") "Besides," she said, "you eat like my son; you remind me of him."

At the queen's toilette there was a sly remark by Madame de Beauvais, who had done so much for the king at fifteen: "Madame, doesn't Mademoiselle make you think of Monsieur? Jesus! What thoughts I have when I look at her!" The queen laughed.

"Where is your brother?" the queen asked the king when he had come in so disheveled-looking after his gallop from Montmédy.

"He's coming in my coach. He didn't want to get on a horse—he was afraid of arriving dirty; he's all dressed up." And as the king said that "he laughed and looked at the queen, as though to indicate that it was all because of me."

And when the queen asked the king "Where was your brother during that skirmish in the wood?" he answered, "He stayed in his coach: he didn't have his boots on."

Monsieur himself, at Sedan, after he had drawn Mademoiselle into the window alcove and kissed her, had hung around her continually. They had danced together; he'd taken her into his room and showed her what he liked best in the world—his collection of jewels; he'd begged her to stay on at Sedan longer; and on the morning of her departure he'd got up before eight to bid her good-by—a "great excess" for him, as this royal adolescent never rose before eleven. All that attentiveness on the part of Monsieur, however, might not have been particularly significant in itself. For Monsieur had always had a liking for his older cousin, even as a little boy, when he'd run up to her in the queen's bedroom in the Palais-Royal after the royal scolding about Saujon and the arch-

duke and kissed her, saying, "I've been for you all along, cousin;
I've been taking your side against everybody." It was what other
people were saying at Sedan that told the story.

During the autumn which followed her reconciliation with the
court Mademoiselle traveled about France visiting a number of
her properties; and then she resettled herself, after five years, in
Paris. This time she lived not in the Tuileries—there was no question of dislodging Monsieur, now five years established in her old
apartments—but in the Luxembourg, where her father had given
orders that his own quarters be furnished for her. "Ordinarily it
would be taken for granted that a father allow his daughter to
live in his house and make use of it as she wished," says Mademoiselle. "That's as it should be. No one would talk about it. But
in my case this was such a favor as I had never before received,
and both his friends and mine spoke of nothing else." Monsieur
called on her at once, beautifully dressed as always, bearing a gift
of Portuguese oranges. And then all Paris descended on her. "Naturally, during the first days of my return my house was never
empty: even if duty and the fact that I'm well liked hadn't brought
people in, everyone would have come anyway, out of simple
French love of anything new. Monsieur came again, and people
told me that he spoke of nothing but how enthusiastic he was
about me. I was glad to hear it: I felt the same about him, and
about everything concerning him. A young prince, handsome,
graceful, brother of the king—he seemed an excellent candidate
for my hand."

During that winter she saw him constantly. She was with him
at theatrical performances in the Louvre, at the ballets and balls
in which he and the king loved to dance in their palaces and in
the homes of courtiers; and this year some of the best balls were
in the Luxembourg—it was the finest place in the world, Mademoiselle discovered, for parties of all sizes. They also spent many
an evening together at the Foire Saint-Germain, the big trade fair
and fun fair held every spring just a few blocks from the Luxem-

bourg; during Lent other festivities closed, but the three-hundred-odd booths of the Foire Saint-Germain offered everything from merchandise to marionettes, from lotteries to magic-lantern shows.

Christina of Sweden, back from Rome, appeared at many of the Paris masquerades that winter, dressed usually as a Turk or gypsy. The king, Monsieur, and the others did not enjoy her presence. She danced badly, and besides, she was in disfavor because of a recent discourtesy. She had stayed in the palace at Fontainebleau for a time on her way from Italy, and had discovered while there that her equerry, Monaldeschi, had committed disloyal acts and had to be punished. "One day, when Monaldeschi was dining in the town"—so Mademoiselle tells the story—"the queen of Sweden sent for him, and said, 'Go into the gallery.' She meant the Galerie des Cerfs. There he found the chevalier de Sentinelli, captain of the queen of Sweden's guards, who said, 'Confess your sins! Here is Père Le Bel.' The queen of Sweden had explained to Père Le Bel, prior of the Mathurins of Fontainebleau, what she held against Monaldeschi, to make the priest understand that to have him stabbed to death in the Galerie des Cerfs was no different, in her mind, from having him beheaded in Sweden. Monaldeschi was extremely reluctant to die. He sent Père Le Bel to the queen, to beg for his pardon and his life. She refused. He tried to jump out a window; they were all locked. Sentinelli had trouble killing him: he was wearing a coat of mail under his shirt and had to be stabbed a great number of times. The gallery was drenched with blood; every attempt was made to clean it, but traces still remain. They buried Monaldeschi in the Fontainebleau cemetery that night. They say the queen of Sweden came to watch the killing; I don't know whether that's accurate."

Actually, Christina did not watch Monaldeschi's murder: she merely listened to it from the next room. Otherwise Mademoiselle's account is substantially correct, though far less bloody and detailed than one written by Père Le Bel himself. "Such putting to death is cruel and barbarous in anyone, especially in a woman," says Mademoiselle. But it was Christina's Gothic insensitivity as shown in her choice of place for the assassination that displeased the French: "Her deed was very much disapproved by the court. She was much blamed for having it committed in the king's palace." Christina was guilty, if a queen could be, of a kind of *lèse-majesté* toward Louis XIV. Long before she left Paris, once again Italy-bound, "everyone was incredibly impatient for her to be gone."

During that winter Mademoiselle found a number of things to notice about Monsieur, that "excellent candidate for her hand." She noticed what he said when Henrietta-Maria's daughter, princess Henriette d'Angleterre, complained of being slighted one evening at court: "We feed those people, don't we? If they don't like it here why don't they go somewhere else?" (The queen reprimanded him.) She found that he couldn't stand being teased. Mademoiselle loved to joke; but to joke with Monsieur was apt to make him sulky; once he sulked "for eight or ten days, until the queen had us make up." And there was something else, something that during her exile Mademoiselle had heard about, but only now saw for herself. At one of the Mardi gras masquerades Monsieur was dressed as a girl. The queen seemed quite pleased with his appearance, and remarked that he looked more like Mademoiselle than ever.

"How are you getting along with Monsieur?" the cardinal asked her one day when they were alone.

"As well as anyone could, with someone as childish as he."

"The queen and I are in despair about him," the cardinal said. "He seems to enjoy nothing except having dresses made for Mademoiselle de Gourdon"—Mademoiselle de Gourdon was one of the queen's maids of honor—"and dressing up as a girl himself. He doesn't ride, or fence, or do any of the exercises young men of his age commonly do; he's going in more and more for a daintiness unbecoming to a man."

Mademoiselle remembered what she had heard. "I thought you

wanted him to behave that way, that you wanted him to lead that kind of a life."

"On the contrary: the queen and I wish passionately that he would ask to go into the army."

"Every day I blame him for not doing just that."

"If you could induce him to, it would be the greatest pleasure you could give the queen."

"I'm told that the queen disapproves of my being with Monsieur so much. If that's true, I wish you'd tell me. I could easily stop going out with him, without telling him I'd been forbidden to."

"Don't believe those who tell you that. The queen likes him to be with you; you're a good influence on him."

"I haven't given him any advice yet. If I do give him some, you may rest assured it won't go against the queen's feelings or yours."

"What advantage would it be to me," the cardinal demanded, "if Monsieur were to turn out badly? It would kill every chance of our getting along well together. If he is worth something, I'm sure he'll do me the honor of loving me."

"I left," says Mademoiselle, "very satisfied with that conversation. I told Monsieur about it, and thereafter we went out together frequently."

Still, when the court accompanied the king north that May, to the siege of Dunkirk, Mademoiselle had no reason to be satisfied concerning Monsieur. Day after day the king was on horseback; the siege was long; the Spaniards, led by Condé and Don Juan of Austria, brought up strong reinforcements; but on June 4 Turenne won a mighty victory. "Have you ever seen a battle lost?" Condé asked the duke of Gloucester that day. "Well, you'll see one now." It was the famous Battle of the Dunes, the end of Spanish supremacy in the Low Countries. And all that time, "while the king was with the army," Mademoiselle records, "Monsieur, instead of being with him, stayed with the queen like a child— and now he was nineteen years old. The queen led her usual life, praying and playing cards. Monsieur went out with her maids of honor, strolled along the seashore, enjoyed splashing them and being splashed, and amused himself buying ribbons and cloth that came over from England."

After the victory the king came down with fever and lay at death's door in Calais. He was given the last rites; the Blessed Sacrament was exposed in the churches of Paris; all France prayed. It was then, with news of the king's death expected hourly, that Mademoiselle discovered her real feelings concerning Monsieur— the only feelings possible in one who was *fille de France*.

"I was greatly distressed about the king, as may easily be imagined. He is my first cousin, he treats me well, and besides, to see a young king die is a terrible thing. I myself was terrified when I thought of the future and the affliction of the queen. I was fond of Monsieur; nevertheless, as he was, I could not feel that it would be to his advantage to be king. He was too much of a child to rule, too much of a child even to know what was good for him. The defects of exalted persons are more apparent than those of others, and I have no wish to exaggerate the defects of those close to me. It isn't that Monsieur isn't very intelligent; but so far he is without solidity, he has neither knowledge nor experience. His habits and his close friends were more calculated to ruin him than help the state. I confess that this redoubled my worries about the king's illness. It wasn't out of self-interest that I was worried: I knew the king would never marry me, and I was sure that kingship would do nothing to change Monsieur. I am so attached to my family that I should like all its members to be able to maintain its dignity and glory as superbly as the king my grandfather. Otherwise, I hope they may never reach the throne."

The king was cured by a provincial practitioner named Du Sausoy, generally considered a quack. Called in as a last resort, he shocked everyone by perching on the king's bed while he made his examination: "He's a very sick boy, but he won't die," was his verdict, and his prescription of emetic wine worked the miracle. However deplorable the political and social consequences of the long reign of Louis XIV, it is difficult to repress a shudder at the thought of his brush with death there in Calais after the Battle of the Dunes. For Monsieur would have succeeded him; and concerning Monsieur and his tastes and way of life Mademoiselle had been right, in her conversation with the cardinal, and the cardinal had, as usual, been far from candid.

As supervisor of the education of the two royal brothers, Mazarin had pursued two separate aims that were really one. The king had been carefully trained in manly pursuits—dancing, riding, arms: it was a kingly version of the culture of the academy attended by Mademoiselle's chevalier de Charny. "He'll go a little slowly at the beginning," Mazarin had commented, observing his young sovereign's progress, "but he'll go further than most others. There's enough stuff in him to make four kings, and a gentleman besides." Besides military strategy and tactics, the royal curriculum included history and mathematics; but intellectual exercises were not stressed: perhaps Mazarin was satisfied that the king *should* go slow, that for the time being the cardinal should continue to be the brains of France. As for Monsieur. . . . The example of the older Monsieur, Mademoiselle's father, haunted Mazarin. The last thing he wanted was another royal younger brother like Gaston d'Orléans, rebellious and interfering, a potential Frondeur. And so Monsieur was formed in a way that would render him harmless to king and cardinal: from his earliest years he was systematically emasculated. This was made the easier by his smallness and prettiness (people whispered that he looked like the cardinal's nieces): he was petted by the queen's women, treated by them as one of themselves. They taught him perverted little songs that he sang in a sweet little voice:

> *"Suis-je une fille, suis-je un garçon?*
> *Ton-ton, tontaine, ton-ton . . .*
> *Peut-être l'un, peut-être l'autre . . .*
> *Voyez, voyez, si ma façon*
> *Convient à l'une ou bien à l'autre."*

Not only at a single Mardi gras masquerade with Mademoiselle had the queen complacently viewed Monsieur dressed as a girl: she had always, on the cardinal's advice, encouraged him in his girlish tastes. Madame de Choisy, the wife of Gaston d'Orléans' chancellor, the lady who during the Fronde had been one of Mazarin's go-betweens with Mademoiselle in the affair of *mon petit mari,* had been encouraged to bring up her son François as a girlish companion to Monsieur. François de Choisy later became an abbé, an abbé who wore women's clothes, and he left memoirs that are among the best known documents of transvestism. "They used to dress me as a girl every time little Monsieur came to our house, and he came at least two or three times a week. I had pierced ears, diamonds, beauty spots. . . . He wore an embroidered corset. . . . I used to visit him at the Palais-Royal and he was delighted to see me because our inclinations were the same. . . ."

It was precisely during the period of Mademoiselle's return from her exile that Monsieur's habits were beginning to harden, his companions becoming less childishly lisping, more coldly vicious, than the young François de Choisy. The marquis de Villequier, the comte de Guiche, the chevalier de Lorraine—he was starting on a series of sinister favorites, each of them deplorable. The queen became displeased when Madame de Choisy began arranging for Monsieur to meet the comte de Guiche clandestinely, "like a mistress," and for a time Madame de Choisy was exiled to one of her estates in Normandy.

As boys, the king and Monsieur had expressed their rivalry as brothers do, though perhaps a little more overtly than is usual—their conflicts took the form of spitting at each other, urinating on each other's beds, throwing soup in each other's faces. Later, Monsieur copied his brother to the point of having some easy feats of arms arranged for himself in the field. But the cardinal's policy must be called a success: Monsieur was never a political danger.

Had the queen and the cardinal really hoped that Mademoiselle

would be Monsieur's bride? With the older Monsieur still awk-
wardly alive, his *apanage* was not yet available for the younger
Monsieur—who was, however, about ready for some kind of endowment: Mademoiselle's money would have been a royal con-
venience. The cardinal had been fractionally sincere with her: apparently he and the queen were dismayed by the *extent* to which
their training of Monsieur had taken. The scenes and stories now
beginning to be frequent scarcely added to the dignity of the
court. Were the queen and the cardinal so fatuous as to think, or
at least hope, that Monsieur's rich, older first cousin, of whom he
had always been fond, could be a kind of older-cousin-wife to *"la
plus jolie créature de France,"* as Monsieur was beginning to be
called, that she could keep him from scandalous disaster, or act as
a dignified screen? At any rate, they did not insist.

To Mademoiselle, of course, marriage with anyone unfit to be
king, or at least unfit to rule, anyone unfit to bear arms, was in-
conceivable; and her reflections concerning the king, Monsieur,
and the house of Bourbon during the king's illness were crucial.
"Monsieur was still perfectly friendly with me," she says, of the
summer that followed, "but he wasn't nearly as enthusiastic about
me as he had been during the first three months of my return to
court. To tell the truth, I didn't much care. The more I knew him,
the more I considered that he was a man who thought more about
his beauty and his dress than about achieving distinction by great
deeds. So I loved him dearly as a cousin, and would never have
loved him at all as a husband."

A little later she records: "Monsieur told me that he had been
to a masquerade dressed as a girl, and that he had found a gentleman there who had said loverlike things to him that he had
greatly enjoyed." Mademoiselle let Monsieur tell her such things
about himself, and she brooded on them no longer now that she
was no longer personally involved—and now that the king was
perfectly well.

In Blois, at the time of Mademoiselle's expensive reconciliation with her father, he had said that the most fitting candidate for her hand was duke Charles-Emmanuel II of Savoy—the son, that is, of his own sister Christine, Madame Royale, dowager duchess of Savoy, established at her court in Turin since before Mademoiselle's birth. "He said that I mustn't get it into my head to marry Monsieur: that that was just the kind of idea I *would* get into my head—that I never wanted anything except the impossible."

Her father had been right about Monsieur, of course, though not in the way he had intended: he had meant that the court would never allow his daughter to marry the king's brother, and in this he may well have been mistaken. One might be tempted to think that it was this paternal disapproval of the match with Monsieur that had caused it to fall through—that the mere shake of her father's head had been as decisive a deterrent as it had been at the moment of the affair with Charles II. But things had changed since then. Her father had tried Mademoiselle too sorely, outraged her too often; with him she now felt some kind of numbness. She calls it "indifference." Our conversations were the most indifferent imaginable," she says, when they met for the first time after her return to court, "like those of two people who were profoundly indifferent to each other." After her father's blackmail, she had found the court, the king's presence, a refuge: in a sense, Mademoiselle had changed fathers. Even before the Fronde the one exception she had made to her disdain for love had been in favor of *mon petit mari:* "I had put more hope in the way the king had been behaving with me, and in the pleasure he had been taking in my company, than in the negotiations of Madame de Choisy: that way of becoming queen was more to my taste than the other." Now, in Louis XIV at twenty, Mademoiselle had found someone who fulfilled her ideals of what a *fils de France* should and could be: in her turning away from young Monsieur, her father's disapproval counted for less than the king's mere existence. Indeed, it might even be said that by now the very resemblances of the younger Monsieur to the older—the same title, the same rank, the same blatant shoddiness —made it easy for her to extend to the one the same "indifference" she believed she had come to feel for the other.

As for her father's recommendation that she marry the duke of Savoy. . . .

Savoy was an important place. It was French policy to keep it strong and friendly, since it separated the Spanish Hapsburgs in Italy from the Austrian Hapsburgs to the north; and now a Franco-Savoyard alliance was indeed being talked about. Not Mademoiselle's marriage to the duke—though that, too, was a possibility— but Louis XIV's to the duke's sister, princess Marguerite. The very October following the king's recovery, the French court set out for Lyons, where they were to meet the entire Savoyard ducal family from Turin: if the king found the princess personally pleasing, Mazarin had arranged, they would be married.

Mademoiselle, though she still felt no inclination toward marriage, looked forward to meeting her Turinese relatives. She enjoyed the progress down through Burgundy and Beaujolais. She often left her coach to ride horseback beside the king in the fine autumn weather; at other times she tactfully left him alone with Marie Mancini—for he was as infatuated with the cardinal's niece as ever, inseparable from her during this trip designed to unite him with another. The king left the Dijon parlement aghast at the amount of money he extracted from the province in return for superfluous official posts he insisted on creating and being paid for; but even so, in town after town the Burgundian citizenry turned out to greet their king in impressively armed array: "They say it's because Caesar spent so much time in the region—martial ways have been handed down from father to son ever since." At Châlons there was a tourist attraction—a woman possessed of the devil; the king and all his suite went to see her—all except Mademoiselle: "I think the devil so evil, whatever aspect he may take, that he will never cause me anything but terror—never will I have the slightest wish to see him; I dread meeting him in this world as much as in the next."

But at Lyons, despite Madame Royale's arrival in a state of semicollapse following her crossing of the Susa pass, despite gorgeous receptions and honeyed words tendered the cisalpine party, the entire trip was quickly revealed to be just one of Mazarin's tricks. Savoy was important, but Spain was more important. The bride the cardinal really wanted for the king was the infanta of Spain. After twenty-five years of war, it was time for Franco-Spanish peace, and since the Battle of the Dunes negotiations had been in progress. The hand of the infanta would be the symbol of the new order; but the king of Spain, dissatisfied with certain treaty clauses insisted on by France, had been playing coy about yielding his daughter. Now, seeing Louis XIV on the point of being affianced to the princess of Savoy, Philip IV dared hold back no longer: he wanted peace badly, and he saw it threatening to elude him. To Lyons, therefore, scene of the Franco-Savoyard engagement negotiations, Philip IV hastily sent an envoy. Louis could have the infanta.

Mazarin had won. When he broke the news to the Savoyards, he was all polite regrets—but politics was politics. Madame Royale, no mean politician herself, saw the situation for what it was; but still she wept with rage and disappointment, screamed, even beat her head against the wall. Princess Marguerite smiled composedly at everyone; her self-control in the face of such humiliation, the French told each other admiringly, showed that had politics allowed, she would have made a good queen of France.

As for duke Charles-Emmanuel, a boisterous fellow, he "galloped his horse several times around the place de Bellecourt, jumped the fences of the mall, and shouted, 'Adieu, France, forever: I leave you without regret!' "

Gossip in Lyons had it that he declared, as he left, "I'm glad to have seen Mademoiselle: now I'm cured of *that* idea." But when the rumor reached him in Turin, he promptly had his ambassador at the French court, the abbé d'Amoretti, call on Mademoiselle to disavow it. "It made him feel desperate, he said, that anyone should want to make him out so ridiculous."

At any rate, there could be no question of a marriage between the duke and one who had witnessed the humiliation of his entire family. Mademoiselle was relieved. She had taken a dislike to Madame Royale, her aunt whom she had never seen before; she was an overmasterful woman, far more masterful even than her sister Henrietta-Maria. As a mother-in-law she would have been impossible: the only words her son was ever heard to utter in her presence were, "May I?"

After the departure of the Savoyards—Anne of Austria contemptuously dismissed Madame Royale's extravagant behavior as histrionics: "She's the world's greatest actress"—Mademoiselle received permission to make, from Lyons, a side trip of her own—a visit of a few days to her nearby principality of Dombes. At Trévoux, its ancient capital, she received the homage of her provincial parlement, clad in red robes: "I hadn't wanted them to come to Lyons for this, lest someone from court be with me at the time and see how pleased I was to be harangued like the queen by my subjects on their knees before me."

Back in Lyons, Mazarin showed that he knew what she'd really been up to in Dombes: "Well, Mademoiselle, you're rich! Your duchy has given you a present: you've created some new offices in your parlement."

Mademoiselle admitted it: "I told him I wished I might have a duchy only five leagues away from every city the king visited: it took care of my travel expenses. It was quite true: I'd appointed a president, three councilors, and other officers." It was, on a smaller scale, what the king had done in Dijon.

The court was back in Paris by February, and a portent of the approaching peace with Spain was the visit of the Spanish general

Don Juan of Austria, son of the king of Spain by his actress-mistress Maria Calderon: Anne of Austria called him "my nephew." Don Juan was on his way back to Madrid from the once-Spanish Low Countries. He was something of a novelty, one of the first high-ranking Spaniards to visit Paris in a generation; but even more intriguing to the Parisians was a certain item in his traveling gear. "Someone asked him for news of his fool, and he said he had left her with his baggage. She arrived in Paris a few days later. She was dressed like a man, with short hair and even a hat and a sword. She's ugly and cross-eyed, but to make up for it she has a lot of wit. She never left the Louvre. The king took a great fancy to her; the queen and Monsieur enjoyed her; so did I: each of us talked with her in turn. She spoke incessantly of the infanta. I don't know whether that displeased Mademoiselle Mancini; in any case, she conceived an aversion for the creature, called her crazy to her face, and couldn't stand her. La Pitore—that's what they called the girl: it's Spanish for 'simpleton'—made some joke in revenge. Mademoiselle de Mancini heard about it and was furious, with the result that the king's friendly feeling for the creature turned to hate. He could no longer bear her presence, and she had to be sent away. Everyone gave her gifts: the queen, Monsieur, and I gave her our portraits in enamel, with diamonds."

Such were the first presents from France to its new friend, Spain. Of course Don Juan's cross-eyed fool La Pitore offended Marie Mancini: with her talk of the infanta she was the first herald, after the envoy the Spanish king had sent to Lyons, of the married state now so near for the king. Negotiations with Spain were proceeding; and soon after the appearance of La Pitore at the Louvre, the king and Marie Mancini were torn apart. It was the cardinal who forced the inevitable break: he mercilessly exiled his niece to Brouage, a seaport on the Channel near La Rochelle. To the weeping Louis she sobbed out some farewell words; legend has given them the noble form of *"Vous êtes roi, vous m'aimez, vous pleurez, et je pars"*; and those, in turn, are said to have given Racine inspiration for lines in his tragedy *Bérénice:*

> *"Vous m'aimez, vous me le soutenez.*
> *Et cependant je pars, et vous me l'ordonnez?"*

The cardinal himself left for Saint-Jean-de-Luz, to work on details of the peace with the Spanish prime minister Don Louis de Haro; and then, in July, began a famous progress—the slow progress of the French court toward the Spanish border, where, when peace was signed, the king was to meet and marry the infanta.

Once again Mademoiselle traveled with the court. This time, all unsuspecting, she was traveling to meet the first apparition of *her* fate.

5

O N ITS WAY SOUTH, the court spent a night at Chambord—
the first time royalty had so honored Gaston d'Orléans
since the Fronde.

It was an honor that Gaston and his family would gladly have
done without. For one thing, there had been irresponsible talk
about Mademoiselle's oldest half sister marrying the king; her
parents and governess had foolishly called her "little queen"; and
now the poor girl, fourteen, awkward, and as chance had it that
day disfigured by insect bites, had to see the husband of her
dreams on his way to marry someone else. Gaston resented the
expense: he found it hard to smile when the king bagged fourteen Chambord pheasants in a single morning. And at dinner at
Blois the next day the court found the food, service, and company
ludicrously old-fashioned and didn't fail to show their feelings.
"The king and queen were in such a hurry to leave that I've never
seen anything like it. It wasn't very polite. I think my father felt
the same: he would have been glad to be rid of us."

Before the court left Chambord, she had had a talk with him.
"He woke me at four in the morning and sat on my bed. 'I think
you won't mind my waking you,' he said, 'since I shan't have a
chance to see you tomorrow. You're going on a long trip. Whatever people say, it isn't so easy to negotiate a peace as they think,
and perhaps there won't be a peace; your trip may last a long time.
I am old and worn out"—Gaston d'Orléans was fifty-one—"I

may die during your absence. If I die, I commend your sisters to you. I know you're not fond of Madame; I know she hasn't always acted toward you as she might. But the girls aren't to blame: look after them for love of me. They'll need you badly: Madame won't be much help to them.' He kissed me three or four times. He aroused my affection: I have a tender heart, and am easily touched when treated properly. I told him how I felt about such things; my words were full of respect, affection, and gratitude for the sincerity with which he'd spoken to me. We parted kindly, and I went back to sleep. If I hadn't remembered that episode very clearly, I might be tempted to believe I dreamed it when I think of everything that went before."

From Blois the court went to Bordeaux and Toulouse. Long stays were made in each city, and town after town, château after château, was visited in between. They were still in Toulouse at Christmas; then they continued south. At Salon Mademoiselle visited the tomb of Nostradamus; and on the stony Provençal plain called the Crau (we know it from a picture by Van Gogh) she passed judgment on the exotic local mutton, nourished on wild thyme and much boasted of for its flavor: she preferred, she decided, plain Paris meat. And on February 2, at Aix-en-Provence, there was wild rejoicing. It was the *fête de Notre-Dame,* but there was another reason: the Peace of the Pyrenees was announced— for the first time in a quarter of a century, France and Spain were no longer at war.

Amid the sound of pealing bells, the singing of the *Te Deum,* the processions, the crowds in the streets, Mademoiselle felt a sudden, overpowering sadness. "I went to the house where I was staying and burst into tears. I couldn't stop weeping for an hour. I said to the comte de Comminges: 'Some disaster must have happened that I know nothing about: this sadness must be a presentiment.'

"He made fun of me: 'It's nothing but meaningless vapors.' "

Her depression continued for twenty-four hours; then she

forced herself to forget it, and took part in the court welcome extended to one of her relations: her old friend and hero Condé.
His pardon and his return to France assured by a clause in the
Peace of the Pyrenees, he had come to pay homage to the cousin
and sovereign he had been fighting for ten years. "He acted at
court as though he had never been away. The king talked with
him about everything he had done in France and Flanders as pleasantly as though it had all been done in his service."

Condé and Mademoiselle had long conversations. "We talked
a great deal about the Fronde, and laughed about the follies we'd
committed. The king took our joking in good part."

Then, the evening of the day Condé left for Paris, "I was doing
needlework in my room. A courier from Blois came in, a crazy
fellow that my father always found amusing. He flung a big
packet of letters on the table, and told me: 'Your father isn't
dead. I don't think he'll die this time. Is the cardinal here? I have
a packet for him, too.' "

Her father had had a stroke, the letters told her; he was dan-
gerously ill. She wanted to rush to Blois at once, "taking from
each city to the next the horses belonging to the governors and
bishops"; but her own doctor told her, after reading a document
sent her by doctors in Blois, that she would never find her father
alive, and the cardinal persuaded her to await another letter in
Aix. She sent off Cabanes instead, the brightest of her *valets de
chambre,* ordering him to return to Aix at once should he learn
on the road that her father was dead. The archbishop of Aix ordered a forty-hours' devotion in the cathedral; parlement shut the
theaters; Mademoiselle spent her days praying in convents. On
Sunday evening she returned to her lodgings and found her entire
household gathered, waiting for her. "I asked them whether Cabanes had returned. They said he had."

Alas! The affectionate, dreamlike scene at four o'clock in the
morning at Chambord was not Mademoiselle's last memory of her
father. Since then he had accused her, purely on hearsay, of hav-

ing spoiled one of her half sister's chances of becoming duchess
of Savoy: someone had told him she had written to Madame
Royale that the girl was a hunchback. Mademoiselle had secured
a written denial of this from Madame Royale herself and had for-
warded it to Blois; but now, learning of the time of her father's
death, she knew it had arrived too late. Gaston d'Orléans' disfavor reached Mademoiselle from his deathbed.

Mademoiselle retired to her study and wept. "At that moment
I felt all the affection that nature inspires on such occasions, and
my only feeling was one of great sadness. Everything that had
happened between my father and myself passed through my
mind: what I felt was not resentment, but regret that he should
always have been surrounded with people hostile to me, and regret at the self-reproach he must have felt at having appropriated
much of what belonged to me." Then, rallying, she sent word to
the king, the queen, and the cardinal, who had all gone to Tou-
lon. She sent to Paris for Préfontaine, whom her father had never
allowed her to rehire; she sent her equerry to Blois with messages
of sympathy to Madame and her half sisters; and the next day
she received the condolence calls of everyone of importance in Aix.

"During the absence of the court, I went out for drives; in the
fine weather I couldn't bear to stay in my room—I disliked it all
the more since it was hung with black. I had my furniture covered with gray; it was the first time a daughter had ever been
known to do such a thing; previously, it had been a custom observed only by widows. It made everyone realize that I wanted to
observe the deepest, the most complete mourning. All my staff
down to the kitchen boys, my servants' servants, wore black; the
cloths on my mules, the trappings on my horses and pack horses—
everything was black. My drives always took me to some convent.
I went often to the Carmelites; and it was in their church that I
had a service said for my father."

The court returned to Aix.

The cardinal first. He spoke to Mademoiselle of her father as kindly as he could; he begged her to believe that he would see her well established (sixteen years earlier that subject had first been mentioned between them, in connection with the king of Spain); he would ease her financial burdens by seeing that all three of her half sisters found husbands. "I had no desire to marry," says Mademoiselle, "but I found everything he said admirable. Since getting to know the cardinal better than I knew him before the Fronde, I have found him quite a just man."

Then came the king, the queen, and Monsieur. All were kind. And in this condolence call Louis XIV, her first cousin, ten years her junior, formerly *mon petit mari,* definitely assumed the new role in which, ever since the end of her exile, Mademoiselle had been casting him: "He told me he wanted to be a father to me: it was his duty."

Everything wasn't so serious in the king's demeanor that day. In Mademoiselle's presence he teased Monsieur. "Tomorrow you'll see my brother in a mourning-coat so long it trails on the ground," he told Mademoiselle. "I think he's delighted by your father's death for that reason: his dignity would never have allowed him to wear such a garment for anybody else. I'm glad your father was older than I: otherwise my brother would have wanted *me* to die so that he could wear it. He thinks he'll inherit your father's *apanage,* too. He talks of nothing else. But he hasn't got it yet."

The next day Monsieur did appear wearing "an extravagantly long coat. He very carefully gave me a number of orders to pass along to my stepmother, lest she overlook some portion of the dignity of her mourning."

But little did Madame, in Blois, care about the dignity of her mourning—or about, as Mademoiselle put it, "the glory of our family." Mademoiselle soon learned, in Aix, of how, the very day Gaston d'Orléans died, Madame "broke up the house": she locked away all the plate and dishes, locked all doors at night so that priests were prevented from coming to watch beside the corpse, and refused to allow oil to be bought for lighting or wood for the fireplaces. Her maids refused to supply a sheet for the dead man's shroud; and wrapped in one furnished by the governess of Mademoiselle's half sisters, the body of Gaston d'Orléans was transported to Saint-Denis "without pomp or expense." And Madame, "instead of remaining for forty days in a room hung with black, as is the custom for widows, left in ten or twelve days for Paris"; and in Paris she went straight to the Luxembourg, dismantled Mademoiselle's apartment, and moved herself and her furniture into it—a circumstance which, when Mademoiselle heard of it in Aix, she knew would have to be drastically remedied "when the time came."

As for her father, Mademoiselle learned that he had died a Christian death. For some time past he had "forbidden anyone to swear in his house and had even rid himself of this bad habit"; he had been administered the last rites while his wife calmly ate her dinner in another room; and he had blessed the three daughters who were at his bedside. But "because of the confusion, those around him neglected to ask his blessing for me; and though they spoke to him about the chevalier de Charny, he made no answer that was at all favorable to him." (Mademoiselle had recently bought her half brother a company in an infantry regiment, and he was at present in Madrid, in the suite of the maréchal de Gramont, the special ambassador sent by Louis XIV to make formal request for the hand of the infanta.)

So that it was a Mademoiselle swathed in black, shocked out of her "indifference" toward her father by the fact and the circumstances of his end, who accompanied the court on the rest of its progress—to Marseilles, Narbonne, Perpignan, back to Toulouse, where Préfontaine rejoined her, and then via Bayonne to Saint-Jean-de-Luz.

And since it was when her father had been distressing her that Mademoiselle always spoke out most strongly against *galanterie*, against passion, against marriage, it is scarcely surprising that now, when he had caused her the greatest distress of all, the unique distress, she should express herself about those things uniquely.

In festively decorated Saint-Jean-de-Luz, cardinal Mazarin, who had sat through twenty-four conferences with Don Louis de Haro in order to negotiate this peace that was the climax of his life's work as prime minister, had collapsed into a fit of the gout. "We went to see him every day," Mademoiselle says, "on our way back from vespers, complin, or benediction. The queen always attended at least one of these services, and often all three. One day I was looking out one of the cardinal's windows, from which one could see the river and the Pyrenees. Madame de Motteville, who was with me"—Madame de Motteville was the queen's first lady in waiting—"gave me an occasion to speak of the solitude of the desert, and we moralized about the happy life one could lead there, away from the fatigues of court and out of reach of the injustices one meets with. . . . We'd have talked longer about this if the queen hadn't come out from the cardinal's room on her way to the theater. I accompanied her and Madame de Motteville as far as the door, and then I went for a stroll on the seashore, where many thoughts passed through my head relating to a community of true hermits. It seemed to me that membership should be restricted to those who hadn't been rejected by the court, but who had themselves rejected it; and as I thought of one detail after another, each better and more practical than the last, I hurried to my room, took pen and ink, and wrote a letter two or three pages long, which I addressed to Madame de Motteville. I had it copied and delivered to her by someone she didn't know. There would be no love-making or even marriage in my desert: I was positive about that."

Madame de Motteville recognized the letter, of course, as being a development of the ideas expressed by Mademoiselle at the cardinal's window, and she sent a letter in reply. During the next year or two there was something of a correspondence between the ladies about "their desert"; two of Madame de Motteville's letter-fantasies, containing "quotations from the Italian and Spanish, from Holy Scripture and the Holy Fathers themselves," were later published in a collection of fragments called *Oeuvres galantes.* Mademoiselle's letters were never published—Madame de Motteville was far more learned than she, she says, and wrote admirably—but it was Mademoiselle, clad in her mourning, who had conceived this plan for an ideal community of solitary, chaste spirits.

Then—it happened very fast, just five months after the death scene in Blois—an experience of a very different kind came to Mademoiselle in Saint-Jean-de-Luz.

Mademoiselle attended both the fantastically ceremonious marriage services that united her French first cousin Louis with her Spanish first cousin Maria-Theresa, there at the Franco-Spanish border. The first, on Spanish soil, she was allowed to witness only *incognita:* it was a purely Spanish affair, the bridegroom was not present, and it was Don Luis de Haro, as his proxy, who exchanged vows with the infanta. At the second performance, in a Saint-Jean-de-Luz festooned and garlanded and noisy, bursting with noble visitors, Mademoiselle was one of the actresses: it was she, as *fille de France,* who handed to the infanta the offering which the bride then presented to the poor; and two of her half sisters, sent for from Blois, were among the bride's trainbearers. The infanta wore "a royal mantle of purple velvet embroidered with *fleurs de lis,* under it a dress of white brocade covered with precious stones, on her head a crown"; the king and Monsieur blazed with gold and diamonds. But among all this, among the companies of Swiss and French guards drawn up in double line, there was something that Mademoiselle noticed especially.

"There was one group of guards that I had never seen before, because it serves only at ceremonies: in earlier days, I'm told, it was very distinguished and fashionable—two companies of gentlemen called *becs de corbin* [crows' beaks] from the shape of

their halberds. The first of these was commanded by the marquis
de Péguilin, younger son of the house of Lauzun, whose members
have always had this command, and the other by the marquis
d'Humières, of the house of Crevant. I don't know why the latter
began to quarrel with the former. In any case, there was a scene,
and Monsieur de Péguilin came off the victor, behaving with extraordinary *hauteur*. He had an air of grandeur about him that
made it clear that he was not born for ordinary things."

"I have all my life," Mademoiselle writes of herself about this
time, "been strongly attached to all the glories that serve to distinguish me from others, although on many an occasion I have
neglected some of them out of a certain freedom of spirit, a certain kind of *hauteur* that put me above bagatelles."

That was true, perhaps. But when, before, had Mademoiselle
ever had the "freedom of spirit" to be impressed by a mere marquis, the younger son of a count?

Very gradually, over the next ten years—very gradually for a
long time, and then with a sudden rush—Mademoiselle was to
bring herself into the orbit of Péguilin, younger son of the house
of Lauzun.

During the Fronde, Mademoiselle had moved in the very cur-
rent of her times. She had lived the Fronde; she had been its
daughter, its mascot, its victim, all in one; with its picture her own
personal picture merges. Then, during her years of exile and even
after her return to court, she had been in eclipse; history had
marched on without her: she had been a quiescent, if not quiet,
background figure. Now her role was to change again. Once again
Mademoiselle was to become news. But this time, in her maturity,
she was to strain every nerve to fashion for herself a unique
womanly destiny, as though trying to match in private life her
earlier uniqueness as a public figure. This time it was against
Mademoiselle's own dearest desires that the situation of Mademoiselle became an affair of state.

Part Three

LOVE UNDER AN ABSOLUTE
MONARCH

1660–1671

1

Péguilin, Péguilain, Péguilien, Puyguilhem, Puy-guilhem: his name was spelled in all those various ways; and Mademoiselle had seen him at least once before the king's wedding.

A year earlier she had danced opposite him in one of the ballets at the Louvre: she had been one of four peasant girls; he, one of four shepherds. The peasant-girl costumes had been highly glamorized—cloth-of-silver with pearls, diamonds and emeralds, and black velvet hats decked with pink, white and flame-colored plumes. The shepherds, too, had been splendidly unshepherdlike. "Never," Mademoiselle reports, "was a masquerade so magnificent." But at that time it was the masquerade that had impressed her: Puyguilhem she mentioned only casually.

He didn't continue to be called Puyguilhem very long. The court found the name a tongue-twister; everyone wrote it and pronounced it differently; Puyguilhem himself spelled it wrong. He and everyone else were doubtless relieved when, on the death of his father, the comte de Lauzun, in 1668, his older brother renounced the title because of the debts that went with it and he, the second son, marquis de Puyguilhem, became comte de Lauzun.

For us, let him be Lauzun immediately.

The natives of Gascony (roughly, the country between Bordeaux and the Pyrenees) are traditionally a bragging, swaggering lot. Dumas' D'Artagnan and Rostand's Cyrano de Bergerac are the two most celebrated fictional Gascons. Lauzun was a *real* Gascon. He was less boastful than ambitious, incalculable, eccentric. His family was an ancient one in its province, well connected, with the usual feudal château; on his mother's side he was great-grandson of the maréchal de la Force, a famous warrior under Henri IV. He was born in 1633, seven years later than Mademoiselle, and christened Antonin-Nompar. One of the names is a claim in itself: Nompar is derived from *non-pareil,* and *non-pareil* means "matchless." As a boy he was a "country cricket," a "grasshopper"; when he was fourteen his family sent him to Paris to be educated. He stayed with relations (he was first cousin of the maréchal de Gramont and nephew of the maréchal de Turenne); they sent him to the academy; then he entered the army and distinguished himself at the Battle of the Dunes. At the home of one of the cardinal's nieces he was presented to the king. Soon he was popular at court: one had to be, to be asked to dance in the king's ballets. Then he was chosen to be one of the cardinal's guards at Saint-Jean-de-Luz during the twenty-four conferences leading to the Peace of the Pyrenees.

Lauzun was small—"one of the smallest men God ever made" —towheaded, wiry, sharp-featured. He had a "pretty leg," and he was debonair: there was something about his blue eyes, his wit, his manner, a strange, piquant mixture of cruelty and consideration, that brought women flocking around him—"too many," says Mademoiselle, "for his own good." In warfare he was intrepid; at court he learned rapidly—he seemed almost to know without learning—how to be by turns humble and haughty, indifferent and attentive, soft-spoken and sarcastic, kind and ruthless. When Mademoiselle was impressed by his air of grandeur as hereditary captain of his company of *becs-de-corbin* at the wedding, he was twenty-seven, and just beginning to climb.

The central figure at that wedding in Saint-Jean-de-Luz, the royal bridegroom himself, was also just about to begin his real career. Mazarin was old and ill; less than a year later he was dead. He left France at peace, and he had kept Mademoiselle's fortune out of the pockets of foreign princes. His own fortune, which by the terms of his will was to go to his nieces and nephews, he obsequiously offered on his deathbed to the king: after all, he said humbly, he had amassed it in the public service, and the king was head of the state. "Your family must have it," the king replied magnanimously—only to discover that the cardinal had left several other fortunes, about which he had said nothing—huge sums in cash, hidden here and there all over France. These Louis XIV appropriated: overnight he became the wealthiest monarch in Europe.

The day before the cardinal's death the king called a meeting of his principal ministers: in the future, he told the startled gentlemen, he would be his own premier. The next evening the archbishop of Rouen sought the king in audience: like everyone else, he was incredulous of the news—France had been governed by cardinals for almost half a century. "It was Your Majesty's order that I address myself to the cardinal on all matters of business. To whom shall I address myself now that he is dead?"

"To me."

It was unequivocal confirmation. The king was twenty-three. His resoluteness was in part, no doubt, reaction—reaction from years of a mother's leading-strings and the cardinal's domination. But the cardinal himself had foreseen it, or something like it: his pupil had indeed, as he had prophesied, gone "a little slowly at the beginning," and now he was about to "go further than most others." Louis XIV was beginning what was to be a fifty-four year span of absolute rule. "I felt my mind and my courage soar," he later wrote of this moment in his life. "I felt completely changed. I discovered in myself qualities I had never suspected, and I joyfully chided myself for having been unaware of them so long. The timidity that had troubled me, especially whenever I had to speak at length in public, quickly vanished. Only then did it seem to me that I was king, born to be king. I had a sense of gratification that is difficult to express."

Some of the ministers bequeathed him by Mazarin he kept, at least for the time being. Le Tellier continued as minister of war, though gradually handing over his power to his son, the marquis de Louvois. "I owe Your Majesty everything," Mazarin had said on his deathbed, "but I feel I pay some of my debt in leaving you Colbert." Colbert was kept, and it was he who revealed to the king the existence and whereabouts of the cardinal's extra money. But there was one rapid, dizzy fall. Nicholas Fouquet, the cardinal's minister of finance, had, like the cardinal himself, amassed a fortune in office. Colbert had pointed out some of Fouquet's irregularities to the cardinal, who ignored them; now he pointed them out to the king. Fouquet blithely built himself a pleasure palace at Vaux-le-Vicomte that rivaled the royal châteaux of Fontainebleau and Saint-Germain, and was so proud and rash as to invite his sovereign to a sumptuous fête. The royal guest saw the grandeur and the fabulous novelties—the fountains playing in the gardens designed by Le Nôtre were the first in France—and he struck down his embezzling, ostentatious servant. Fouquet was arrested, taken to Vincennes, then to the Bastille. Colbert became minister of finance. And after a trial that was a merciless farce despite his undoubted offenses—less a trial than a grim lesson to ministers and courtiers—Fouquet was sentenced to perpetual banishment and confiscation of his fortune. The king found the sentence too mild: he changed it from perpetual banishment to perpetual confinement in the prison-fortress of Pignerol, isolated and inaccessible in the Alps near Turin. To Pignerol Fouquet was taken in a carriage by Charles de Baatz, seigneur d'Artagnan, lieutenant of the king's musketeers, with an escort of armed musketeers in attendance. The prison gate closed on him. Still imprisoned in Pignerol, nineteen years later, he died.

And when he had destroyed Fouquet, the king began what was to be a never-ending search for new men, men of ability and loyalty. He preferred them to be not of the highest birth—he feared the bluest bloods as potential Frondeurs—but rather of the lesser nobility and the bourgeoisie: men who would find their glory in serving him. Within a few years there was at court a new elite of officeholders, a core of sixty "king's men" granted a new, exclusive right: the right to wear the *justaucorps à brevet,* the "king's jacket." Blue, lined with red and bright with gold and silver braid, its model changed every year, the ranks of its wearers constantly purged, the *justaucorps à brevet* was coveted as eagerly by the men around Louis XIV as the blue ribbon of the Order of the Saint-Esprit had ever been sought by the old nobility. It brought with it the privilege of "following the king in all his pleasure outings, without asking permission": the sixty gentlemen could freely ride with the king, walk with him, hunt with him, attend spectacles with him. The jacket was an identification, a passport, a token of the king's trust.

Lauzun was one of the sixty original wearers of the king's jacket. The king had made him captain of his dragoons.

Mademoiselle saw him constantly about the court, clad in the precious garment. Then, at an official function that surpassed even the royal wedding in splendor, she saw him costumed still more gorgeously. Within a year after Mazarin's death the queen of France gave birth to a son. This baby prince, as befitted the heir of Louis XIV, was called not only the Dauphin, as his father had been, but often the Grand Dauphin; and to mark the great dynastic event, the king ordered the performance of a "Carrousel"— a kind of mock-tournament, or ballet on horseback. An amphitheater was constructed in front of the Tuileries—the spot is called the Place du Carrousel to this day though the Tuileries itself has long since disappeared; Monsieur de Gissey, designer of the royal ballets, set to work; and for two days early in June, 1662, before ten thousand spectators—it was the only royal spectacle of the reign that the populace was allowed to watch—there unrolled a series of cavalry games. The jousting was preceded by five "quadrilles," or parades of costumed mounted nobles, each led by a prince of the blood. The first was led by the king himself, fantastically garbed in flame-color as "king of the Romans," bearing on his shield the emblem he had taken as his own—the sun. The second was led by Monsieur, "king of the Persians." At the head of the third, the "Quadrille of the Turks," was Condé, no longer a proud rebel, but the most assiduous of courtiers; and it was in Condé's suite that Mademoiselle once again saw Lauzun in glory. This time he wore blue satin, embroidered with silver; on his head was a blue turban, with blue and silver plumes; and on his shield was a flower, shown turned toward the sun. There was a motto: *Ne despice amantem*—"Scorn not him who loves you." Never had courtier appealed more directly for monarch's favor.

Mademoiselle, however, made a mistake about the shield Lauzun carried at the Carrousel. Her memory played her false when she wrote about it later in her memoirs. "The words on his shield were in Italian or Spanish," she says, "I don't remember which. The emblem was a rocket, mounting to the skies, and the words were: 'I go as high as one can climb.' I thought it extraordinary." It is an amusing, telltale error. Lauzun's sunflower had been turned toward the king: but the rocket—how clear it becomes from everything that follows!—is aimed at Mademoiselle.

Two years later there was another *fête galante,* this one at Versailles, to inaugurate the newly planted gardens and the newly dug canals—the beginning of the masterpiece of landscaping ordered by the king from Le Nôtre as though in deliberate intent to surpass Fouquet's Vaux-le-Vicomte. This first fête at Versailles, called *Les Plaisirs de l'ile enchantée,* lasted more than a week, and included ballets, fireworks, gondola-maneuvers by a group of imported Venetians, and performances of two plays by Molière, with the author playing some of his own roles. *Les Plaisirs de l'ile enchantée,* it was commonly thought, was given to honor the king's mistress, Louise de La Vallière.

She was a shy, pretty girl from Blois—"the violet," people called her—who had begun her career at court as a screen. Shortly after Mazarin's death Monsieur had married: married the very princess Henriette d'Angleterre, Charles II's sister, about whom he had said, "We feed those people, don't we? If they don't like it here, why don't they go back where they came from?" He had married her eagerly, for the king, wanting a link with the newly restored Stuarts, had promised him part of the *apanage* of the late Gaston d'Orléans as a wedding present. Not all of it: Monsieur was never to be made *seigneur* of as much of France as Gaston had been; but with his marriage he did become, like Gaston, the duc d'Orléans; and Henriette, his duchess, was called Madame. (We too shall call her that from now on. The older Madame, Mademoiselle's stepmother, continued to bear the same titles as Henriette; but she was of no concern to anyone, and ailed and aged in the Luxembourg, which Mademoiselle had reluctantly consented to let her share.) The king, who seldom missed a chance to jeer at his brother, mocked him for being so willing to embrace "the little bones of the Holy Innocents," as he called Henriette, so thin and forlorn had she always seemed at court in her role of penniless exile. But now the new Madame began to bloom—she was only seventeen; and before long Louis XIV was infatuated with his brother's bride. It was to screen this affair, which now began and continued with Monsieur's full approval—like everyone else, Monsieur was proud to share to what extent he could in the king's favor—that the king pretended an interest in Louise de La Vallière, one of Madame's maids of honor. But it wasn't long before she, too, captivated him. During the next ten years the king took noticeable pleasure—much more than Monsieur—in the frequent pregnancies of his sister-in-law; and his children by her maid of honor, whom he made a duchess, he eventually legitimized and ennobled.

There were eight hundred guests at the fête for Louise de La Vallière in the newly planted gardens of Versailles, and Lauzun was one of them. Mademoiselle was not. Mademoiselle was absent, at the king's request. "I would spend my life in solitude rather than submit to the slightest humiliation, even if my fortune were at stake," she had written of herself at the end of her four and a half years at Saint-Fargeau. Now she was being given a chance to see whether she really believed those words she had written, a chance to see what this new age—this age of Louis XIV being inaugurated along with the gardens of Versailles—was like.

2

THE MARÉCHAL DE TURENNE—uncle of Lauzun, battlefield rival of the flamboyant Condé—was celebrated for his matter-of-factness, his impassivity. He was a man who lived simply and spoke directly. Very early one morning, as one of his domestics passed, in a corridor, someone whom he took to be a fellow servant, a figure clad in nightshirt and nightcap, back turned, leaning on a window sill breathing the fresh air, he landed a tremendous friendly slap on his supposed comrade's "lower back"—as the French are sometimes polite enough to say. The victim wheeled around: it was Turenne. The slapper fell on his knees: "Monseigneur! I thought it was Georges!"

"Even for Georges," was Turenne's only comment, "that was hard."

With some of the same dryness about a very different matter, Turenne, calling on Mademoiselle one day in her apartments in the Luxembourg, told her that he had something to discuss with her.

"Since I too am brusque and impatient by nature," Mademoiselle tells us, "I asked him, 'What's up?' "

"I want to see you married."

"That won't be easy." Mademoiselle laughed. "I'm happy as I am, and determined not to change."

"I want to make you queen. Listen to what I have to say: then you can talk later. I want to make you queen of Portugal."

"Fi!" cried Mademoiselle. "I have no wish to be that!"

[187]

"Young women of your rank," retorted Turenne, "must have no wishes except the king's"—a statement as matter-of-fact as "*L'État c'est moi.*"

"Did the king send you to me?" Mademoiselle demanded.

Turenne denied it: he had come on his own.

But he was clearly the bearer of a message from someone, and Mademoiselle let him talk. He told her a story she knew already: a story about Luiza, the clever old queen of Portugal, widow of the late Don João of Braganza. With French military help she had led a revolution twenty years before which had freed Portugal from Spain and put her husband on the throne. Since his death she had ruled as regent. She had recently made a powerful alliance with England by making her daughter what Mademoiselle had refused to become—Charles II's queen; now, before retiring, she wanted an alliance with France. Her son Affonso was old enough to rule: he needed a wife, and Mademoiselle was her choice. Affonso, Turenne told Mademoiselle, was "a boy who had never had any opinions except his mother's." He was accustomed to do what he was told. His mother would place the power in Mademoiselle's hands, and Mademoiselle would be absolute mistress of Portugal. And he described the husband he was proposing as being "quite good-looking, blond, with inclinations that were neither good nor bad."

Mademoiselle didn't mention certain of Affonso's "inclinations" she had heard about. She continued to listen, and Turenne told her that Louis XIV intended to send French troops into Portugal again, as a precaution against any Spanish attempt to regain the lost territory. "The maréchal said I could take anyone I wanted with me to Portugal. Before leaving France I could choose the principal officers and even the commander, who would be under my orders. I'd be in complete charge: the king"—the king of France, Turenne meant—"was in full agreement."

"But you told me it wasn't the king who sent you to me!" Mademoiselle cried. "And here you are, disposing of his troops!"

Turenne said nothing.

"I'd consider it a hideous thing to be part and parcel of an eternal war between France and Spain," said Mademoiselle. "It's shameful to think of France supporting a king who's a rebel against his own true king. Besides, I'm sure I'd no sooner arrive than there'd be peace: the Spaniards would only wait for the French to leave, and then they'd cast the so-called king out. After he'd eaten up all my money, he'd come to France and beg alms of the king, and what would I be? A wretched 'queen' in some little French town. I'd rather be Mademoiselle in France with 500,000 livres a year, and ask nothing of the court, and be esteemed for my person as much as for my rank. Believe me, when you find yourself in that situation, as I do, good sense tells you to stay in it."

"You forget one thing," Turenne reminded her. "You may be Mademoiselle, with the rank and riches you mention, but you're still the king's subject. The king can will as he wishes. If another's will doesn't coincide with his, he scolds; the whole court feels the weight of his displeasure. Often he goes further. He banishes anyone he takes it into his head to banish. He sends him from one end of the kingdom to another. If he's well off where he is, he sees that he's moved elsewhere. Or he imprisons him in his own house. Or he sends *her* to a convent. And after such punishment you still have to obey. You do perforce what you refused to do voluntarily. Think about what I've just told you. What do you say?"

"That people like you don't threaten people like me," retorted Mademoiselle. "If the king said to me what you've said, I'd think about how to answer him. But I have nothing to say to you, no explanation to make whatever."

Turenne impassively left her. A few days later he brought up the matter again. She answered as before, and once again he departed.

Mademoiselle's friends to whom she repeated the conversations told her she'd been rash. Didn't she know that the king was determined on the Portuguese marital and military alliance against Spain, despite the Peace of the Pyrenees? Probably Turenne had been telling the truth in saying that the king hadn't "sent" him to her: the king enjoyed giving an order at several removes, allowing someone close to him—Le Tellier or Louvois or Colbert—to mention to someone like Turenne the possibility that someone like Mademoiselle. . . . That didn't make it any less an order.

Disquieted, Mademoiselle wrote to the king. She didn't mention Portugal, but she said she'd come to feel it was time for her to marry, and she begged him to find her a husband, or rather an establishment—one that would be useful to him and agreeable to her. Her aim, she tells us, was to "make the king speak." But he didn't speak. He didn't answer her letter. When she saw him he seemed ill at ease. When she told the story to Anne of Austria, who as a Spaniard naturally hated the Portuguese, the only answer she received was: "If the king wishes it, it's a terrible pity. But he's the master. I can't advise you."

And when she went so far as to hint to the king one day that a match could probably be arranged between her and the duke of Savoy whom she had *not* become engaged to during the trip to Lyons—he was now a widower, having married one of Mademoiselle's half sisters who died almost at once—the king replied sharply: "I'll see that you're married wherever you'll be most useful for my service."

Not a word passed between the king and Mademoiselle concerning Portugal. But now she learned that one of her letters had been intercepted and shown him—a letter she had sent the chevalier de Charny, who was still serving in Spain, by a fellow officer who had unluckily died and whose effects had been examined, a letter in which she had made "a few sarcastic remarks" about the Portuguese king: "She wished he'd be hanged," was one of them. And one October day when she was at her château of Eu, in Normandy, she was told that someone had arrived to speak with her: the marquis de Gèvres, captain of the king's bodyguard. He was shown in. "I was in my room with a number of people. I asked them to leave. As soon as he was alone with me he said: 'The king has commanded me to tell you that he orders you to go to Saint-Fargeau until you hear from him further!' "

Mademoiselle wrote to the king, to Monsieur, to the queen-mother. Turenne had not presented the Portuguese marriage as a royal order, she protested: she had intended no disrespect to the king. Her letters were not answered. The queen-mother told some-one, "I've never seen the king so angry against anyone as against my niece."

Mademoiselle went to Saint-Fargeau.

In January Turenne had someone write her, to ask her two ques-tions. Had she reflected on what he had said to her about Portugal? Had she changed her mind about a proposition that would be so useful for the king's service, so advantageous for her own establish-ment? Mademoiselle's reply was in her best vein. This separation from court which she was now suffering, she said, made her realize more acutely than ever how painful it would be to separate herself from it for the rest of her life.

And only from Saint-Fargeau does she lift, for our benefit, the curtain on what Turenne had called the "inclinations" of Affonso, king of Portugal. She does so quite casually. One of those wander-ing monks who play such entertaining minor roles in her life called on her one day at Saint-Fargeau. He had just happened to be pass-ing by, he said, and he had stopped in because he wanted to see her: he had recently been in a country where he had heard much about her—in Portugal. "He told me a thousand marvelous things about the old queen of Portugal and her son. The queen had often spoken of her wish that I marry him; she had sworn that she would retire and leave everything in my hands." Portugal was the most beautiful country in the world, the monk told Mademoiselle. "I asked him," she says, "if he had heard about the man the king of Portugal had killed from a window. He answered very seriously that the king hadn't done it 'on purpose.' But I knew the truth, which was that he'd shot a Frenchman, standing on a ship just arriving in Lisbon harbor, aiming at him from a window as calmly as if he were firing blanks. 'You've probably heard also that he roams the streets at night, killing everyone he meets,' he said. 'But it's not true.' However, I got plenty of stories about the king out of him—even more than I'd heard before."

Indeed, Affonso of Braganza wasn't the most attractive of Mademoiselle's proposed husbands—not if a description of him sent to Paris by the French envoy in Lisbon, the abbé de Saint-Romain, is to be believed. He had been born considerably paralyzed in body, and apparently much damaged in brain. At twenty-three, he still couldn't read or write. On his good days he had the habit of tweaking the ears of those around him and pulling out their hair; in more morose moods he struck them, kicked them, lunged at them with his sword. The sword was particularly busy at night: he hid in dark corners of Lisbon with hoodlums and common criminals, darting out at passers-by and running them through. He was a fat glutton, usually drunk, usually vomiting after meals. He dressed strangely, wearing six or seven suits of clothes one on top of the other and piling his head with hats and hoods. "His body," the abbé wrote, "has a naturally bad odor, and his skin hangs in great ulcerated stinking folds. Out of fear, he always sleeps in a room with sixteen others, and as a final sweet-smelling touch there is his chair—a certain type of very useful chair, which stands day and night beside his bed."

Such are some of the more printable details concerning the king of Portugal.

Mademoiselle spent a year and a half in exile for refusing him.

Turenne sent a messenger to Saint-Fargeau in further attempt to persuade her, and she sent Turenne a second answer as good as her first. "It would ill become me to allow your messenger's eloquence to prevail over yours."

After about a year she secured the king's permission to move to Eu to benefit from the sea air. "I founded a school for the education of the poor children of the town, and I passed my life in marvelous tranquility. I saw no end to my exile, and didn't care." The establishment of a school for poor children was an unusual, imaginative form of philanthropy for a lady of rank in those days. Mademoiselle called the place Saint Anne's, after her own patron saint, mother of the Virgin. (Mademoiselle was called by her title so exclusively that one tends to forget she had names—Anne-Marie-Louise—like anyone else.) The teachers were Sisters of Charity.

When she learned that the queen was pregnant again she thought it would be "a good excuse to write to the king. I thought: Perhaps the king would like me to petition him. To be eighteen months or two years without writing was really neglecting the court too much. I'd have to return sometime: I might as well try now. So I wrote him, rejoicing in the queen's pregnancy, emphasizing very sincerely the desire I felt that God might give him another son. I also spoke of my sorrow at being so long distant from him, of my longing to have the honor of seeing him."

The letter brought forgiveness: apparently even Louis XIV was capable of shame.

This time Mademoiselle's reunion with the court was at Fontainebleau, just after *Les Plaisirs de l'île enchantée* had been given at Versailles. The king led her onto a terrace, and when she began to speak of the Portuguese affair, he stopped her by kissing her. "But tell me the truth," he said. "Confess you were bored."

Just like the last time, Mademoiselle stoutly denied it. "I told him that often when I was busy at Saint-Fargeau and Eu I said to myself: 'They're fooled at court: they think I'm in despair, and I'm more peaceful and happier than they.' "

When they rejoined the queen and the rest of the company the king made a brief announcement: "My cousin and I have just kissed."

It was all the court needed. "At this moment of return everyone was my friend—but I was convinced of the opposite, for in my exile no one had shown the same interest. That's how people are at court: it's up to everyone to know where he stands."

The king now negotiated for Mademoiselle's marriage with the duke of Savoy, but the duke was still averse to one who had witnessed his family's humiliation at Lyons, and besides, he indicated a preference for someone younger. The king awarded him, instead, a niece of the fishwives' darling, the Frondeur duc de Beaufort—Mademoiselle de Nemours, twenty-one and pretty. For her sister, Mademoiselle d'Aumale, nineteen and even prettier, he made a still more brilliant match: lacking the absurd scruples of Mademoiselle, she readily consented to marry Affonso, king of Portugal. She found her husband "delightful," she wrote from Lisbon to all her friends; she was "utterly happy." But it wasn't long before everyone knew the sequel. The new queen of Portugal fell in love with her brother-in-law, the delightful Affonso's younger brother Pedro; together they had Affonso declared incompetent and his marriage with her annulled by papal bull. He was locked up on an island, Pedro became king, and following a new marriage service—her second with a reigning Portuguese monarch —Mademoiselle d'Aumale became queen of Portugal again.

Mademoiselle heard the news with a certain cynicism: Pedro, while unquestionably an improvement over Affonso, was known to have his own eccentricities. "She's in the position of having two husbands, of having married two brothers," Mademoiselle remarks. "But even if mental derangement is sufficient reason for annulling a marriage, she won't be able to leave her present husband to marry a third brother, because there isn't one."

A year or so after the king forgave Mademoiselle with a kiss, Lauzun had *his* first taste of what the new age could be like.

Among the relations with whom he had grown up after coming to Paris was a pretty cousin, Catherine-Charlotte de Gramont; affection, then passion, sprang up between the two young people;

but about the time Mademoiselle saw Lauzun at Saint-Jean-de-Luz Catherine-Charlotte was married to Louis de Grimaldi, prince of Monaco. When she left for her new principality, gossip at court had it that the infatuated Lauzun stayed close to her, following her across France to the border disguised now as an old woman, now as a servant. (Most stories about Lauzun sound like gossip, yet some of them are true. "Other people's dreams can't compare with Lauzun's life," someone once said. "It's like a novel, except that it lacks verisimilitude.")

In any case, shortly after Mademoiselle's return to court from exile at Saint-Fargeau and Eu, the princesse de Monaco returned to France. She was alone, on a political mission for her husband. The king became infatuated with her: she was an enjoyable momentary change from Louise de La Vallière. Lauzun, lusting after his cousin, lost his head when he saw her slip out of his arms into the embrace of his sovereign. He reminded her that some of the letters she had been writing him were politically indiscreet, and he threatened to show them to the king. She complained to her royal lover that Lauzun was persecuting her out of jealousy, and the king sent for Lauzun and gave one of his oblique orders: wasn't it time for him to go down and inspect his regiment of dragoons, quartered near the Pyrenees?

Lauzun's wild reply is the first indication of the degree of eccentricity that accompanied his character of courtier: he'd resign his commission, he cried to the king whose jacket he was wearing, rather than obey.

The king's three-word comment surpassed in phlegm any of Turenne's warnings to Mademoiselle: "You are unwise."

A few days later came an official court announcement: Lauzun had shown "excessive zeal in defending a lieutenant of his dragoons guilty of conniving in the escape of a bandit in the Pyrenees." And Lauzun received a politely worded royal message—a message that in these early years of the age of Louis XIV was becoming an increasingly well-known formula: "It is my intention that you betake yourself to my château of the Bastille."

Lauzun betook himself—the very permission to do so was proof of the high consideration in which the king held him: ordinary offenders were taken to the Bastille by a guard—and he stayed there six months. He let his beard grow: his looks were nothing to him, he penitently proclaimed, as long as he had the misfortune to be in the bad graces of his sovereign. And when he was released he hastened to court, beard and all, to prostrate himself at the king's feet. The beard made the king laugh, and all was forgiven. Louis XIV was capable of laughter—he so relished the comedies of Molière that he gave the dramatist an honorary post in his household—but he didn't laugh easily; a laugh usually conferred favor. The marquis de Vardes, exiled from court for twenty years for interfering in the king's love affairs, had the wit to return wearing the same costume, now ludicrously outmoded, in which he had departed. "When one displeases Your Majesty," he informed the laughing monarch, "one is not only wretched, but ridiculous." Vardes was back in favor from that moment.

Lauzun, after his release, behaved anything but contritely. He bribed a chambermaid in the royal château of Saint-Germain, locked from the outside the door of a bedroom in which the king was awaiting the princesse de Monaco, threw the key down a nearby privy, and hid in the privy himself, enjoying the frustrated words the baffled lovers exchanged through the locked door. And one day at Saint-Cloud, when the princess was sitting on the floor with a group of ladies, Lauzun suddenly broke into a graceful pirouette: how horrified he was when the princess screamed and he found that his high wooden heel had ground into the very center of one of her hands! He was ready to fling himself out a window, he cried in mortification.

The king, presumably kept in ignorance of the privy incident (if it really occurred), dismissed the outraged princess's complaint that Lauzun had crushed her hand in deliberate revenge. It could only have been an unfortunate accident, he said. And he dismissed the complaining princess herself, as well: he'd had enough of her anyway. Lauzun's pirouette, thus furnishing an occasion for the exit of an outworn mistress, turned out to have been in the service of the king. Officers sent to the Bastille were often relieved of their commissions. Not Lauzun: from captain of dragoons he was promoted to colonel. And in the military campaign that now soon began in Flanders and the Franche-Comté—the Peace of the Pyrenees scarcely outlived the king of Spain, dead five years after it was signed—Lauzun was one of the heroes. These early expeditions of Louis XIV brought under the French flag many of the border cities to the north and east: Lauzun was associated, in the king's mind, with these triumphs, these conquests of Courtrai, Lille, Dôle, and other key places. Everywhere Lauzun was valiant; when he led his dragoons at Lille, his garments and boots were flapping, slashed by enemy sabers. The king promoted him again: in the dragoons he created for him a new grade, the grade of colonel-general.

And the king promised him something else—one of the most coveted commissions in the army, the "grand-mastership of artillery." This was a title that brought with it privilege and prestige at court, and wealth as well—for to the grand master of artillery was awarded, as his personal property, every iron and copper object found in every city that capitulated. The post was sought by many others, some of them the protégés of ministers; the king warned Lauzun to be silent concerning the promise: he himself would announce the appointment when the right moment came, not before. But Lauzun broke: an hour before he knew the king was to reveal the news at the close of a council-meeting, he spoke of his expectation to a palace steward. Such was the court grapevine that within that hour Louvois, minister of war, was informed. Already displeased by Lauzun's rapid rise, Louvois protested to the king; and when the king left the meeting he not only issued

no statement, but greeted the eagerly waiting Lauzun with cold-
ness.

Now the king had recently added another lady to his household. In her role as acknowledged royal mistress he forced Louise
de La Vallière to accept a partner: Athenaïs, marquise de Montespan, who had been lady-in-waiting to the queen. She was a
voluptuous, intriguing, imperious beauty, and in two respects she
resembled the cast-off princesse de Monaco; she had a husband,
and she had a past shared with Lauzun—who had helped her rise
by inflaming the king with hints of her accomplishments. Madame
de Montespan's triumph shocked the staider courtiers. Previously,
the king's affairs with married women had been decently screened.
The open liaison with the maidenly La Vallière involved only one
adultery—the king's own, scarcely to be criticized; blatant double
adultery was something new, an affront to God if not to the marquis de Montespan. Only the marquis was absurd enough to consider it an affront to himself. He draped his coach in black in
mourning for his wife, decorated it with antlers in token of his
own cuckoldry, and paraded under the very eyes of the king. But
the Montespans were soon declared divorced by royal decree, and
the tactless cuckold was exiled from Paris. The king ordered him
to accept a royal gift of 100,000 écus. He could now be said—and
was said—to have sold his wife; but it had been a forced sale.
The king never created Athenaïs de Montespan a duchess, as he
did Louise de La Vallière: perhaps that discrimination against her
was his own peculiar homage to the marriage laws, or perhaps he
shrank from raising a self-avowed cuckold to dukedom. But he
imposed the company of both ladies equally on the queen, who
had to receive them, converse with them, and at times see them take
precedence over herself.

In his dismay at the prospect of losing the grand-mastership of
artillery, Lauzun begged Madame de Montespan, whose career he
had so aided, to intercede for him with the king; she promised to
do so, then swore she had done it. But when there was no news

about the grand-mastership, Lauzun became suspicious. One day
he implored her to speak to the king again that very afternoon
(the schedule of the royal amours was known to all the court);
once again she promised; and, once again bribing a chambermaid,
Lauzun once again hid in a place of vantage. Not in a privy, this
time, but under the lovers' very bed. There (the incredible scene
is recounted in the memoirs of Saint-Simon, in the sober pages
of Michelet) he had the pleasure of hearing his old friend speak
of him to the king in sarcastic terms. The king had had a narrow
escape, she said. She knew Lauzun well. He was a troublemaker.
As grand-master of artillery he would have picked quarrels with
Louvois, caused more trouble than all the rest of the army put together. She was probably right, the king agreed. That evening, at
a ballet, Lauzun allowed Madame de Montespan to tell him *her*
version of her talk: she had done her best, she said, but hadn't
got very far. Then, leading her gracefully out to join the dance,
he repeated to her word for word the conversation as he had heard
it. And then, covering her with fierce whispered insults, he turned
on his heel and left her alone on the dance floor, "half-fainting,
more dead than alive." The next morning he was once again summoned before the king. This time he replied to royal expressions
of displeasure by breaking his sword. Never again, he swore, would
he serve a monarch capable of breaking his word to a gentleman
on the advice of a whore. Louis XIV made one of his inimitable
gestures. He went to the window and tossed out his cane—"lest,"
he said, "he have to reproach himself for *striking* a gentleman."

"It is my intention that you betake yourself to my château of the
Bastille": once again Lauzun received the polite formula.

This time his stay was even shorter than the last. Madame de
Montespan interceded for him: she knew the king really valued
him and liked him. Lauzun, she pleaded, had merely "gone crazy for
a moment." For his part Louis XIV acceded easily: he himself, he
said, "would rather have enough spirit to be wicked"—though he
hoped he might refrain from being so—"than be spiritless out of

stupidity." And, again out of the Bastille, Lauzun became not grand-master of artillery—that post he had to see go to Monsieur de Lude, first gentleman of the king's bedchamber—but one of the four captains of the king's personal bodyguard. "Our knowledge of his courage," the king decreed, "our esteem for his person, and our confidence in his conduct and loyalty are our reasons for raising him to a post suitable to his birth and his good qualities." Like the other commission, this one too brought with it innumerable privileges and benefits. Among them was a considerable degree of independence. The four captains of the king's bodyguard, each of them on duty three months a year, did not depend on the minister of war. Louvois, who had been Lauzun's master as long as he had been an officer of the dragoons, who had kept him from the grand-mastership of artillery, now had no control over him whatever. Closely attached to the king's person, the comte de Lauzun took orders only from the king.

Such, then, were the situations of the two characters whose personal drama was about to begin. Both had been chastised and rechastised. Mademoiselle, forgiven *Frondeuse,* purged of more recent disobedience by a year and a half of exile, restored to favor by a royal kiss; Lauzun, twice imprisoned in the Bastille for offenses regarding the king's mistresses, but steadily promoted. Mademoiselle, immensely proud, but "with a tender heart, easily touched," a spinster in a court of concubines. Lauzun, intrepid soldier, courtier on the make, a little mad. Both of them close to the king: one by blood, the other by ambition, loyalty, professional duty.

Mademoiselle was among those who congratulated Lauzun on his new distinction. "He told me," she records, "that he was very conscious of the honor I did him in thus associating myself with the king's kindness. I now began to think of him as someone quite extraordinary, very agreeable in conversation, and I was glad whenever I had an opportunity to speak with him. I found that he had ways of expressing himself very different from those of other people."

As for the court that was to form the background of the drama, it had changed from the old days when Anne of Austria, Mazarin, the king and Monsieur all lived and moved about close together in the Palais-Royal or the Louvre. Now the survivors had separated. The king and queen were in the Tuileries, which had been handsomely remodeled by Mademoiselle's architect Le Vau; Monsieur and Madame were in the Palais-Royal, with suburban quarters in the palace of Saint-Cloud; the queen-mother had her own court in the Louvre. But the king stayed in Paris as little as possible: he hated the city, with its memories of the Fronde. Even Saint-Germain he disliked: he complained that it had too good a view of Saint-Denis, his final resting place. These were the years of the rebuilding, the vast enlargement and transformation, of the old palace, little more than a hunting lodge, at Versailles. To Versailles, eventually, the king, the courtiers, the ministers, the officials, all would move. Already it was the scene of fêtes and picnics, royal weekends and holidays to which selected groups were asked.

Soon after the death of her brother the king of Spain, Anne of Austria died, destroyed by cancer: the long description of the last days and hours of her aunt, her godmother, her *petite-maman,* her old friend and enemy, is one of the showpieces of Mademoiselle's memoirs. The old queen had farewell words for almost all who crowded round her deathbed—except two: "I was surprised," says Mademoiselle, "that she said nothing to the prince de Condé or to me—we were both present." Anne of Austria had never really forgiven the Frondeurs. There had been periods, of late, when she had not been on speaking terms with the king himself: the extent of his adulteries appalled her. But her last words to him covered an even broader field: "Exterminate heresy, my son."

The extermination of heresy—the revocation of the Edict of

Nantes and the persecution of the Protestants—was to come later. At present, not the prestige of the church, but the prestige of France and of himself was the king's great concern. On the battle-field, at sea, in diplomacy, France and its king must never take second place: the Pope himself sent a special legate, his own nephew, to Paris to apologize for a slight to the French ambas-sador's servants in the streets of Rome. Colbert, far more than a mere finance minister, was achieving the great and longest-lived creations of the reign: the navy and the colonies, the network of roads, canals and aqueducts across France, the Observatory, the Royal Library, and the great industries—those hand products, the silks of Lyons, the tapestries of Beauvais and the Gobelins, the glass, that remain supreme today. The reign depended for its support, based its power, on the prosperity of more and more artisans, more and more merchants—no longer on the nobility, which had shot its last bolt in the Fronde. The moment would come when the powerful French bourgeoisie would no longer be content to be merely the support of a reign, but that moment was a hundred years off. From the very beginning the industries and commerce that Colbert created were looked on as sources of tax revenue, and much of the revenue was lavished on fêtes and favor-ites. One of the king's presents to Madame de Montespan was the entire proceeds of the tobacco tax: in a single evening she lost 700,000 écus of it at cards.

Mademoiselle continued in the Luxembourg, sharing it with her stepmother. They lived in separate wings. The old Madame's wing was known chiefly for its medicines and its priests; the wing be-longing to Mademoiselle, who in Saint-Fargeau had "begun to enjoy books," was the scene of the most agreeable salon in Paris. Madame de Sévigné, Madame de Lafayette, the duc de la Roche-foucauld were her frequent guests; and there was never a hint of dryness and stiffness, for an adjoining room was usually filled with young people dancing to the sound of Mademoiselle's vio-lins. One thing was forbidden: card playing, or any form of gambling. *Le jeu* was the rage in the Tuileries and the Palais-Royal, but it bored and displeased Mademoiselle: at gaming tables in this same Luxembourg she had too often seen her father losing his money—and hers.

Mademoiselle's fêtes in the Luxembourg were not the least distinguished pleasures of the reign of Louis XIV. The first three acts of Molière's *Tartuffe* had been given as part of *Les Plaisirs de l'île enchantée,* the inaugural fête at Versailles that Mademoiselle had missed because of her exile at Eu; but the last two acts and all public presentation were suppressed at the request of the church, and for the next five years the play was known only by readings given by Molière himself before small groups. Now, in 1669, just when she was beginning to speak to Lauzun whenever she could, Mademoiselle invited an engaged couple she was fond of—Mademoiselle de Créqui and the comte de Jarnac—to celebrate their wedding in her apartments; and before the ceremony, which took place at midnight, the entire *Tartuffe,* with Molière himself in the leading role, was played for the first time before the assembled guests.

Molière, Racine, Boileau—the king enjoyed these literary men, and he respected them and recognized them and their fellow artists as contributing, like victories in the field, to the country's and his own prestige. Mademoiselle's hospitality to Molière shed luster on her family. Lauzun, wearer of the king's jacket, captain of the king's bodyguard, but very much a parvenu, a "new" man, was acutely aware that it was a very great lady indeed, a *fille de France,* the king's first cousin, who was "glad whenever she had an opportunity to speak with him." He had every appreciation of the difference between them. He, like Mademoiselle, knew "how people are at court."

3

A FEW MONTHS AFTER the performance of *Tartuffe* in her apartments, Mademoiselle left Paris to spend the summer in her château at Eu.

"Before leaving," she says, "I spoke a few polite words to Monsieur de Lauzun about how much I'd miss such agreeable company as his. I had formed the habit of talking with him, and I used to seek him out for that purpose whenever he came to see the queen. I say that I sought him out, because he acted toward me with such dutiful respect that he would never have come near me if I hadn't spoken to him first. After I had paid him the compliments I have just mentioned, and he had given me several deep bows in reply, he said that even though he could scarcely boast the honor of being among my acquaintances, he was one of the men in the world most eager to carry out my orders if I would do him the honor of giving him some. He said it so spontaneously that I felt he was sincere. When we had exchanged a few more courtesies, he told me that he was much touched by the confidence I had shown in him, and said again that he would be most zealous in carrying out any orders I might give him."

Such was the first of the conversations between herself and Lauzun which Mademoiselle records; and from now on he becomes, next to herself, the chief character in her memoirs, a character with whom she speaks constantly in dialogue.

The following winter the court spent at Saint-Germain, and

Mademoiselle, greatest of *Parisiennes,* found Paris, for the first time in her life, not to her liking. "I went to Saint-Germain, where I spent the winter without coming in to Paris as I usually did. I mean, I had previously always spent two weeks in Paris after every five- or six-day stay at court; this winter, scarcely knowing why, I couldn't bear Paris and couldn't tear myself away from Saint-Germain. I was in Paris briefly when one of my maids of honor came down with smallpox; this kept me from going to court for four or five days; I spent them very listlessly in Paris, and I remember how delighted I was when I was told I could return to court. There I kept seeing Monsieur de Lauzun in the queen's apartments, and took the greatest pleasure in talking with him. Every day I found him more intelligent and agreeable, more so than anyone I had ever known. He continued to be reserved, displaying dutiful respect in his own inimitable way."

It was during that winter of 1669–70—eleven years after she had danced shepherdess to Lauzun's shepherd, ten after she had admired his *hauteur* at Saint-Jean-de-Luz—that she became aware of what had happened to her. And the consciousness of love bursts out, in her memoirs, in a long soliloquy.

"It is God who determines our estate: he lets each of us enjoy his own within the limits of our varying dispositions. He had allowed me to consider mine the most fortunate I could have chosen: I had been content with my birth, with my fortune, with all kinds of advantages that allow one to live without being a burden to oneself or to others. However, as I have already said, without knowing the reason, I found myself disliking places that I formerly liked and partial to others that had once left me indifferent. I was fond of the company of Monsieur de Lauzun, though it hadn't yet occurred to me to attach any precise meaning to my fondness. After long agitation I tried to probe myself, to sort out what pleased me and what caused me pain. I realized that I was in the throes of a preoccupation which was entirely new to me: I saw that I should be happier married. To make someone's fortune, to raise him in the world, would win me his gratitude; he would be touched, he would conceive an affection for me, seek to please me in every way.

"Hitherto, I had been offered great establishments that would have raised my rank but not increased my happiness. This, I saw now, I could attain only by devoting myself to someone who, in turn, would care for me. My heirs, I recognized, considered my property their own: their greatest wish could only be for my death. I turned all this over in my mind, well aware that what begins as inclination may turn to aversion. But I saw that of all the courses open to me God had seen fit to show me that I would find comfort in marrying a person to whom I could bring such great fortune that he would value it for the rest of my life and his own—a person with whom I could spend my days in tranquility, in the union of perfect affection. Then, at last, I understood that my restlessness had had a definite cause. The merit I had perceived in Monsieur de Lauzun, the distinction of his conduct as compared with other men's, the elevation of his soul above the common, and the charm of his company and of a million special traits he possessed, made me realize, or rather feel, that he was the only man who would be equal to the high position to which I would elevate him, the only person worthy of my choice, the one best suited to be my husband."

And Mademoiselle's "self-probings" continued.

"I reflected that all my life I had never received marks of affection from anyone. There is a pleasure in being loved: I knew him to be a man of feeling, and I thought of the joy that would come of living with a really good man whom I could consider a friend, someone capable of sharing my joys and sorrows, someone whose company, I was beginning to realize, I enjoyed more than I had ever enjoyed anyone's before. All my present happiness, I saw clearly, came from my pleasure in speaking with him. My neglect of all my other affairs, the repugnance I felt for society, my bore-

dom whenever I was away from the queen—everything revealed
to me what had been hidden before."

This discovery—so feminine, so belated, so unlike anything
that had gone before—made her more agitated than ever. "I
couldn't stand anyone; I wanted only to be alone in my room, or
to be meeting him in the queen's apartments or in the Cours-la-
Reine, whether by chance or appointment: simply to see him
calmed me. I reflected on the difficulties that might arise: I was
eager to put my problem before the king, to open my heart to him
and ask him to advise me on how to conduct myself. I was dis-
consolate because Monsieur de Lauzun's ever-dutiful, ever-respect-
ful attitude showed that he suspected none of my feelings for
him. And so the task that seemed to me most difficult was to suggest to him how fortunate he was: I couldn't help thinking, sometimes, of the difference between his station and my own."

She knew from her readings in history that many men of lesser
rank and merit than Lauzun had married ladies of royal blood,
and she remembered that some of Corneille's heroines had strug-
gled with problems similar to her own. She sent to Paris for all of
Corneille's works, and the moment they arrived, she found and
learned by heart a marvelous passage about lovers whose union
God Himself has predestined. Then a fear came over her—the
fear that the feelings she was experiencing might really be light
and vulgar, "mere *galanterie"*: how, in her inexperience, could she
know? She resolved never to see Lauzun without a third person
present. But she found that on such occasions she couldn't utter
"three consecutive words that made sense," and that the more she
tried to avoid him the more she craved his company! She prayed
and prayed for guidance; and one day, at a novena with the queen,
"I realized, from the state in which I found myself, that I should
remain unhappy all my life long if I persisted in trying to drive
out of my mind an idea that had taken such strong root." Just
then a rumor came to her that the king was planning to marry her
to prince Charles of Lorraine. She was accustomed to hear such

rumors about herself, but this was one that might prove useful: she could ask Lauzun his opinion of it.

In the queen's apartments she found him talking with the comtesse de Guiche, and approached them. "My I finish telling Monsieur de Lauzun what I have to say?" the countess asked her. "I can't always be sure of finding him; whereas you have only to give the order and he comes."

The countess's words were no more than a reference to Mademoiselle's rank, superior to her own; but the implications made Mademoiselle "tremble." "My heart pounded so violently that I thought he must notice it, and I even wished that he *might* guess my feelings, and realize that what I had come to tell him was far from disagreeable."

"When the comtesse de Guiche left him, I went to a window and he followed me. His air was so lordly that day that he was positively superb: he seemed to me like the master of the entire world. I controlled my trembling. 'You once told me that you were interested in everything concerning me,' I said. 'I don't like to do anything without asking the advice of such a faithful friend, a man of such good sense.' "

Lauzun assured her with many compliments that he would try to deserve her good opinion of him. Had he heard of the rumored match between her and the prince of Lorraine, she asked? He had not; but he was convinced that the king would do nothing unjust, he said, or against her wishes.

"Persons of my age," said Mademoiselle—she was almost forty-two—"are not married off against their wishes, like young girls. I have had many proposals. I have listened to all of them. Some would have raised me very high indeed, but I would have been desperately unhappy if I had had to accept them. I love my country. I am a *grande dame:* my conduct is governed not by ambition, but by reason. We must all have some happiness in our lives, and I am convinced it's not to be found in a marriage with someone unknown to us. Such a partner may turn out badly; then you can only despise him."

"But you're so well off as you are," said Lauzun. "Why should you think of marrying at all?"

She *was* well off, Mademoiselle admitted; but there was one thing that made her consider marriage. And she now confided to Lauzun, with clear intent, one of the thoughts that had formed part of her troubling soliloquy—her awareness that there were people waiting for her to die so that they might inherit her fortune. She didn't identify them; she merely said she disliked having to think about them, and would be happy to disappoint them.

The matter was well worth reflection, Lauzun agreed, and he promised to reflect on it.

The queen appeared just then and interrupted them.

The next day Lauzun greeted Mademoiselle with "a charming smile." He could fill a book, he said, with all the thoughts he had had overnight, but he was afraid they were fantastic thoughts, "castles in Spain." It would be best if she were to tell him what she had in mind, and he would reply in all frankness.

"I've been building as many castles in Spain as you," she said, "but mine are built on firm foundations. I'm glad you're willing to talk with me seriously, like a true friend, for the affair I want to discuss with you is the most important in my life."

He laughed. "I'm very proud of being your chief adviser."

"You're my *only* adviser," she corrected him. "Let's go back to where we were yesterday."

He consented willingly. "In your place I'd feel just as you do," he told her. "It's pleasant to be alive, and most distressing to know that there are people who wish you dead. It's quite comprehensible to me that you should think of marriage for that reason alone. Still, when I look around, I don't see any suitable partner for you. So I find it difficult to advise you. I can only sympathize with you in your predicament. You're quite right to want to get out of it. Otherwise, what is there for you to wish for? Rank, fortune, the king's affection—you have everything. If you were queen or empress in a foreign country, you'd be bored to death."

"I told him he was right," says Mademoiselle. "I told him I saw that I hadn't been mistaken in choosing him as my adviser. 'My rank and fortune could be used best,' I said, 'to elevate some Frenchman of merit. That's what I'd prefer to do: that way I could always stay near the king. And the king would be delighted to have me elevate one of his subjects and provide him with a fortune to be used in his service.'"

Lauzun was half-mocking, half-serious. "How right you were to say you'd been building castles in Spain, like me! You were right, too, when you said they had better foundations than mine. Everything you've just said is quite feasible: I see all kinds of advantages in it for you. You'd have the pleasure of elevating a man above all the sovereigns of Europe and the joy of knowing that he'd be grateful to you forever and love you more than his own life. Best of all, you'd stay near the king.

"So much for the foundations," he said. "But now for the castles in the air. Where will you find a man of proper birth, proper inclinations, proper merits, proper virtue? You must have known in advance," he said, "that I'd consider it impossible to locate such a man for you."

It was Mademoiselle's turn to smile. "You said yourself that the project is feasible. Leave it to me to find the man."

Once again the queen appeared and interrupted them.

"I admit that I was very satisfied with everything I had told him," says Mademoiselle, "and with all his answers. I concluded that he had grasped my meaning perfectly."

But a few days later, when she broached her "project" again, Lauzun was discouraging. "I foresee so much unpleasantness for you, so much difficulty, that I advise you to forget it once and for all," he told her. "You're well off as you are. I'd be unworthy of your confidence if I didn't urge you to stay that way."

Those words wounded her, Mademoiselle says, but had no effect on her determination. She realized that in his position he could not afford to be frank. In his very diffidence she saw further proof of his understanding, and this was a source of comfort: she was getting somewhere, after all.

Still, when she tried to press on, he was adept at tantalizing sidesteps which left things squarely up to her. "I well understand that a woman, whatever her rank, can't possibly spend her whole life in a state of indecision about her condition," he said. "At the age of forty one shouldn't indulge in the pleasures suitable for girls in their teens and early twenties. And so it's my duty to tell you that if you don't marry, you should follow one of two courses: enter a convent, or simply lead a pious life. If you choose the latter, you must dress modestly and renounce all worldly pleasures. You might go to the opera once a year, I suppose, to pay your respects to the king. You must never miss High Mass, vespers, benediction, or sermons. You must attend charity functions, visit hospitals, help the poor and the sick. As for the alternative of marriage—of course that allows you to take part in all festivities and dress well, for it's a woman's duty to please her husband. But a husband isn't an easy thing to come by. Suppose you do find one to your taste: mightn't he prove to have unsuspected defects that would make you miserable? You see: I really can't advise you on this matter."

On this double-talk Mademoiselle put the most favorable interpretation possible. "He was more concerned for my good reputation than for his own advantage."

4

Now, WITH THE SPRING, there was talk of a court visit to
Flanders, to inspect the conquests of a few years before—
and, doubtless, to explore the approaches to Holland,
Louis XIV's next projected victim. No war was raging at the
moment, but the king was by now so accustomed to traveling with
troops that he assembled an army corps as escort, commissioned
Lauzun lieutenant-general in the regular army, and appointed him
commander.

Perhaps this promotion came to him as a reward for a non-
military operation he had recently carried out with signal success
and luck as captain of the king's personal bodyguard. The night
of March 30 Madame de Montespan had given birth to a little
son, later known as the duc du Maine, in her bedroom at Saint-
Germain. Decency demanded that this fruit of double adultery be
removed from the royal palace as quickly as possible. There was
no time even to wrap the infant properly in swaddling clothes;
it was hastily swathed in a coverlet, and Lauzun, tucking it under
his cloak, took it out to a waiting carriage, terrified as he walked
through the palace lest it betray its presence by a wail.

In any case, Mademoiselle sought out the new lieutenant-
general to congratulate him. She could not bear, she found, to
absent herself from court to spend Holy Week as usual at her
château of Eu, and her decision brought its reward: at Tenebrae
on Good Friday, in the palace chapel at Saint-Germain, she found

herself next to Lauzun. They spoke of pious matters. "He has such a universal mind that he can talk amazingly well about anything. He sermonized more impressively than the best preachers." On Easter, in Paris, they met by chance in the street. "I cannot express the joy I felt when I saw his carriage approaching mine, and I greeted him most civilly. It seemed to me that his greeting, too, was more cordial than usual."

The next time they met at Saint-Germain, he laughed to hear her say that Paris bored her. "Of course it bores you," he said. "You used to enjoy it when you had nothing on your mind. Now even one day there is too much: you're full of a project that you can discuss only with me, and it's natural that you should want to come back here and find relief in talking about it. Take my advice," he said. "Find yourself another confidant, one in Paris. Then you won't be bored there. I confess the role of *sole* confidant honors me more than I deserve."

"He kept up that kind of banter until we set out for Flanders," says Mademoiselle, "refusing to be drawn into my serious conversation."

"You'd make a good wife," Madame de Puysieux, a lady in waiting, suddenly remarked to Mademoiselle one day, apropos of nothing, while Mademoiselle was being bled in preparation for the trip. "The man you married would never regret it."

Madame d'Epernon, also present at the bleeding, expressed the opinion that Mademoiselle would never marry—she had turned down so many wonderful proposals.

"It isn't to a king that I'd like to see her married," retorted Madame de Puysieux. And then, turning to Mademoiselle, she demanded, "Am I right, Princess? Wouldn't you rather elevate some deserving gentleman?"

And when Mademoiselle said she would, Madame de Puysieux abruptly advised, "Marry the prince de Condé's nephew, Monsieur de Longueville. He's a very fine man indeed."

"Oh," said Madame d'Epernon, "if you're proposing that kind of a match to Mademoiselle, let me mention my candidate: she should marry *my* nephew, Monsieur de Marsan."

"I wasn't at all sorry," says Mademoiselle, "to let them gossip that way about my marrying. It seemed a good way to get people accustomed to the idea."

"Will my dilemma remain unsolved until after the trip?" Mademoiselle asked Lauzun as soon as she could, when the long train of court coaches, baggage-wagons and cavalry was finally on the road. "You said you sympathized with me in my predicament: is it to continue all this time?"

Lauzun, who "had a thousand things to do," said that for the time being they must think only of the trip.

Mademoiselle did her best to do so. "We left Saint-Quentin in terrible weather. Uncomfortable though I was, I was glad to be of the party, because not a day passed without my seeing the two persons I loved best in the world. The king has always been, and still is, my greatest passion; Monsieur de Lauzun, the second. I don't hesitate to say that for Monsieur de Lauzun, too, the king came first, as I well know from all the affection and devotion he displayed toward him at all times, and from the pleasure we both took in speaking of him." It was obvious that the king returned Lauzun's esteem, and this filled her with joy and encouragement. "It seemed to me that my taste couldn't be bad, since it conformed to the king's.

"The bad weather and horrible rain played havoc with our entire cortege, but the only thing I minded was the sight of Monsieur de Lauzun, bareheaded on his horse, speaking to the king through the window of his coach. 'Tell him to put on his hat!' I could never resist calling to the king." When Monsieur and his friend the marquis de Villeroy, comfortable in their coach, snickered at the sight of Lauzun in the downpour, "his hair all pushed up under his hat," Mademoiselle thought that bedraggled as he was, he looked better than they. But that night, when they stopped at Landrecies, Lauzun himself scolded her for her constant intercession with the king on his behalf: he advised her to control herself in the future, and Mademoiselle, recognizing the value of the suggestion, was grateful for it. That same night Mademoiselle's maids of honor complained to her about Lauzun: he had held up their carriage, they said, held up his very troops, to make way for the coach containing Mademoiselle's chambermaids. Mademoiselle was enchanted to learn it: how many men would be thoughtful enough to realize that at night her chambermaids were far more necessary to her comfort than her maids of honor?

At Avesnes, he himself encouraged discussion of the subject he had told her was in abeyance for the duration of the trip. She had complimented him again on his new command, and his reply was somewhat strange. Of course he valued it, he said, but only as a token of the king's good will. "To tell you the truth," he confided, "in my present state of mind I feel more like becoming a hermit than playing a part in the world. I'd be better off. The only thing is, people ignorant of my motives would think me a madman."

"I've told you about my concerns," said Mademoiselle. "Why don't you tell me about yours?"

"I have none."

"Wouldn't you like to marry? Has no one ever broached the subject to you?"

He had had offers, he said. But if he were ever tempted to marry, it would be solely by the *virtue* of the lady in question. "If I were to find her blamable in the slightest degree, I would reject her no matter how rich she might be." And suddenly he said something that advanced matters with a rush: "Even if it were a question of you," he said—he was still speaking hypothetically, of course, but he said it—"you, great lady that you are, I wouldn't marry you if you weren't virtuous and if I felt no affection for you."

"Are you telling me the truth?" cried Mademoiselle, enraptured. "If you are, my opinion of you is higher than ever."

"Yes," he swore. "I'd rather marry a chambermaid, if I loved her, and if she was virtuous, than any queen you can think of. I'd go off with her and we'd live alone, by ourselves: it would be a mistake in the world's eyes, but I wouldn't consider myself dishonored."

"Then you'd find *me* acceptable!" Mademoiselle couldn't help crying. "I fulfill all your conditions."

Lauzun looked at her reproachfully. "I beg you," he said, giving every evidence of being offended, "don't be facetious when I'm talking about something very important to me."

"Very well then. Since you want to be serious, won't you advise me how to put an end to the situation you sympathized with me about? Tell me how you feel about it. Tell me what to do, and I'll do it."

But they were interrupted by the marquis de Rochefort, one of Lauzun's fellow captains in the bodyguard.

Only two or three days later, at Le Catenet, could they resume the conversation. Now it was Mademoiselle who advanced with a rush.

"I began by telling Monsieur de Lauzun that I was completely determined: I wanted to marry. I had examined and solved all the difficulties he had pointed out, I said, and had even chosen the man he had told me he thought I could never find. Only Monsieur de Lauzun's approval of my choice was lacking. I made him 'tremble,' he replied: he urged me to think for 'a whole century' before making a decision that would determine my future happiness or unhappiness. I told him that when a woman is forty and wants to commit a folly, she cannot afford to think as long as that. Moreover, I said, I was so sure of my choice that I intended to speak to the king about it as soon as there was a break in the trip: I wanted to marry now, in Flanders."

And as though to keep step with her acceleration, Lauzun increased the tempo of his own side of the dance figure, his pattern of advances and recoils. He spoke solemnly, almost in alarm: "Since you've chosen me as your chief adviser, I feel obliged to tell you that you must *not* speak of it to the king. I'm opposed to your hurrying matters: you'd spoil all your chances. As long as you do me the honor of asking my advice, I'm honor-bound not to let you make a mistake."

Mademoiselle fenced with him. "I find it comical that you should dissuade *me* from marrying just because *you* have an aversion to marriage."

"It's true that I'm against it, though a horoscopist once said that I'd acquire very great wealth by a marriage," Lauzun parried. "A person who loved me had my horoscope cast, and was in despair when she learned what I just told you."

"In that case she can't have loved you!"

"On the contrary—it was because she did love me and didn't have the wealth to give me that she was in despair."

He shook his head when Mademoiselle asked him the name of the "person"; her curiosity was to be satisfied only later. "Let's talk about something else. Let's forget astrology and fairy tales."

"I ask you for your advice and am willing to follow it," said Mademoiselle. "Why don't you trust mine? In my opinion you shouldn't overlook that forecast. Believe me, you are in a position to aim high. Without being an astrologer, I can assure you that you will succeed. I beg you: don't lose them."

"In discussing futilities we're losing time this very minute," Lauzun retorted. "At least I am. I have things to do. I must go to the king."

The retreats with which he followed his advances were at once Mademoiselle's despair and her fascination. It was only during that conversation at Le Catenet, he told people later, that he had finally lost all doubt concerning the nature of her intentions. And Mademoiselle, learning that he said this, told everyone "in order to conform to his story," that only at Le Catenet had she made up her mind—"although I had really made it up some time before."

The very next day he let her know in a macabre, oblique way that he, who had advised her to think "a whole century" before acting, was just as conscious as she of the passing of time. Everybody was discussing the sudden death, as the result of an accident in Saint-Quentin, of one of Mademoiselle's favorite servants, her steward Cabanes, who when a young *valet de chambre* had brought to Aix the news of her father's death; and Lauzun took the occasion to discourse on mortuary themes. When he ended, he turned to Mademoiselle: "I know you fear death," he said. "I'm determined to remind you very often that some day you must die. I want you to accustom yourself to the idea." And for the rest of the day, each time he came near he said: "Think of death!" Or, "Remember: some day you'll die!" It served as a reminder, too, of her waiting heirs.

Even the crudest of his eccentricities didn't displease Mademoiselle. A few days later, at Tournai, he played her a practical joke as she was about to step out of her carriage. She held out her hand, asking him to help her; but "he walked away, and I, balanced on one foot as I was, almost fell on my face. He was always doing that sort of thing, which must have seemed ridiculous to those who noticed. But I was so sure that he had his reasons for acting this way that I wasn't angry."

In his entire behavior she saw proof of his great respect. "He realized, I was sure, that if I were to change my mind and the affair were to become known, it would create an embarrassing situation for me, and for that reason he wanted me to preserve my freedom of action. Such modesty and foresight were unnecessary in view of my feelings for him, but I appreciated them: no one else would have been capable of such magnanimity. My esteem for him was greater than ever. I considered him the most extraordinary being I had ever known. He fully understood that with someone of my station, one must not press ahead at the same pace as with an equal."

On days when she couldn't speak to him, she never failed to go to a window to see him mount his horse as he left the king. "I always managed to say something in a loud voice, or to make some other noise, to attract his attention and make him look at me. It made me happy just to have him turn his head toward my window."

One day Mademoiselle returned to the subject of the lady who had Lauzun's horoscope cast. "Tell me: was it the princess of Monaco?"

"No," came the surprising answer, "it was the queen of Portugal."

And, indeed, Mademoiselle learned that the two sisters, Mademoiselle de Nemours and Mademoiselle d'Aumale, had both loved Lauzun passionately, "but they weren't rich enough to marry him unless one of them gave up her fortune to the other and became a nun, so they drew lots, and Mademoiselle d'Aumale won, and had herself proposed to Lauzun." But for some reason the match hadn't gone through. It was on the rebound from Lauzun that Mademoiselle d'Aumale had married the "delightful" Affonso whom Mademoiselle had refused.

The trip took the court as far as Courtrai, limit of French Flanders, and then it turned back. During the southward journey Mademoiselle's dreams of future happiness were disturbed by rumors. At Calais, where the French ambassador to England joined them to pay his respects to the king, Monsieur acted mysteriously. He teased Mademoiselle: he knew something about her that he couldn't tell, he said. But the king himself let her know what it was. Charles II was dissatisfied with his queen; she seemed unable to bear children, and he was thinking of sending her back to Portugal. Once again Mademoiselle was being talked of as his bride. This was frightening news. The king was eager, just now, to please Charles: he wanted him as an ally in the war he was planning against Holland. During this very trip Madame —Henriette, that is, Monsieur's wife, Charles's sister—had been shipped off to England to make overtures to her brother. At the thought of this obstacle to her plans, Mademoiselle burst into tears. "It's just a rumor, so far," the king said. "Nothing to cry about."

"It's the thought of leaving Your Majesty that upsets me," said Mademoiselle.

"It gave me an opportunity to make a display of affection to the king," Mademoiselle tells us, "and at the same time to show Monsieur de Lauzun that I esteemed him above all the kings and emperors in the world. I told him about the rumor, and he said he had heard about it, and knew that I had wept. I was right, he added, to be overcome with grief at the thought of leaving the king. He himself adored him, and was delighted to see what very great affection I had for him. He was well aware, he said, that that had been the *only* reason for my tears. Apart from that, I could only have been proud to marry a king who put away his wife in favor of me. He himself could only have congratulated me."

But back in Paris the rumor about Charles evaporated. He decided not to send away Catherine of Braganza. She bore him no children, but she was placid, he had plenty of children by others, and he had a brother to succeed him. And even if he had consented to divorce Catherine, he wouldn't have made Mademoiselle his queen. He had wooed her only indifferently, at his mother's insistence; but that didn't prevent his remembering that in his exile she had rejected him.

And at this same time there was another short-lived bit of gossip: Louis XIV was tired of Louise de La Vallière, people said, and he was planning to rid himself of her by marrying her to Lauzun. "I think it was Monsieur de Lauzun's enemies who started that rumor," says Mademoiselle. "He would scorn to marry anyone's mistress, even the king's. No worse slander could have been devised for him, after the distinction that *I* conferred on him."

S O NOW THE WAY WAS CLEAR. Nothing stood between Mademoiselle and the step she must take as *fille de France:* the visit she must pay to the king, her "father," head of her family, to ask his permission that she marry.

A few days before the end of June—June 30 was a Monday—she told Lauzun at Versailles that she would speak to the king. "I want everything settled before the first of July," she said. "After that you'll be on duty with the king and won't have time to give me advice: you're still the only man from whom I'm willing to take it."

He begged her to wait only a few more days. "I'm going to Paris tomorrow," he said. "I'll be back here Sunday without fail. I'll listen to everything you have to tell me and I'll advise you as a faithful servitor should. Believe me, I long to see your worries at an end."

On Sunday, June 29, she was talking with Lauzun's sister, Madame de Nogent. During recent months Mademoiselle had cultivated her friendship; she had often confided to her that she was not happy as she was, that she wanted a change. Now she went further: "You'd be quite surprised, I suppose, if I were to tell you that I'll soon be married? It's true, though. I'm going to ask the king's permission tomorrow, and everything will be decided in twenty-four hours."

Madame de Nogent "listened with great attention."

"Perhaps you're wondering whom I'll marry," suggested Mademoiselle. "I shouldn't mind if you guessed."

As Mademoiselle herself tells us, "it was impossible that Madame de Nogent shouldn't have known what was in the wind." But she was as foxy as her brother. "I suppose it's Monsieur de Longueville?" she asked.

"No, it's a man of rank, of infinite merit, whom I've liked for a long time. I haven't kept my intentions from him. He knows what they are, but out of respect for me he has said nothing. Look around this room," said Mademoiselle. "Mention any names you like. I'll say 'Yes' if you come to the right one."

But when Madame de Nogent had mentioned "everyone of proper rank present," and Mademoiselle had steadily said "No, no, no," Mademoiselle called an end to the game. "You're wasting your time," she confessed. "He's in Paris. He'll be here this evening."

And she had barely said those words when the comte d'Ayen, Lauzun's colleague, captain of the king's bodyguard then on duty, came rushing in with terrible news: "Madame is dying!"

It was true. An hour or two before, in the palace of Saint-Cloud, Madame, who had recently returned from her mission to her brother the king of England, had asked for a cup of chicory water; no sooner had she swallowed it than she screamed that "her stomach was on fire"; her pains were excruciating; already everyone was whispering, "Poison." The king, the queen, and Mademoiselle hurried from Versailles to Saint-Cloud in the king's coach. "Halfway there we met Monsieur Valot, the king's physician, on his way back; he told the king it was only a colic, that Madame's illness would be neither long nor dangerous. When we arrived at Saint-Cloud, we found almost no one who seemed concerned; Monsieur appeared very surprised that we had come. But then we saw Madame, on a little bed that had been made up for her in a corner of the room. Her hair was all disheveled; her suffering had been so continuous that there hadn't been a moment to dress her hair for the night. Her chemise was all disordered. Her face was pale, her nose sunken; already she had the look of someone dead. 'You see what state I'm in,' she said to us.

"We began to weep. Mesdames de Montespan and La Vallière arrived. She was making terrible efforts to vomit. 'Try,' Monsieur kept saying to her. 'Try, so that you won't choke on your own bile.'

"I could see how distressed she was by the carelessness of almost all who were present: the state she was in should have filled everyone with pity. She spoke to the king for a few moments in a low voice. Then I went up to her and took her hand. She pressed mine: 'You are losing a good friend,' she told me. 'I was beginning to know you and to love you.' My tears were my only answer.

"She asked for an emetic, but the doctors said it was unnecessary, that this kind of colic sometimes lasted nine or ten hours, never more than twenty-four. The king tried to argue with them: 'Surely you won't just let a woman die without trying to save her!' They just looked at each other and said nothing.

"People in the room were talking, coming and going, even laughing, as though Madame were perfectly well. I spoke to Monsieur: 'No one seems to realize that Madame is dying, that someone should speak to her of God.'

" 'Whom could we find,' Monsieur asked, 'whose name would look well in the *Gazette* as having been with her at the end?' I told him that at such a moment the chief requirement of a confessor was that he be a good man, fit for his task. 'Ah, I know!' Monsieur said. 'The abbé Bossuet. Madame has talked with him occasionally. He's the man.' He proposed the abbé Bossuet to the king, who told him that he should have thought of it sooner, should have seen to it earlier that she received the Sacraments. 'I'll wait till you've left,' Monsieur said. 'With you here too many formalities have to be observed.' [By custom, a French monarch absented himself whenever possible from the sight of death, disturbing reminder of his own mortality. Louis XIV had retired to an adjoining room as his mother had approached her end.] By now Madame had been placed in her regular bed. The king kissed her and bade her farewell. She spoke to him affectionately, and to the queen too. I stood weeping at the foot of the bed; I couldn't bear to speak with her again. We returned to Versailles. . . ."

At Versailles they found Lauzun. Mademoiselle spoke to him in a low voice: "This is a misfortune that won't leave *me* unharmed, I fear."

"I'm sure of it," he answered. "I think it will spoil all your plans."

"I told him," she says, "that it could only postpone their execution. Whatever happened, I wouldn't change my mind."

Madame died at three that morning. It was probably peritonitis that killed her, but at the time poison seemed a certainty. Monsieur had cared nothing for her. He had married her only to get his *apanage;* he had been jealous—not of her relations with the king, but of the attention paid her by some of his own male favorites. Once, when she had been unwell in a coach, Mademoiselle had heard Monsieur comment: "A horoscopist once told me I'd have more than one wife. I begin to think he was right." The king demanded to be told whether there was any evidence that it was Monsieur who had poisoned her. He was much relieved by the answer: the poison, it was thought, had been sent from Italy, without Monsieur's knowledge, by the chevalier de Lorraine, one of Monsieur's favorites whom the king had exiled. The news of her death was brought to Mademoiselle as she lay in bed. "It caused me real sorrow," she says. "I hadn't slept all night, thinking that if she died, and if Monsieur took it into his head to marry me, I'd be in difficulties. But whatever happened, I determined to persist in my resolve. I'd have to let some time pass before definitely refusing Monsieur, and a little more before disclosing my intentions.' The idea of the delay made me desperate."

And indeed, that very morning, when the king was discussing

with her details of Madame's funeral, he said to her, " 'Cousin, here is a place to be filled. Are you willing?'

"I turned pale as death, and said, trembling, 'You are the master. I shall never have any will but yours.'

"He pressed me hard, but that was all I would say. He asked, 'Do you feel an aversion for it?'

"I still didn't answer.

" 'I'll think about it,' he said, 'and speak to you.' "

It was a terrible situation. Not that she would obey the king if he ordered her to marry his brother—she had defied him before and would do so again: *nothing* would induce her to marry anyone but Lauzun. The danger was in—and for—Lauzun himself. How could she expect him, count and younger son of a count, to court utter ruin—loss of office, imprisonment, perhaps worse—for seeming to compete with a prince of the blood for the hand of a *fille de France?* It would amount to *lèse-majesté*—disloyalty to the very king whose person he guarded. That Monsieur would now want to marry her was a tragic probability. For all his worthlessness she retained an affection for him—she had never been able to forget the love he had shown her at a time when she'd needed it: "I've been for you all along, cousin; I've been taking your side against everybody." But lately, even with Madame alive, he had been displaying a certain new interest that disquieted her: he had become in her mind the chief of her would-be heirs, those hopeful ghouls whose depressing effect on her spirits she had mentioned to Lauzun as her chief reason for wanting to marry. As Monsieur, as duc d'Orléans, as the king's brother, as her first cousin, who— he had been hinting—was more qualified than he to be the heir of his first cousin, daughter of Monsieur, daughter of the duc d'Orléans, daughter of a king's brother? And with Madame gone . . . why should Monsieur wish to wait to inherit?

The next few days saw her worst fears well on their way to fulfillment. With Madame still unburied, the entire court was gossiping about her probable marriage to Monsieur. And Lauzun spoke to her precisely in the way she had dreaded. "He told me that he was 'delighted' to hear that I was going to marry Monsieur. I replied that I had no expectation of doing so. 'You'll have to,' he said, 'since the king wills it. At least, I'll still be able to refer to myself as a friend of Madame. The late Madame did me the honor of being kind to me; I hope you may do the same!' "

"The match you mention will never take place," Mademoiselle insisted.

"I tell you it will. And I add that I shall be very pleased. It means that I'll no longer be your confidant, but I place your grandeur above my private interest. I know of no better way of acknowledging my obligation to you than by saying this: 'I scorn my own advancement when your glory is at stake.' "

His words had the utter correctness, even the nobility, of a loyal subject of the king who was at the same time her own loyal servant: how could she complain of them, yet how could they cause her anything but despair?

Later that day he spoke to her again. "The king wishes you to marry Monsieur. You must obey. You did me the honor of giving me your confidence; you must do so now more than ever. I can't give you better proof of my sincerity than to tell you a thousand times that you must do as the king desires. It's not up to you to reason: you must follow your duty blindly. Think only of that, and you'll find yourself well off. Think of who and what Monsieur is! Only the king and the Dauphin are above him. Above you will be only the queen. The king will esteem you. Every day he'll give you new marks of his favor. The whole court will come to you: you'll have music, balls, ballets, plays———"

Mademoiselle cut him short. "You forget that I'm more than fifteen. You speak to me as though I were a child. I have the honor to be the king's first cousin—I want no grandeur or elevation beyond that. I have my own plan; I know what I have to do to be happy. Do you think I've forgotten the past? Do you think I don't remember everything I've told you?"

Lauzun was firm. He was so mindful of his duty, he said, that he had forgotten everything she had ever told him. Now he was entirely engrossed in the pleasure of thinking of her as Madame. "I used to spend my time thinking of the stories you told me about your plans concerning someone. The only person I pity in everything that's happened is that 'someone.' Since you've never told me his name, I don't even know whose misfortune it is that I lament. And so I prefer to think of nothing but your establishment."

"He said all that so freely and naturally," says Mademoiselle, "that I should have been beside myself with grief if I hadn't realized what he was doing. He was doing something that under the circumstances was very wise: he was trying his best to conceal his true feelings."

After Madame's funeral Lauzun twisted the knife—still in the cause of discretion and advantage. The time had come, he said, for her to stop speaking to him. In the past he had already incurred Monsieur's displeasure, merely by being useful whenever he could to Madame. Now there were going to be difficulties. Monsieur was going to ask for Mademoiselle's hand; Mademoiselle was going to demur; and even under the best of conditions he, Lauzun, was almost certain to be blamed. For these reasons, he begged her to speak to him only if she wanted to make use of him in his capacity of royal bodyguard: he always stood ready to transmit messages from her to the king. Otherwise they must not communicate, even through others.

Once again Mademoiselle recognized his wisdom, his shrewdness both for himself and for her. But she implored him to put a time limit on his prohibition. "I want you to tell me this: 'If you're not married to Monsieur in six months, I'll speak to you.'"

He refused: "It's not up to you or me to put a time limit on something that's in the king's hands. I can't afford to be rash in an affair that concerns you. Therefore I have nothing to say—except that I shall continue to pity the unfortunate 'somone,' and shall never forget the honor you did me in choosing me as your confidant."

"He made me a deep bow. He had never, he said, given me greater proof of his devotion, or felt greater respect for me, than at this moment."

"You're going?" Mademoiselle cried. "Is it possible? I'll not be speaking to you again?"

And when he silently withdrew, she went to her room and wept. "Though I was crazed with grief over my situation, I thought of his. I condemned his conduct, and yet I admired it."

The summer that Mademoiselle had thought would be the season of her happiness was an interval of pause and tension, calling for patience and astuteness. When she took leave of the king before going to Forges, her usual watering place, he gave her the news she expected: "My brother has been speaking to me like a man eager to marry you. It wouldn't be decent to marry so soon after the death of Madame, but he'd like the contract drawn up and signed before you take the waters. Then you can be married this winter."

Mademoiselle replied with a clever reference to the chevalier de Lorraine, the favorite of Monsieur's whom she knew the king hated most. Monsieur would never marry without the chevalier's approval, she said, and since there would be a delay because the chevalier was at present in exile in Italy at the king's order—she well knew the rumor that it was he who had sent the poison that had killed Madame—mightn't any decision be postponed until after she returned from Forges?

The king consented easily.

When she returned from the waters she said nothing to Monsieur, who seemed a little embarrassed in her presence; and with the king she used the weapon of ridicule.

"My brother has been speaking to me again about the matter," the king said to her in Paris, "and he wishes, in case you and he

have no children, that you leave all your property to his daughter
by Madame. He indicated that he'd just as soon have no more
children if he could be sure that his daughter would marry my
son and become queen of France. I told him I couldn't promise it,
that he'd better hope for children."

"I began to laugh," Mademoiselle says, "and told the king that
I thought this was the first time a bridegroom had ever said that
he hoped for no children." "Furthermore," she said, "it seems
ridiculous for Monsieur to insist that *his* daughter have *my* money
for the purpose of marrying *your* son: the Dauphin of France
doesn't give me the impression of being a boy who'll be dependent on a girl for his financial well-being."

The king laughed too: Mademoiselle was happy to see the affair take a mocking turn. Indeed, the king began voluntarily to
talk to her *against* Monsieur as a husband: "If you marry my
brother, you must never hope he'll have the governorship of a
province, for I'll never give him one. I tell you this so that you
won't be disappointed, and so that you won't advise him to ask me
for any favors for his friends. As for money, I'd give him some
only if you asked for it, so that he'd have you to be grateful to."

This was more than Mademoiselle had hoped for: with Louis
XIV it was always advantageous, almost essential, to be able to
say that you were following *his* ideas. "I replied to the king that
what he had just done me the honor of telling me had given me
a great distaste for the marriage, and that it wouldn't be long before I asked him to bring all talk of it to an end."

"By the way," the king said, "I forgot to ask you: is it true
that the day following Madame's death you were planning to
come to me with another marriage proposition?"

Mademoiselle was taken aback. "If someone told you that," she
said evasively, "it must be true." The king didn't press her, and
she went on: "I think that if I chose a good man, one who would
be useful to you, you'd have the goodness to approve my choice,
and that you'd never force me into a marriage repugnant to me."

"Certainly," said the king. "I'd let you do what you wanted, and would never want you to do anything that would upset you."

"Then I humbly beg Your Majesty"—Mademoiselle dared use the broadest irony—"arrange my marriage with Monsieur at once. If you don't do it soon I'll have reason to complain that you think little of me."

"We've talked enough," the king said, smiling. "Let's go to dinner."

A few days later he told her that Monsieur had been after him again to draw up the contract. "But I suggested to him that we wait until we get back from Chambord. Do you approve of that?"

Only now did she finally dare be sincere. "The longer we wait," she said, "the more pleased I'll be."

During the hunting at Chambord she saw Lauzun every day. She was surprised that no one commented on their lack of conversation, but apparently they had hidden their intimacy better than she could have believed. One evening she couldn't resist asking him to tie one of her ribbons, but he begged to be excused, saying he was too clumsy: most of the time he didn't even look at her. She made a point of being seen with Monsieur de Longueville, and tongues wagged about that. It was probably the chevalier de Beuvron, another favorite of Monsieur's, who unwittingly won her her final victory. "It's to the advantage of the chevalier de Lorraine and me to approve your marriage to Monsieur," he airily told her one day. "Because if we do, I'm sure you'll show us your gratitude, since you know we could prevent it if we wanted to."

Mademoiselle didn't fail to report his words to the king, and amid the royal scorn and indignation that they caused, she made her humble prayer: "I beg you: allow me to say that I honor Monsieur extremely, that I have all conceivable gratitude for the honor Your Majesty has done me in wishing to marry me to him. But for a thousand different reasons I should be unhappy. I beg you with all my heart: let this marriage be spoken of no more."

"What you ask," the king said, "is that I tell my brother you wish never to marry?"

"No, Sire; merely that I wish not to marry *him*. We'll always get along well as first cousins, but never as husband and wife."

"I will tell him," the king said, "what you wish."

"The next day he summoned me to the queen's apartments to tell me that he had spoken to Monsieur. The announcement had greatly surprised him, especially what I had said about my resolve never to marry applying only to him, indicating that I might have someone else in mind. Monsieur had said that there were people at court who were my friends but not his, and that it was they who had spoiled the match. 'I wasn't so inquisitive as to ask him who they were,' the king said, 'because I don't like to cause anyone trouble. I think he'll be sulky with you, but I advise you to pay no attention.'"

"I can't imagine who it is that Monsieur suspects," Mademoiselle said, with an innocent air. "I know that since the death of Madame the only people I've had private conversations with have been Rochefort and the archbishop of Rheims."

It was over.

It had taken her three months, not the six she had begged Lauzun to set as a time limit. She had worked hard. She had allowed the king to express his own contempt of his brother, his own low appraisal of him as a husband; she had freed herself with the king's blessing; she had given the king warning that she might be thinking of someone else.

Now the way was clear again.

6

L AUZUN, so close to the king, must have heard the interesting
news at once, but he scrupulously avoided being the first to
mention it, or even seeming to be eager to: it was three days
before Mademoiselle managed to corner him. "It's all over between me and Monsieur," she whispered hastily as they came together for an instant in a doorway at Saint-Germain. "Don't you
think we should have a talk? I'm sure I have much to tell you."

His discreet reply—"I'm completely at your disposal"—told
her that his caution would continue to the end. And once again
she recognized its appropriateness: if there was no longer a question of his competing with a prince of the blood, he could still be
accused of seeking to take his place.

They met the next day in the queen's apartments at the hour
Mademoiselle set. She was entirely resolved, she said, to carry
out her original project. She was sure it was the right thing for
her to do: it was in conformity with God's will.

Once again he warned her to go slowly, and—here was a new
twist—he begged her above all not to reveal to the "someone"—
whose name he still didn't know—that it was Lauzun who was delaying his happiness by giving her such advice. "You might make
'someone' my enemy, whereas I hope someday he'll be my friend:
someday he may realize that my advice was good."

But Mademoiselle, "naturally impatient," found that she could
not endure further delay. The next time they met, she pushed him
in his own new lead. "I am absolutely determined to carry out my

[233]

plan," she told him. "And I have made up my mind to tell you the name of my choice."

"You make me tremble," said Lauzun. "If I don't approve your taste, you'll shun my company. My very eagerness to preserve your friendship forbids me to listen to a confidence that might make me lose it. I beg you: speak no more about the whole thing."

"The more he insisted on not hearing his own name," says Mademoiselle, "the more I craved to utter it. But I confess that I was embarrassed to say, point-blank, 'It's you.' "

"I am absolutely going to tell you the man's name," she said one Thursday night.

He seemed in a panic. "Have the goodness to wait till tomorrow!"

"I said that I wouldn't, because Fridays were always unlucky for me. 'If I had a desk and some paper here,' I said, 'I'd write the name for you: I confess it's beyond my strength to say it. I'd like to breathe on a mirror and write the name in large letters on the clouded glass, so that you could read it.'"

As they continued to banter, midnight struck. "It's Friday," said Mademoiselle. "I won't say another word."

"The next day I wrote on a slip of paper the words *It's you.* I sealed it and put it in my pocket. I met him at the queen's: 'I have the name in question in my pocket,' I said. 'But I won't give it to you on a Friday.'"

"Let me have it," Lauzun coaxed. "I'll put it under my pillow and won't read it before tomorrow. You may be sure I'll keep myself awake, and read it as soon as the clock strikes midnight."

"You might make a mistake in the time," said Mademoiselle. "I'll not give it to you until tomorrow night."

But she didn't see him until Sunday. "I was alone with him beside a fireplace. I took out the paper and showed it to him several times, each time putting it back in my pocket or in my muff. He kept urging me to give it to him, saying that his heart was pounding: he had a premonition, he said, that he was on the point of doing 'someone' a bad turn by disapproving my choice and my intention."

The game went on for some time. "Each of us," said Mademoiselle, "was as embarrassed as the other." Finally she said, "Here is the paper. I give it to you on condition that you write your answer on the same sheet: there's plenty of room—my message is brief. Give it back to me tonight at the queen's."

He took it away with him.

"That night, at the queen's, I saw Monsieur de Lauzun come in. He came up to me silent, his eyes averted: the sight of his embarrassment increased mine. I knelt in front of the fire; he was just beside me. 'I'm paralyzed with cold,' I said."

"I'm even more paralyzed by your note," Lauzun replied quickly. "Don't think I'm so stupid as to fall for such a trick as that. You're having fun at my expense: you wrote what you did in order to avoid giving me the real name. But I'll never insist on your giving me a confidence you'd rather withhold."

Brutal though that sounded, Mademoiselle accepted it for what it was: the extreme of caution. She didn't flinch. "The two words I wrote speak nothing but the truth," she said. "And I shall not swerve from my purpose."

"He made no answer," says Mademoiselle, "either because he had no time or because he was overcome."

The words he had written at the bottom of her note were as prudent as those he had spoken before the fire. But guarded though they were, they thrilled her. "He told me on the one hand that he was counting on nothing, and on the other that he would always be obedient to my commands. It was his way of saying that he would do what I wanted."

A few days before, she had written three names on a card and handed it to Lauzun's sister, Madame de Nogent:

> *Monsieur*
> *Monsieur de Longueville*
> *Monsieur de Lauzun*

"Guess which of these three men I want to marry," she said. Madame de Nogent flung herself at her feet: it was, she whispered, the only reply she could possibly make.

For two days following the exchange of messages, they didn't meet. Then: "Who'll begin?" Mademoiselle asked him when they found themselves walking in the queen's drawing room.

"You," said Lauzun, "unless you order me to."

And Mademoiselle formally declared her love. As in the plays by Corneille which she had ordered from Paris, emotion was no less pulsating for being clad in reason.

"I've explained to you why I want to marry," she said. "I'm convinced that of all the reasons I've given you, the best is the esteem I have for you; and I've often ventured the opinion, when talking about other things, that if esteem continues long enough, love is born of it. You are free to think what you wish: for my part I choose to believe that your feelings match mine. And so I have good reason to think that we'll be happy together."

"Against my better judgment," answered Lauzun, "I'll reply as though I believed you were speaking seriously. Is it really possible that you want to marry one of your first cousin's servants? For make no mistake: nothing in the world will induce me to leave the king. I am so attached to his person, my duties give me such pleasure, that in all candor he will always be my first concern. My second, I need scarcely say, will be my gratitude to you."

"Do you forget that my first cousin is my master as well as yours?" Mademoiselle chided. "Instead of minding your being his servant, I can imagine nothing more honorable. Indeed, if you didn't have a position at court, I'd buy you one."

"You forget that I'm not a prince, and that a prince is what you should have. I'm merely a gentleman of fair rank: you need something more."

"What you are is enough for me to make you the greatest lord of the kingdom: I have wealth and titles to bestow on you."

"I must remind you of something else. When you marry, you should know a person's character. Now, no one knows my good and bad qualities better than myself. I'm not much of a talker: you seem to have a passion for conversation, so in this I don't suit you at all. I shut myself up in my room three or four hours every day. I refuse to see anyone, even my own servants: I'd beat them, I think, if they came in when I wanted to be alone. The rest of the day is taken up with my duties for the king, and I expect to be so busy at this in the future that I don't see what time I'd find to spend with a wife, supposing I were to marry. Would you like a husband who wouldn't share your amusements, who'd do nothing to keep you entertained? The only thing I can offer you is the promise that I'll never give you cause to be jealous, because I hate women as much as I used to love them." If those words were equivocal, they were followed by a clear contrast between himself and Monsieur: "Nor will I ever ask for a higher position than the one I have now: I'll never want to be governor of a province, for example. For I never want to be separated from the king's person." And then: "All these strangenesses of mine may put you off. Besides, for all I know I may have some personal defects that you'll find objectionable."

"For a man who's not much of a talker, you've said a good deal today," Mademoiselle laughed. "But I'll tell you briefly that I find your manners very pleasant, and as regards your person, my only complaint is that too many ladies have taken too much pleasure in it. Now tell *me* something: isn't there anything about me that you dislike? Do my looks offend you? I believe I have only one flaw—my teeth aren't good. That flaw runs in my family. But I imagine my inherited family failings displease you less than they might another: you love the head of my family, and, as you see, a certain lesser member isn't indifferent toward you."

But his reiterated refusals to believe that she was speaking in earnest, the new barriers he erected each time she broke one down, finally changed her pleasantries to a cry of anguish: "Your incredulity will be my despair!"

"I think we would have stayed there the rest of our lives," said Mademoiselle, "I saying 'yes' he saying 'no,' if I hadn't grown so numb with cold that I had to find a warmer place. My maids of honor, who had all that time been near a window, were almost frozen to death: I can imagine that they weren't too pleased with either of us for keeping them there. As he left, he saluted them: 'Aren't you warm, ladies?' he said. 'As for me, I feel on fire in this drawing room!' " Mademoiselle says that she imagined the joke was lost on the maids of honor; but it meant something to her.

And that evening he came up to her after the queen had had her supper. "Do you know," he said, "there are times when I try to persuade myself that everything you tell me is *not* an illusion?"

During the next few days they had several conversations, hypothetical and tentative, about their future. When Mademoiselle told him of her plans to beautify her château at Eu, he lamented the fact that it wasn't closer to Gisors, where one of his brigades was stationed. "I'm sure that a fine house and estate must afford much pleasure, but I can take mine only where I can be useful to the king." He admitted that he occasionally indulged in daydreams. "If this project were to be carried out soon," he said one day, "I could afford to refit my company for the review scheduled for next March. Sometimes I dream of buying Spanish horses for one brigade, barbs for another, Croatians for the third, and good racers for the fourth—they'd cost a hundred pistoles per mount. Think of how the guards would look in their buff jerkins, with gold and silver braid!" He even sent his sister to Mademoiselle to obtain her advance consent that after their marriage he retain his room in the Louvre, because of its proximity to the king. She agreed at once, but asked him, when they next met, why he hadn't put the question himself. "Because I didn't dare," he said. "To anyone but you my request would have sounded suspicious. I know you want me to remain near the king. You know that I always see him to bed, and never leave him before two in the morning, and have to be up again at eight to be there when he wakes. If I had to come home to the Luxembourg every night, I'd never get to the Tuileries in time in the morning. Therefore I'll always sleep at the Louvre. I'll come to see you when I'm off duty, as often as I can."

"You know I go to the Tuileries every day," said Mademoiselle. "Whenever the queen's busy at her prayers, I'll come to see you in your room."

"Would that be proper?" asked Lauzun. "Wouldn't people talk?"

Mademoiselle said they wouldn't. "He was always so worried lest he make a misstep," she says, "that I was always having to decide things for him."

And indeed, though he certainly seemed to expect to marry— whatever his peculiar vision of marriage was—he was so resolved to avoid any appearance of pushing himself forward that Mademoiselle had to force him to agree to the crucial step: her formal petition to the king. "He kept putting me off from day to day, refusing to give his consent. Finally, after I had pressed him very hard and scolded him for insisting on delays that he must know were painful to me, I wrote my letter. I was in such a hurry, fearing that he might change his mind, that I didn't take the time to make a copy: I think I didn't even read it over."

Lauzun approved it—it stated her case eloquently, invoking Lauzun's great merit and their joint attachment to the king—and she sent it off. In it she pointed out the difference between her case and that of one of her half sisters, whose recent marriage to a man beneath her—a minor Guise, of the house of Lorraine—she herself had urged the king to prohibit: Lauzun was infinitely superior to Guise as a man, she said, and moreover was a member of the French, not foreign, nobility. "The king returned a very kind reply. He said that he was somewhat surprised; that I mustn't do anything lightly; that I should think carefully. He didn't want to thwart me in any way, he said; he loved me; he would give me tokens of his affection whenever occasion presented itself."

In the midst of a great reception that Mademoiselle gave for a group of envoys from Holland, Lauzun came to the Luxembourg; and there, when the guests had left, she showed him the royal response. She was very displeased, she said, that it wasn't an outright approval. "How could you expect him to be any kinder?" demanded Lauzun. "You want something that's unsuitable; he realizes this, gives you his opinion, begs you to think it over, and at the end assures you of his affection."

But Mademoiselle was uneasy. She had asked the king to keep her request secret, even not to refer to it explicitly in his reply. Both she and Lauzun were careful to confide in no one except Madame de Nogent, who served as their post office the days they couldn't meet. They knew there were plenty of people who would oppose the match. A premature disclosure could spoil everything. "I avoided speaking to my servants," says Mademoiselle, "because I distrusted them. To escape importunates, I went to bed early."

"If any of my servants speak of you with less respect than they owe you, after our engagement is made public," she told Lauzun, "I'll dismiss them all and hire a new staff."

Lauzun said that wouldn't be fair. "You must forgive them their first impulse," he said, "because they'll have good reason to disapprove. After that, those who serve you well will become my friends because I'll intercede for them with you; the rest you can dismiss at the end of their term."

7

B UT SOMEBODY TALKED.

"One day, on leaving church, Lauzun said to my equerry: 'I must speak to Mademoiselle.' He took my hand and whispered that Guilloire, my steward, had discovered our plans and reported them to Monsieur de Louvois. 'I'll tell you more,' he said, 'when I can speak to you alone.'" And that evening she learned from him what her unfaithful servant had said to the powerful minister of war. "He told him that he wasn't sure whether the king knew of my plan to marry Monsieur de Lauzun, and that he thought something had to be done about it." Mademoiselle was for punishing Guilloire with instant dismissal, but Lauzun told her that that was precisely what she should *not* do. "But you must speak to the king at once," he said.

"What shall I say to him?" asked Mademoiselle. "Advise me."

"I advise you to say: 'Sire, the shortest follies do the least harm. I have come to thank Your Majesty for your thoughtful advice, and to tell you that you have made me change my mind. I have abandoned my plans.'"

"What!" cried Mademoiselle. "Is that what you want me to say to the king?"

Lauzun was never more self-effacing than in response to that challenge. "I want nothing," he answered her. "If you have to speak to him, follow your own heart, not my counsel. Above all, you must speak for yourself, not for me."

That night the king was at his gaming table until two in the morning. Mademoiselle saw the queen to bed, and waited in her bedchamber. "You must have important things to say to the king, to sit up so late," the queen said.

"I have indeed," said Mademoiselle. "Something crucial to me is going to be discussed in council tomorrow."

"What!" said the king, when he finally came in. "You still here, cousin? Don't you know it's two o'clock?"

He was a little dizzy, perhaps from wine and lack of sleep, and Mademoiselle's heart was "pounding so violently" that all she could say for a moment or two was "Sire, Sire." Then, with a rush: "I've come to tell Your Majesty that I am still resolved to do what I told you of in my letter." And she begged the king to give her his approval, despite Lauzun's lower rank. She pointed out that she had come to esteem him only after the king himself had distinguished him: for her to elevate him still further would be but a continuation of the king's own work. "After I have Your Majesty's approval," she concluded, "and when the world remembers my past life and considers my reasons for wanting a calmer one in the future, I don't think my action will be held amiss. I can be criticized only for not being ambitious; but I have found the ambition I want: to contribute to the elevation of a man as extraordinary as Monsieur de Lauzun."

"I must admit that I was taken aback by your letter," the king said, "especially considering how violently you disapproved of your sister's marriage to Monsieur de Guise. Don't misunderstand me: even as he is, Monsieur de Lauzun is the equal of any foreign prince, and you would raise him much higher; I have no objection to him on the ground of rank." But he still refused to commit himself. "I don't want to give you any advice: people would think that the match was my idea. You are old enough to know what is good for you. I merely ask you to think seriously before deciding. And I have one more caution: keep your plans secret until your mind is made up. Many persons sense that something is going on;

my ministers have mentioned it to me. Monsieur de Lauzun has enemies: act accordingly."

"Sire," said Mademoiselle, "if Your Majesty is for us, no one can do us harm." She tried to kiss his hands, but he raised her up and embraced her: no one, not even the queen in her bed across the room, had overheard them.

People were indeed gossiping. Two days later Louise de La Vallière spoke to Madame de Nogent at Versailles: "Let me congratulate you on the news about your brother." Madame de Nogent pretended not to know what she meant. People hinted to Mademoiselle that there would soon be a sensational event at court. And when Mademoiselle played ignorant, she was told more explicitly that the event would be an astonishing marriage. Madame d'Epernon told Mademoiselle she had heard a rumor that Mademoiselle was going to marry Monsieur de Longueville. "What! Mademoiselle marry, at her age?" Madame d'Epernon had retorted to the gossip-monger. "And to Monsieur de Longueville, of all people? I don't believe it."

"Madame, people marry at all ages," said Mademoiselle. "If I were to marry Monsieur de Longueville, there'd be nothing extraordinary about it." And Madame de Thianges teasingly asked Mademoiselle if she didn't think Monsieur de Lauzun and Mademoiselle de Retz would make a splendid couple.

So much talk about marriage was troubling: Mademoiselle and Lauzun held a council of war. There was no time to lose. "We decided that the duc de Créqui, the duc de Montausier, the maréchal d'Albret and the marquis de Guitry should call on the king the next day, and ask him in my name to be good enough to let me carry out my plan." Mademoiselle had had a different idea. "Why shouldn't the two of us go to the king ourselves?" she had asked Lauzun. But he persuaded her that a delegation would be more respectful and efficient. She had approached the king directly by letter and again in person: in neither case had she won her point.

The gentlemen could speak more freely; and to a delegation representing Mademoiselle's clear wishes the king could scarcely reply, as he had twice replied to Mademoiselle herself, that she should "think things over."

Once again Lauzun proved a clever strategist. The duc de Montausier came to Mademoiselle and reported success. "I see that Mademoiselle has made up her mind," the king had said to the four gentlemen after listening to their plea. "When she spoke to me about this matter herself, I advised her as a father might have. Now I have no choice but to consent." And, the duke said, the king had stuck to his decision even in the face of the violent opposition of Monsieur, who was present at the interview and went so far as to accuse the king of having instigated this monstrous *mésalliance.* "So," the duke told her, "your business is settled. But I advise you to delay as little as possible. In your place I'd get married this very night."

Mademoiselle heartily agreed, and asked him to give his news and his advice to Lauzun if he should see him before she did.

The king had given his consent; Monsieur had been apprised: now it was time to inform the queen. That evening Mademoiselle flung herself on her knees before her in her bedroom. "I think Your Majesty will be surprised to hear that I have made up my mind to marry."

"Indeed I am!" The queen repeated those words "two or three times in an acid tone." And then she demanded, "What's come over you? Aren't you happy as you are?"

"I'm not the first person to marry at my age, Madame. Your Majesty approves of marriage for others: why should I be the only one to stay single?"

"Whom are you marrying?"

"Monsieur de Lauzun. He is not a prince, but apart from the princes of the blood, the kingdom has no grander *seigneur.*"

"I disapprove strongly, cousin." The royal voice was icy. "The king will never consent."

"Pardon me, Madame: the king has no wish to coerce me—he has given his word."

The retort to that was savage. "You'd do far better not to marry, cousin, and to keep your money for my son the duc d'Anjou."

So the name of another would-be heir was out in the open! The duc d'Anjou was the Dauphin's younger brother. "Ah, Madame! How can Your Majesty speak so?" cried Mademoiselle reproachfully. "I am ashamed for you: respect forbids me to say more."

The queen, daughter of a Spanish Hapsburg and of Mademoiselle's own Bourbon aunt, had been asked by a member of the French court at the time of her wedding, "Surely men of your own country have sought Your Majesty's hand?"

"How could they?" she had answered. "The only king in Spain is my father." Foreign nobles visiting Spain were treated exactly like commoners unless on diplomatic mission: how could the Spanish queen of France find Lauzun palatable as a first cousin by marriage? She rose, and the conversation was over.

Mademoiselle hastened to tell Lauzun about it, and to remind him of Montausier's advice. But Lauzun refused to be hurried. It was imperative, he said, that the king not be given the impression of a bridegroom intoxicated by good fortune, of a bride showing childish impatience. He would play cards with the king that night as usual; and he would find an opportunity to thank him for the favor he had done them. The king himself must be allowed to set the date of their marriage.

Probably it was a continuation of his policy of modest caution that kept Lauzun from following the duc de Montausier's advice to marry Mademoiselle that very night. Some have suspected that the reason may have lain in the exactly opposite quarter—in the fiancé's ambitious pride; that he considered a hasty, quiet marriage as lessening the greatness of his glory; that he was willing to wed his royal princess only with all the éclat to which she was entitled. But his strategy of not pushing had so far proven effective—it had been crowned with the success of the king's consent—and apparently he saw no reason to change it. Or perhaps he expected Mademoiselle to force his hand, as she had done earlier, especially in the matter of her letter to the king. But for Mademoiselle, the king's consent spelled the end of her active role. She now had an officially approved fiancé, and she allowed him to take the reins. In effect, she, as well as he, was waiting for the king to act. The king could not possibly retract his word. The day he gave his permission, Monday, December 15, 1670, and the two days that followed, were the happiest days of Mademoiselle's life.

All Paris was buzzing with the news.

That very night Mademoiselle's friend Madame de Sévigné, always one of the first to know the gossip at court, wrote her cousin Coulanges in Lyons a letter that has become famous.

"Now I'm going to tell you a piece of news that's most amazing, most surprising, most marvelous, most miraculous, most triumphant, most dazzling, most unheard-of, most singular, most extraordinary, most incredible, most unexpected, the biggest and the littlest, the rarest and the commonest, the most public and until today the most secret, the most brilliant, the most envy-arousing, a thing we can scarcely believe in Paris, so how could you believe it in Lyons? A thing that makes everybody cry 'Mercy!', a thing that will take place on Sunday, when those who witness it won't believe their eyes, a thing that will take place on Sunday and will perhaps still be waiting to take place on Monday. I can't bring myself to tell it. Three guesses: do you give up? Well, then, I must tell it. Next Sunday, in the Louvre, Monsieur de Lauzun will marry—whom do you think? I'll give you four guesses, I'll give you ten, a hundred. I can hear Madame de Coulanges say: 'What's hard about that? It's Madame de La Vallière.' Not at all, Madame. 'Then it's Mademoiselle de Retz?' Not at all: you *do* live in the woods! 'Ah, how stupid of us!' you must be saying. 'It's Mademoiselle Colbert.' You're even further from the truth. 'Then

it's surely Mademoiselle de Créqui.' You're still wrong. So I have
no choice but to tell you: next Sunday, in the Louvre, he is to
marry, with the king's permission, Mademoiselle, Mademoiselle
de . . . Mademoiselle—guess the name! He is to marry Mademoiselle—yes, I mean Mademoiselle, the Grand Mademoiselle, daughter of the late Monsieur, Mademoiselle granddaughter of Henry
IV, Mademoiselle d'Eu, Mademoiselle de Dombes, Mademoiselle
de Montpensier, Mademoiselle d'Orléans, Mademoiselle the king's
first cousin, Mademoiselle destined for the throne of France,
Mademoiselle the only match worthy of Monsieur. What a subject
to talk about! If you scream, if you're beside yourself, if you say
that I'm lying, that it's false, that I'm making fun of you, that it's
a joke, that's it's a silly fancy, in short if you hurl insults at me,
I'll think you're right: I did the same when I heard it."

The next day some threatening notes crept into the happy excitement. Amid the compliments and congratulations—the archbishop of Rheims asked for the honor of officiating at the marriage—were some alarming reports. Mademoiselle learned that
the queen had spoken against her and Lauzun to the king, and
that, being rebuffed, she had "wept all night." Monsieur had taken
the duc de Montausier to task for approving Mademoiselle's elevation of a gentleman, and had expressed the opinion that Mademoiselle should be locked up in an insane asylum; the king, hearing of this, was greatly displeased with his brother. The duc de
La Feuillade "thanked the king on behalf of all the nobility of the
kingdom." That was scarcely discreet: nothing was further from
Louis XIV's mind than a wish to honor his nobles *en masse.* The
duc de Montausier warned Lauzun of a mischievous move of Monsieur's: he had told the king that Mademoiselle was saying to
everyone that she was marrying Lauzun only to please the king—
that the marriage was the king's idea. The king was upset, said
Montausier; and Mademoiselle thought it prudent to give her
sovereign the courtesy of her own official denial. She had herself

summoned by him before the council, and in a passionate tirade branded the story a lie: far from ordering her to marry Monsieur de Lauzun, the king had urged her to reflect, she told the assembled gentlemen, and he had finally acceded only to her reiterated requests. The council complimented her on her lucidity and eloquence, and the king spoke to her affectionately. Nevertheless, the queen's entire household was up in arms to thwart the match, and Mademoiselle's stepmother wrote the king to protest. The hostility Mademoiselle resented the most came from Condé. With him, she discovered, the blood of the Bourbons took precedence over old friendship; this time his pride flashed out even against her who had saved him and his army at the Porte Saint-Antoine, and he added his voice to the chorus of opposition.

But Mademoiselle put the cabals out of her mind: what did they all amount to, as against the king's word? The incredible had happened: Lauzun was talking confidently, even affectionately, of their future together. "When I think that I'm to be master of the Luxembourg," he mused, in one of their rare moments alone, "I need all my self-control to keep my head from turning. But you know you'll always continue to be mistress there."

"Most of the time I won't want anyone with me there except you," said Mademoiselle.

"If you don't tell me that again, I won't believe it." He smiled. "So tell me: you won't be bored with me?"

He warned her that in the war with Holland that was undoubtedly coming, he would have to display extraordinary bravery, take extraordinary risks, to justify her choice of him in the eyes of the world. If he were to be killed, people would say, "Mademoiselle was right to think so highly of him." Such talk made Mademoiselle weep, and he took such pleasure in her tender tears that he often returned to the same subject.

"I know," he said, one day, "that whenever you're angry, you won't fail to remind me of the difference between our ranks, and that will always be unanswerable."

"Not at all," she said. "If I ever bring that up, I give you permission to reply: 'If I were king or emperor, I'd not have married you, because you're forty-three years old.' That way we'll be quits."

They took pleasure even in the prospect of their future quarrels. "When someone comes to you with a bad story about me, you won't tell me who it was," said Lauzun. "You'll stick to your resolution for a couple of days, sulking all the while, and then after worrying me to death, you'll reveal the person's name. We'll make up easily, and then we'll be perfectly peaceful together until the next slander." And he proceeded to depict himself as bad-tempered, choleric, and violent.

"I'm just like you," said Mademoiselle happily. "So I imagine we'll quarrel and make up very often."

"When are you planning to marry?" Rochefort asked them, coming upon them together. Like happy children, they said they didn't know. "If you take my advice, you won't delay," he said. "You'll do it today rather than tomorrow. You're happy because you've got what you wanted: for that very reason you should observe all precautions. If you could both see yourselves in a mirror, you'd see the very picture of happiness."

"I'd hate to see that I looked happier than Monsieur de Lauzun," said Mademoiselle.

Rochefort laughed. "I see you're being pampered as well as elevated," he said to Lauzun.

"Mademoiselle's making fun of us," said Lauzun. "I assure you my luck hasn't gone to my head yet. When she talks to me like that, I just make her a bow in return."

The morning of Wednesday the seventeenth, Mademoiselle was told on waking that Montausier and Lauzun were waiting to speak with her. She hurriedly arranged her hair and had them sent in.

The duke was agitated and severe. "I've come to scold you," he said sternly. "I've been scolding Monsieur de Lauzun already, but he puts the blame on you. Why are you still unmarried? Do you intend to have a great ceremony, as though it were a wedding of two crowned heads?"

Mademoiselle protested that in failing to follow the duke's advice to marry immediately she had given in to Lauzun. "He's cleverer than I am," she said. "As for me, once we had the king's consent, I'd like to have got married very quietly. Then we could have simply announced that we were Monsieur and Madame de Montpensier."

"You're right," said the duke. "That's what I want you to do." And seeing Lauzun engrossed in the pictures hanging on the walls of Mademoiselle's bedroom, where he had never been before, he burst out angrily, "Are you planning to set up an art gallery, or to get married? Let's talk about the best way not to lose any more time."

They thereupon discussed plans. Mademoiselle thought it would be well for them to go quietly to Saint-Fargeau or Eu for the ceremony, but Lauzun said that both places were too far away. He suggested a country house belonging to his friend Monsieur de Richelieu, close enough to Paris so that he could return the next day to his duties.

"But I don't know Monsieur de Richelieu," Mademoiselle objected.

"It's enough that he's one of my friends," retorted Lauzun.

"Don't start quarreling," begged the duke.

"The trouble is," said the irrepressible Lauzun, "we're both old. Mademoiselle is opinionated, and I'm not docile either. Neither of us is willing to change his character. At least it's a good thing for us to know each other's faults so that later we can't accuse each other of deception."

When the duke left, Lauzun apologized for having spoken so sharply. It was ridiculous of him even to mention it, said Mademoiselle; they had far more important affairs to attend to. He asked her to instruct her servants to admit no general company that evening: it was important that they not be disturbed.

It was important indeed: that evening Mademoiselle's lawyers came to the Luxembourg and drew up various documents relating to the disposal of portions of her property. By one of them she transferred to her future husband the duchy of Montpensier and the principality of Dombes, two magnificent morsels that insured his appearing with ducal rank in the marriage contract and in the banns. Leaving the lawyers to their verbiage, the couple joined a few intimates who had been waiting in an adjoining room. "I present to you the duc de Montpensier," she told them. "From now on I beg you never to call him by any other name."

Lauzun left the Luxembourg at eight that evening. They were to marry the next day; not in Monsieur de Richelieu's house after all—his wife, it turned out, preferred not to offend the queen— but at Charenton, in the home of the maréchal de Créqui. Even so, the new duke refused to stay for supper. He declined on grounds of delicacy. "If our plans were to fall through," he said, "I would never forgive myself for having done something that might discredit you."

8

THURSDAY MORNING Mademoiselle rose gaily and early, but at ten o'clock Madame de Nogent arrived with dampening news: the work on the contract had not been completed, and there was no choice but to postpone the marriage until the next day. "I said," Mademoiselle tells us, "that in that case the ceremony would have to take place after midnight, as I refused to marry on a Friday. This delay distressed me: it seemed a bad omen."

That afternoon the engaged couple had another tête-à-tête. "Please promise me," said Lauzun, "that if you feel the slightest repugnance to going through with our marriage, you'll break it off, even though we be standing in front of the priest."

"And I beg you," Mademoiselle answered, "to stop saying that kind of thing unless you yourself prefer to break it off because of lack of affection."

"I am all that I should be," he said cryptically, "and I'll tell you nothing that I shouldn't."

"What! Do you mean you don't love me?"

"That's the very thing I won't tell you until we leave the church; I'd rather die than reveal my feelings for you before the time comes."

They made their final arrangements. Mademoiselle was to go to confession Friday afternoon, and be at Charenton by six; Lauzun, too, would make his confession during the day. In the meantime

Colbert was to submit the marriage contract to the heads of Mademoiselle's family—the king, the queen, and the nine-year-old Dauphin; it was thought better to by-pass Monsieur and her other relatives in view of their hostility. The queen had said she wouldn't sign it, but the king would doubtless persuade her. The archbishop of Rheims, they learned, had made some disobliging remarks about them, so despite his request, they wouldn't be married by him but by the curé of Charenton. "Since you're extraordinary in everything," said Mademoiselle, "I expect you to go directly from the church, after the ceremony, to attend the king's going-to-bed." Lauzun laughed. He wouldn't promise, he said, to do so. As he left, Mademoiselle burst into tears without knowing why; he too suddenly seemed dejected. Everyone present laughed at their behavior.

At eight o'clock that night came a messenger, summoning her to the king.

Trembling, filled with premonitions, she had herself driven to the Tuileries. In the king's dressing room she was told to wait; and as she waited, someone whom she was not allowed to see was ushered into the king's bedroom adjoining. But a moment later, when she, in turn, was ushered in, she found the king alone: the mysterious person who had preceded her, she knew, must be hidden somewhere. The king looked upset and sad. "It breaks my heart to tell you what I have to," he said. "Everyone is convinced that I'm ready to sacrifice you to benefit Monsieur de Lauzun. Such a story would do me great harm abroad. I cannot permit you to make this marriage. You have every reason to think harshly of me—"

"Ah Sire!" shrieked Mademoiselle. "What are you saying?"

"Scream at me," the king said. "Strike me, if you will. How could I blame you?"

Mademoiselle flung herself at his feet. She begged him to kill her—kill her, rather than forbid her to marry the man in whom she would find "her repose and salvation," the man who would inspire her each day with "new reasons for affection." She implored him again: "I beg you, kill me rather than forbid me to marry Monsieur de Lauzun! From now on, he would not be safe: the same enemies who oppose his elevation might well decide to take his life."

The king raised her up, but once again she flung herself down, and this time he knelt and embraced her. "For three-quarters of an hour we remained speechless in each other's arms, our cheeks touching; the king wept as I did."

"Why did you give me time to change my mind?" the king reproached Mademoiselle. "You should have done it quickly."

"Alas, Sire! You have never broken your word to anyone: how could I expect you to begin with me and Monsieur de Lauzun? I shall die! I long to die! Never before in my life have I loved anyone; now I am in love, in love sincerely and passionately with the truest gentleman in your kingdom!"

She protested her devotion to her sovereign, and Lauzun's fidelity to him. "I began to scream: 'Kill me! I forgive you my death, but not separation from all that I love in the world! Let me live with Monsieur de Lauzun! Or be responsible to God for an act of terrible cruelty!' "

At that moment Mademoiselle heard someone cough behind the door leading to the queen's apartments. "Who is it you're sacrificing me to?" she demanded of the king. "Could it be Condé? I saved his life once: does he want to deprive me of mine by separating me from a man who recognizes no master but you?"

"Ah, cousin!" the king cried. "Only obey me, and I'll grant your every wish."

"My only wish is to marry Monsieur de Lauzun. What will those foreign princes say when they learn that you have broken your word?"

The king raised his voice—it was obvious that he wanted to be heard on the other side of the door: kings, he said, very distinctly, had to follow public opinion.

"Those to whom you sacrifice me will jeer at you!"

"It is late," the king said. "You have nothing more to tell me, and I shall not change my mind."

He wept again.

(One wonders whether Louis XIV thought, during that scene with Mademoiselle, of his own early, thwarted love affair. After he had married his queen, Marie Mancini had sullenly consented to marry a prince Colonna in Rome, and the lovers she took in her lovelessness were—like the king's mistresses—the talk of Europe.)

"He embraced me and wept. 'You weep with compassion,' I said. 'My happiness is in your hands; you pity me, and yet you lack the courage not to sacrifice me to others. Ah, Sire! You are condemning me to death, and you are doing yourself the greatest harm in the world.'

"I left without seeing anyone, and hurried home to be alone with my tears."

On the way back to the Luxembourg she gave way to hysterics; in the violence of her frenzy she shattered the windows of her coach; and although visitors waiting to see her were dismissed by tactful footmen, some of them lingered long enough to see her arrive, crying and gesticulating, her hair streaming, a tragic fury.

She was not left to weep alone. Into her bedroom came Montausier, Créqui, Guitry and—Lauzun. "When I saw him, I began to scream. Nothing mattered to me, I cried. If I couldn't live with him, I wanted to die."

Montausier began to transmit a message from the king. It was the king who had sent Lauzun to her at this moment, "to thank her for the honor she had wanted to do him." And the king expressed thanks for her submission, and promised rewards to both her and Lauzun. "How can you resign yourself to seeing me in this state?" Mademoiselle demanded of Lauzun through her tears.

"And where will you find the strength to bear such a blow yourself?"

Lauzun seemed in perfect command of himself. "If you take my advice," he said evenly, "you'll dine tomorrow with the king, to thank him for breaking off a marriage that you would have repented of in four days."

"Leave us alone together," Mademoiselle begged the others; and when they had withdrawn she was comforted, for Lauzun's bravado melted and he wept with her. He couldn't utter a word. "Does this mean I'll not see you again?" cried Mademoiselle. "If so, I'll die of despair."

And when he too left her she went to bed, where she stayed "twenty-four hours without speaking, so numbed by grief as to be almost unconscious."

The next day the king visited her. "When he entered, I began to sob and cry. He embraced me, and held his cheek against mine. 'How can you embrace me?' I wept. 'You're like those monkeys who hug their young to death.'"

The king repeated his regrets. His hand had been forced, he said; he had had to disappoint her because the rumor that had begun to circulate had been too vicious to be ignored. He had nothing but sympathy for her and Lauzun, and would do "wonderful things" for him. But Mademoiselle was not to be consoled. "Everything you say and everything you promise is nothing but words," she said. "My pain is real, and very sharp."

The queen paid her a visit of "condolence," as did Monsieur, who had the tact to speak of nothing but perfumes; Mademoiselle refused to receive her triumphant stepmother and her half sister who had been allowed to marry Monsieur de Guise. The two royal mistresses came separately to express sympathy. Lauzun returned the deed of gift transferring to him the duchy and the principality. "He was so entirely devoid of greed," said Mademoiselle, "that he refused even to accept that token of my affection."

After several days she began to tell herself that the king, touched by her submissiveness, might eventually reconsider: the thought kept her from wanting to die. But the agony of grief continued. "No one ever suffered as much as I: God alone knows what such sorrow is."

It was Lauzun who insisted that she begin to show herself again at court. She had thought it more tactful to stay away from the king "because the very sight of my grief would be a reproach to him"; and indeed, the first time she returned to the Tuileries she almost fainted as she passed the scene of the terrible interview. Walking with the king in one of the galleries, she was suddenly overcome by such weeping that she had to withdraw to a window to avoid making a spectacle of herself; the king, too, seemed close to tears, and from this she took comfort. That Christmas Eve, for the first time in her life, she stayed away from Midnight Mass: "I wasn't composed enough to attend to my devotions."

Louis XIV was certainly telling Mademoiselle the truth when he said that in breaking his promise he was yielding to irresistible pressure. Mademoiselle's grand design, purely personal though it seemed to her, could not have been carried out without offending everyone who counted in this new age of rising absolutism. Monsieur and the queen were determined that their cousin's great fortune should not pass outside the royal family; and they were seconded in their opposition by Condé—it had indeed been he behind the door—and by foreign sovereigns, who resented the slight to their blood implicit in the bestowal of a royal princess on a mere gentleman. The interests of the middle class, as represented in their growing importance by such ministers as Colbert and Louvois, went toward maintaining as wide a gulf as possible between the nobility, which had left them in the lurch during the Fronde, and the royal power needed to keep the nobility in check. Lauzun's only allies were the class in decline—the nobles like himself; and their indiscreetly expressed joy at his rise undoubtedly helped alert his enemies.

Once the king was made to realize the political implications of the affair, he had no choice. If his memory of Marie Mancini increased his sympathy for Mademoiselle, it may well also have confirmed his decision that she should sacrifice personal happiness, as he had, to the higher interests of the state. And, as we shall see, the woman now closest to the king, Madame de Montespan, had once again put the weight of her influence on the side of Lauzun's enemies. Apparently she remembered her old grudge against him more vividly than even his most recent service—his help the night she gave birth to the duc du Maine.

Only by presenting the court and Paris with an accomplished fact, before the implications of their marriage had had time to crystallize in everyone's mind, could Mademoiselle and Lauzun have been successful. The king's cry, "Why did you give me time to change my mind?" has an authentic ring. The warning not to wait had been given—given not only by shrewd courtiers like Montausier and Rochefort, but also by a subtle connoisseur of the human heart. "I called on Mademoiselle at nine o'clock Thursday morning," Madame de Sévigné wrote at the end of December to her cousin Coulange, "having heard that she was going to be married in the country. That had been decided Wednesday night. Mademoiselle was writing; she told me to come in, finished her letter, and asked me to come close to her bed. She told me to whom she was writing, and why, and what wonderful presents she had given the day before, and the title she had bestowed. She said that there was no foreign prince she wanted for a husband, and that she wanted to marry. She told me word for word a conversation she had had with the king, and she seemed enraptured at the thought of making a man happy. She spoke tenderly of Lauzun's merit and gratitude. Thereupon I said, 'Heavens, Mademoiselle, I see how happy you are, but why didn't you finish the matter once and for all last Monday? Don't you know that such a great delay gives the whole kingdom time to talk, and that to prolong so extraordinary an enterprise is to tempt God and the king?'

She said that I was right, but she was so full of confidence that my words made only the slightest impression. . . . That same evening, you know what happened. The next day, a Friday, I called on her again. Again I found her in bed. When she saw me her lamentations redoubled. She called me to her, kissed me, and showered me with her tears. 'Alas!' she cried, 'Do you remember what you said yesterday? Ah, how horribly right! How right!' She wept so much that she made me weep too. I have seen her twice since. She is in great distress, and treats me like someone sympathetic with her grief. She is not mistaken: she inspires me with feelings one seldom has for persons of her rank."

If the news of the king's consent to Mademoiselle's marriage had caused a sensation, so did the news of its withdrawal. Only the stanchest friends of the couple voiced, among themselves, dismay at the king's breaking of his word; but the king himself thought it necessary to justify his conduct to the whole of Europe. The entire French diplomatic corps abroad received a royal circular giving his version of the affair. As might be expected, this document is less forthright than were his words to Mademoiselle. He had been opposed to the marriage from the beginning, he claims; his consent had been extorted only by the insistence of Mademoiselle's delegation of four, who had represented that his opposition would be an intolerable insult to the entire nobility of France. "I finally agreed to give at least my tacit consent, shrugging my shoulders in amazement at my cousin's infatuation, and saying only that she was forty-three years old and could do as she wished." His letter made no mention of the part played by Condé or the intervention of Madame de Montespan; it spoke only of the harmful rumors which attributed to him the very idea of the match, the wish to elevate Lauzun. "I sent for my cousin. I told her that I would not tolerate this marriage, but that if she chose any qualified nobleman in France, with the sole exception of the comte de Lauzun, I myself would lead her to the altar." (If the king did say that to Mademoiselle, so infatuated with Lauzun, he surely knew he risked nothing!) And he contrasted her hysterical behavior with Lauzun's ready obedience: "It is superfluous to describe the grief with which she received my words, how copiously she wept and sobbed. She flung herself on her knees. I had given her a hundred dagger blows in the heart; she longed to die. I resisted everything." As for Lauzun: "I can say that he received my decision with all the constancy, submission, and resignation I could wish for."

Madame de Sévigné, too, in still another letter to her cousin, emphasized Lauzun's manliness in the face of disappointment. "By now you know the whole romantic story of Mademoiselle and Monsieur de Lauzun. It is a true tragedy, in which all the dramatic rules are observed. We were arranging the acts and scenes the other day; we took four days instead of twenty-four hours, and it was a perfect play. Never before have so many changes been witnessed in so little time; never before has there been such universal excitement; never has news been so extraordinary. Monsieur de Lauzun played his part to perfection. He bore his misfortune with a firmness, a fortitude, and at the same time a grief mingled with profound respect, that aroused everyone's admiration. What he lost is beyond price; but the king's good graces, which he has preserved, are beyond price also."

9

IT WAS ONLY a little thing that Mademoiselle had wanted, a little personal happiness, and when it was snatched from her she could not console herself. "I was sure that you would not disapprove of a step that violated neither my honor nor my conscience," she wrote in a broken-hearted letter to her friend the former Mademoiselle d'Epernon, the Carmelite. "Only my ambition would have been wounded; but my ambition had so long possessed me, and caused me such suffering, that I had resolved to abandon it for the sake of my own peace."

Such was her despair that even in front of the king, whom it was indiscreet to remind of his broken promise by the slightest reference to the affair, the slightest show of grief, she could not always control herself. "I became so accustomed to tears that not a moment passed without my shedding them, and each time I saw Monsieur de Lauzun I could not refrain from crying."

Lauzun himself deplored her behavior. "If you continue to act this way, I'll avoid you."

But even this threat was of no avail. One evening, in the midst of a Vincennes house party which she was reluctantly attending at the king's request, "I was dancing a courante with the duc de Villeroy, when I was suddenly so overcome by weeping that I stood still in the middle of the floor. The king rose and came over to me; he held his hat in front of my face to conceal my tears. 'My cousin has the vapors,' he told everyone."

She forced herself to attend all the court ballets, but usually she sat beside the queen, her coifs lowered so that she might weep unobserved. In the Luxembourg her life was a continual lament. She received a stream of visitors who condoled with her but hastened to spread accounts of her grotesque behavior. She was acting like a bereaved wife, people said. On one occasion, lying in bed bewailing for the thousandth time her bitter loss, she struck the vacant place beside her and cried hysterically: "He would have been here, here!" Poor Mademoiselle was soon more laughed at than pitied. In a society of scoffing courtiers, accustomed to sacrifice personal feelings to any opportunism, the depth of her attachment was considered freakish. She dismissed all members of her household, including the steward Guilloire, who had displayed hostility to Lauzun. She learned with bitterness that her lawyers and businessmen had deliberately delayed the drawing-up of the marriage contract: to "protect her interests" they had helped prevent her marrying on Thursday. And when she consented at Lauzun's request to become reconciled with Condé and his family, she had the courage to show the king a letter, written to them, in which she spoke of Lauzun with affection.

She grew thin; and then her feet, her hands and her cheeks began to swell. "My doctors kept telling me that it was nothing, that my indisposition came from my grief, the blackness of my mood. I easily believed it. The state in which I had been and still was would have upset even a stronger person than I." Her swellings, which caused charitable souls to say that she was dropsical and "wouldn't live six months," didn't keep her from participating in another court progress to Flanders. As usual, the company included the queen and the royal mistresses. It also included Lauzun; and since the king not only permitted, but encouraged her to see the man he had forbidden her to marry, apparently hoping that he would infect her with his atttitude of calm resignation, she was able occasionally to lay aside distress and enjoy the passing moment. Sometimes hope and despair must have been strangely confused in her mind when she and Lauzun addressed each other as they had in the past, before her three days of deceptive triumph.

A rumor suddenly sprang up during the trip: the duchess of York was dead, and Mademoiselle was to replace her. "If you want to marry the duke of York," Lauzun said to her one evening, "I'll beg the king to send me to England tomorrow to negotiate the marriage. There is nothing I wish for more in the world than your glory, and I'll never be happy until you are. All I'm good for," he said, "is to render you what little service I can. I'd be ungrateful and despicable if I neglected such an occasion as this. What do you think?"

"What do I think?" cried Mademoiselle. "I think only about you. My only wish in the world is to find a moment to speak to the king, to tell him that after everything that has happened and after the way everyone has seen me behave, he shouldn't fear that the public and individuals will believe that by letting me marry you, he'd be sacrificing me. I am sure that my words will touch him. That is what I think about, Monsieur."

"He flung himself at my feet and stayed there some time without speaking. I was tempted to raise him up, but I conquered my desire and withdrew to a corner of the room. He stayed where he was, on his knees, and said: 'This is how I should like to spend my life, to thank you for what you have just said, but I am not fortunate enough to be able to do so. I have no hope that the king will do as you say, so I have only death to wish for.' I began to weep, and he went away."

If he offended her, she had only to see him to forgive him. "If I felt like scolding him, he disarmed me by a demeanor so extraordinary that it passed my understanding." He stood for everything breathlessly beautiful; masterpieces of nature and art made her think only of him. One day he left for Brussels without being able to bid her good-by, and during his absence she spent a day visiting, with Monsieur, the famous garden of Condé's château of Enghien, just over the present Belgian frontier. They were enchanted, and spoke of the garden "as of a miracle"; and when Lauzun, on his return, apologized for his precipitate departure, she could only say, forgetting all her resentment, "You're like the garden at Enghien: it fascinates everyone who sees it; its beauty can't be imitated or even comprehended."

Lauzun's very smallness, his trimness, seem to have awakened all her dormant motherliness, which during these months expressed themselves strongly. In an aristocratic convent at Mons she caressed two little seven-year-old canonesses, "who were very pretty and who wanted to come away with me, they took such a liking to me. I wanted to put them in my pocket, to take them with me to the French court." The day of the visit to Enghien she had the joy of a visit from a certain young officer, now stationed near by, who had been one of the first people ever to make her feel motherly: the half brother whom she had elevated—the chevalier, now comte, de Charny, whose good looks earned him many compliments from Monsieur. And when the trip was over, and she learned that Lauzun was to spend some time at Fontainebleau, she begged him to keep out of the dangerous evening damp.

In her continued infatuation, in her grief over her shattered hopes, she approved certain aspects of Lauzun's behavior which were causing comment among the courtiers and which should have given her pause. If there was any chance that the king would one day be moved to lift his ban on the marriage, much would depend on Lauzun's way of conducting himself. The first impression he made on the king was excellent, but as months passed it became more and more apparent that his resignation had been only formal, concealing a resentment that occasionally exploded to the dismay of his friends and the delight of his enemies. Mademoiselle seems to have fanned his latent rebelliousness.

In promising Mademoiselle to do "wonderful things" for Lauzun to compensate him for his disappointment, the king had obviously been sincere. On March 30, first anniversary of the birth of the duc du Maine, he granted Lauzun a sum of money, the privilege

of *les grandes entrées*—admission to his presence at all times—
and the governorship of the province of Berri, which brought an
annual income of twelve thousand écus. For all this Lauzun professed himself grateful; but Mademoiselle seized the occasion to
declare to him, in a whisper, "I shall never be satisfied with what
the king does for you until he gives you to me: till then all your
promotions will leave me unmoved." A little later, when the king
offered to make him duke and maréchal de France, he proudly declined; he had done nothing to deserve such military distinction,
he said, and preferred to wait for the honor until he had really
earned it. Mademoiselle considered this "sublime," but there was
a buzz of disapproval—and indeed, Louis XIV was not a man
who liked to have his favors refused. "This incident was used
against him," says Mademoiselle. "He was criticized for excess of
pride, and indeed, his association with me had made him prouder
than ever: it seems to me that he had good reason."

Far from doing anything to conciliate his powerful opponents,
of whose identity he was well aware, Lauzun actually sought occasions to affront them. He was lavish with indiscreet remarks, all
of them of course repeated to those whom they concerned. In
meetings of the war council he consistently contradicted Louvois
himself, and the fact that the king sometimes took Lauzun's side
scarcely improved matters. With Madame de Montespan his indiscretion was all but incredible. When the marriage still hung in
the balance, she had promised Lauzun to support his cause. Quite
naturally he hadn't trusted her, and this time, instead of hiding in
a privy or under the royal lovers' bed, he had bribed a servant to
eavesdrop, and knew that once again she had spoken against him
to the king: "Sire, a great king may feel free to break his word
when the interests of his country and the honor of his family are
at stake." Knowing nothing of the bribery, she swore to Lauzun
that she had done her best. He kept quiet for a time; but as the
months passed his self-control wore away. He picked quarrels
with the favorite, and finally burst out. "You're a liar and a com-

mon whore!" he shouted at her one day; and as he had done once before he repeated to her, like a record, her own words to the king about him. When the king ordered him to "give satisfaction to Madame de Montespan within five days," he sent, instead, a memorandum to the king justifying his behavior. Madame de Montespan was more than outraged; she was a superstitious creature, and was terrified by Lauzun's apparently uncanny knowledge of her secrets. She told everyone he must be allied with the forces of hell. So long as this devil was around, she came to feel, she had no safety. Whether Mademoiselle approved of Lauzun's defiance of the king's mistress as "sublime" we do not know: she claims to have been deliberately incurious concerning reports of Lauzun-Montespan "differences."

Nor did she pay much attention to a particularly dangerous rumor circulated by their enemies—the rumor that she and Lauzun had been secretly married. "It was only my close friends who dared mention this to me, and I didn't even take the trouble to deny it. I let them believe what they liked, convinced as I was that the king would never believe that Monsieur de Lauzun and I had acted against his orders."

Only one thing shook her out of her fool's paradise—a report that came to her one evening in Saint-Germain that Lauzun had been arrested in Paris. She quickly learned that the news was false, but from then on, she maintains, she suffered from a mysterious malaise. "I was troubled without knowing why. I didn't know what I was doing or what was the matter with me; I was so anguished that I couldn't remain long in one place." She shuttled constantly between Saint-Germain and the Luxembourg.

On the evening of Wednesday, November 25, 1671, *"jour de la fête de Sainte-Catherine"*—patron-saint of French spinsters—she was having supper in the Luxembourg with Madame de Nogent and her ladies in waiting. "A valet came and whispered something to Madame de Nogent. She left the table, followed by the other ladies. I stayed behind a little, talking with my servants.

In my bedroom I found the comtesse de Fiesque. [Mademoiselle had long-since forgiven "the countesses."] 'Monsieur de Lauzun . . .' she began.

"I thought she was telling me that he was there, that he had been shown into my study through the dressing room. I hurried in that direction, saying aloud: 'How like him! I thought he was at Saint-Germain, and he turns up here.'

" 'No,' said the comtesse de Fiesque. 'What I was trying to tell you was that he has been arrested.' For half an hour I was speechless; only then did I realize that Madame de Nogent was lying there half-conscious."

This time the news was true. The king's guards had taken Lauzun into custody at Saint-Germain.

For a month, Mademoiselle was told no more than that. As far as she was concerned, Lauzun had simply vanished.

Urged by her friends, she appeared at court as usual the following Friday and saw the king at supper. "I looked at him with tears in my eyes; he seemed oppressed and ill at ease with me. I thought it proper to say nothing to him, and the next day I learned that he approved my conduct."

The next day Monsieur arrived at court, bringing with him his new German wife, Elizabeth-Charlotte of Bavaria, princess Palatine, niece of the older princess Palatine who had been one of Mazarin's go-betweens with Mademoiselle in the affair of *mon petit mari;* and once again Mademoiselle listened to the advice of friends and attended the reception given to honor the new Madame. As she watched the ballet—it happened not to be a new one, but was made up of old numbers that she and Lauzun had often danced—her mind was on her absent lover. "I recalled seeing him at just such gatherings, and my heart tightened at the thought of how grieved he must be to have displeased the king, for whom I knew he had such affection. I was worried by the snow and the cold of the night, wondering where he had been taken. I was torn by a thousand agonies; the sight of others enjoying themselves filled me with despair. I told myself that the king would take into account the sacrifices I was making by attending a spectacle that would have been intolerable to me if I hadn't thought that my presence might inspire him with some pity for Monsieur de Lauzun. That was my only thought. I resolved to be assiduous at court, in the hope that I could thus be useful to him."

The year before, she had been too shattered by her disappointment to be able to attend Midnight Mass on Christmas Eve. This year she forced herself to go, and it was on this occasion, in the royal chapel at Saint-Germain, that she learned Lauzun's fate.

Escorted by d'Artagnan and an entire company of musketeers, he had been taken in a carriage to Pignerol, the isolated prison in the Alps near Turin to which Fouquet had been conducted by the same d'Artagnan eight years before and from which he had never since emerged.

"How do you like what has happened to Monsieur de Lauzun?" Madame de Sévigné wrote her daughter. "Do you remember the sensation he was a year ago? Would we have believed it if someone had told us then that within a year he would be a prisoner? *Vanity, vanity, all is vanity!*"

Part Four

MADEMOISELLE OR MADAME?

1672–1693

1

IT WAS, OF COURSE, the way Mademoiselle had been accustomed to being treated by her father most of her life. The king's broken word and his imprisonment of Lauzun formed one of those designs of great princes that like the mysteries of the Holy Faith are not to be probed into. The only hope was that the great prince might be induced to reverse his design.

That was now what Mademoiselle looked forward to; once again she had a clear purpose. The king's heart (Mademoiselle was sure he had one) must be moved somehow; and in her grief she resorted to what might be called the method of the mute appeal. There was no question of direct pleading, nor dared she proclaim her feelings by absenting herself from court. On the contrary, she must be present at all times, displaying her grief as tactfully as possible, seizing whatever occasions presented themselves to refer obliquely to Lauzun. This course she patiently pursued.

When her stepmother lay dying in the Luxembourg in April, 1672, five months after the arrest, Mademoiselle did not go to see her. "This is neither Christian nor heroic of Mademoiselle," Madame de Sévigné wrote her daughter.

But Mademoiselle's behavior was deliberate. "I told the king that Madame was ill, that I hadn't seen her, and that he knew the reason better than anyone else. I was glad to be able to remind him of Monsieur de Lauzun: he couldn't have forgotten that it was at the moment we were to be married that my stepmother had offended me most grievously. He said I had done right." The old Madame died the next day, and Mademoiselle did not accompany her body to Saint-Denis.

In 1675, during a court trip to Alsace and Lorraine, after visiting in Nancy the convent chapel in which her father had been married, she prayed at the shrine of Saint Nicholas near Lunéville. "They showed us the chains of a man who had made a vow to Saint Nicholas while held captive by the Turks; he escaped, and presented to the saint the chains he had worn on his hands and feet. Those who realize to what extent I was affected by the imprisonment of Monsieur de Lauzun will judge how fervently I prayed God, through the intercession of Saint Nicholas, to restore his freedom. I didn't fail to tell the king about the miracle of the slave's escape; I clasped my hands together to indicate how he must have thanked God and Saint Nicholas." This was supposed to indicate to the king that she, too, stood ready to give proof of gratitude in return for a miracle: three years after Lauzun's arrest this was still as far as she dared go in suggesting a purchase of his freedom.

At Brisach, "the château where we spent the night is gloomy; everything about it is like a prison; the rooms are dark and the windows barred. I asked the king several times whether the place didn't give him the vapors. 'As for me,' I told him, 'the very sight of anything that looks like a prison is enough to kill me.' And I expatiated on the horror that prisonlike surroundings must inspire in anyone."

In general, the court acted as though Lauzun were dead. "Once, at supper, there was discussion about a horse. The king said, 'I remember: it belonged to . . . and without finishing his sentence, he looked at me, blushed, and stopped short. Everyone noticed that he had refrained from uttering the name of Monsieur de Lauzun, to whom the horse had belonged, lest I be hurt." However, a few days later, as though to show her that the name didn't

frighten him, the king brought it into his conversation deliberately, almost defiantly, apropos of an acrobat who had been one
of Lauzun's servants.

Only foreigners, ignorant of the situation or unbound by court
etiquette, dared speak to the king of his prisoner. The duke of
Buckingham, who had been a friend of Lauzun's, did not hesitate
to express surprise that one who had been so loyal a servant
should be "ruined." "He isn't ruined," the king replied. "It's
simply that he hasn't yet paid his full penalty."

And the aged German bailiff of a village near Strasbourg, who
had known Lauzun during a stay in Paris, asked the king about
him in affectionate reminiscence. " 'What has happened to little
Puyguilhem, who was such a good-looking boy? I hear he's now
called Monsieur de Lauzun.' Everybody looked at everybody else
without saying a word, and the silence discouraged him from further questioning."

Only in private could Mademoiselle pour out her heart. She
went to great trouble to obtain eye-witness reports from d'Artagnan
about Lauzun's trip to Pignerol; she talked endlessly with Madame de Nogent about the scraps of news that reached them by
roundabout ways from the prisoner. For the first five or six years
Lauzun was allowed to communicate only with Louvois, the minister of war, but certain details leaked out. One of his trusted
servants was discovered in Turin, arrested, and taken to Pignerol
himself, where he cut his throat in despair. Lauzun, digging his
way by night up through the flue of his fireplace, suddenly appeared before his astonished fellow prisoner, Fouquet. The ex-
minister of finance, whose memory was of an insignificant, provincial young Puyguilhem, listened incredulously to his sooty-faced
guest's narrative of his rise in the king's favor and his near marriage to the king's first cousin. At first Fouquet assumed him to
be a lunatic; but from then on they visited regularly. In 1676
Lauzun almost succeeded in escaping: with incredible labor he
dug a long tunnel and emerged in the prison courtyard, where,

with only one gate between himself and liberty, he was stopped by a guard who happened to be passing. The next year, Madame de Nogent was allowed to visit her brother to discuss testamentary matters following a death in the family. He was ill, she reported on her return: he badly needed a change of air. When she heard this, Mademoiselle was finally driven to write to the king, begging for clemency, and as a result Lauzun's living conditions at Pignerol were improved. Of course he had been stripped of his commission as captain of the king's bodyguard: from his prison he protested violently to Louvois against this "offense to a gentleman," and Mademoiselle too considered it the greatest of his misfortunes.

But little of Mademoiselle's time could be taken up with Lauzun. There was seldom anything she could do for or about him, and she filled her life as best she could. At Choisy, on the banks of the Seine near Paris, she built a country house, designed for her by a member of the famous Gabriel family of architects (it was a Gabriel who designed the buildings on the Place de la Concorde). "Since I intended to live there in summer, I made sure that from the house I'd be able to see the river even when it was at its lowest. From my very bed I can look out at it and watch the passing boats." Just as she had done at Saint-Fargeau, she filled Choisy with portraits of her ancestors and relations. In her memoirs she mentions most of them again: "I am over one of the fireplaces," she ends the passage, "holding the portrait of my father."

She means, of course, that over a fireplace hung a portrait of herself in which she was shown holding a likeness of her father— holding a portrait within a portrait. At least two pictures answering this description still exist, both of them at Versailles; and one of them—perhaps the one that hung at Choisy—is extraordinary. It is by the painter le Bourguignon, and shows Mademoiselle garbed as Minerva, Roman goddess of wisdom, war, and the liberal arts, motherless daughter of Jupiter. In the foreground a few books are to be seen, but it is the martial aspect that is emphasized

—even more so than in the earlier portrait by Mignard. Here, as in the Mignard picture, Mademoiselle carries a lance, but here she wears Minerva's bronze helmet, complete with plumes and owl. On the ground beside her lies Minerva's shield, embossed with the head of Medusa; and held by her left hand is the portrait of Gaston d'Orléans. He is shown not as Jupiter, but as himself, in royal robes and armor decorated with the lilies of France. His portrait is oval, and in the context it seems almost a second shield: it seems almost as though Mademoiselle-Minerva has discarded Medusa only to brandish another face, equally calculated to strike terror to the human heart. Mademoiselle-Minerva herself stares away from Gaston, as though well aware of his petrifying power. In such grotesque guise are father and daughter united for posterity.

And all over the house at Choisy hung likenesses of Mademoiselle's other great paternal protector. "There are pictures of the king everywhere." The king, refusing to give Mademoiselle the one gift she longed for, gave her another: he had constructed for her at the shipbuilding center of Le Havre, and floated up the Seine to her very water stairs at Choisy, a painted and gilded boat, "upholstered in crimson damask," in which she could glide up and down the river between her summer house and Paris.

When she was in the city, she spent much time praying in one or another of the Carmelite convents, and she saw something of the austere abbé de Rancé, reformer of the Trappist monks. With him she felt a bond, for it was he, as a younger man, almoner in her father's household, who had given the dying Gaston the last rites. "People told me that he longed for me to become a Carmelite, but he never mentioned the subject to me. He was too intelligent not to know that persons of my rank can do more good in the world than out of it."

At Eu she busied herself with her children's school: "I often go there to watch the nuns teach; I'm careful to see that the place is well run." She built a seminary for the nuns, and a hospital where some of them nursed.

And at Eu, in the summer of 1677, Mademoiselle took up once again an occupation she had let lapse—the writing of her memoirs. Seventeen years before, in 1660, the year her father died, the year she saw Lauzun at the wedding, she had put aside the manuscript she had begun during her first exile at Saint-Fargeau: she had found herself too "distracted by the brilliant society of the court, by travel, by new exile, and especially by a certain person" to be able to keep it going. Now she began to write again: "I hope to amuse myself in my old age—if God in his mercy grants me long life—by looking over what I did in my youth: it will give me greater insight into the wickedness of the world and confirm me in my renunciation of it. And I have another purpose in writing. Though I was born to great rank and wealth, though I have never harmed anyone, God has allowed my life to be afflicted by a thousand scourges. Such an example seems to me a worthy subject of reflection."

With her reflections, with her memoir-writing, with her prayers and good works, with the riverside pleasures of Choisy, Mademoiselle filled the years of Lauzun's imprisonment. Assiduous though she was in her attendance at court, she seemed somehow outside court life; it flowed past her; she felt herself a spectator, and others felt her the same. Madame de Sévigné, writing to her daughter in 1674 of a ball at the Tuileries, noted that "the Grand Mademoiselle dances no longer"; and she adds the words "thank God"—Mademoiselle was approaching fifty, and her determined gallantry in her bereavement was becoming, for someone of Madame de Sévigné's sensitive perception, almost too painful. Other courtiers naturally found her merely comic, as they had from the first moment of her grief.

There were changes at court. For years Louise de La Vallière had been begging the king for permission to withdraw from her position of co-mistress and retire in repentance to a convent; once or twice she had run away from him to the Carmelites only to be brought back; in 1675 he finally let her go for good, and she became Mère Louise de la Charité. That same year her former partner began to see her supremacy threatened: Madame de Montespan saw Madame Scarron, a needy widow whom she had made governess of her children, created by the king marquise de Maintenon and brought to live at court. 1674 saw the last of Molière. In 1675 the sixty-four-year-old Turenne was killed in battle on the Rhine; Condé, ten years younger, took over his old rival's command and then retired, gout-ridden, to his château at Chantilly. From 1672 to 1678 battle followed battle in the war with Holland. The scene was ever-shifting.

Throughout everything Mademoiselle continued her technique of the mute appeal. And throughout everything it failed to make the slightest impression on the king.

But in 1680, when Lauzun had been in Pignerol eight years, there was evidence that it had begun to make an impression on someone else.

In the ten years since Lauzun had spirited the little duc du Maine out of the birth chamber and out of the palace, Madame de Montespan had borne the king five more children, three girls and two boys. The king doted on all six; it was his visits to them in the care of their governess that had aroused his interest in that worthy lady and brought about her advancement. All six had been legitimized; all six were visited and fawned on by courtiers who sought the favor of the king. And all six were visited by Mademoiselle, who not only sought the favor of the king but loved children.

The duc du Maine appealed to her especially. He was the oldest, he was handsome, he was bright, he was associated in her mind with Lauzun, and he aroused her pity, for he had been crippled in a leg by some accident of infancy and his limp had grown worse after a Dutch quack had treated him. Mademoiselle saw a good deal of the boy, and whenever he was absent at a watering place for a "cure," they corresponded. His return of her affection seemed sincere, but Mademoiselle wasn't unaware that it was also encouraged. There was evidence that her enthusiasm for children in general, and for the little duke in particular, was being fanned and played upon. In 1680, Madame de Montespan finally began to hint. "Think of something you might do that would please the king," she several times urged Mademoiselle when they were with the boy. "Something that would move him to grant your dearest wish."

A gentleman named Pertuis, a friend of Lauzun's, came to Mademoiselle—sent, no doubt, by an interested party—and spoke more openly. "If only you could give them some hope that the duc du Maine might be your heir!"

His use of the word "them," Madame de Montespan's words about pleasing the king, and similar remarks she made from time to time, told the Mademoiselle the story. It wasn't a new story to her; it was almost a repetition of the story of Gaston d'Orléans and his blackmail at Saint-Fargeau. The king and Madame de Montespan, Mademoiselle knew, were thinking of her possessions. And she came quickly to her decision. "I decided to make the duc du Maine my heir, on the condition that the king would recall Monsieur de Lauzun to Paris and allow me to marry him."

She approached Madame de Montespan. "I have a lot of things I'd like to talk to you about," she said. "But we ought to have time to talk at leisure. We're always being disturbed."

Madame de Montespan showed the opposite of impatience. "She is shrewder than I am," Mademoiselle says, "and eager as she was to achieve her objective, she knew that I was even more eager to achieve mine. So she preserved her cool head and displayed far greater prudence than I."

Somehow Madame de Montespan was never available. Mademoiselle was unable to obtain the private interview she desired.

But when she sent an emissary—a gentleman named Barrailh,

who had been an officer in Lauzun's company of guards—he was received at once; and when the two ladies next met Madame de Montespan thanked her kindly for the proposals he had delivered. She was sure that the king would be pleased by her generosity to the son he loved, she said, and she had little doubt that in return he would do everything Mademoiselle wished. It was a vague answer. It was, Mademoiselle recognized, nothing more than an expression of Madame de Montespan's opinion. Mademoiselle pressed her to obtain Lauzun's immediate release. "After all," she said, "you know you can count on my word now that I've given it."

Madame de Montespan promised to speak to the king about it, and to arrange for an interview between him and Mademoiselle. "But when you speak to the king," she warned, "say only that you wish to benefit Monsieur du Maine because you love him and because you wish to please His Majesty. Don't mention Monsieur de Lauzun. For all we know, the king may be as eager for his release as you are, but his enemies are so numerous and powerful that it would be unwise for the king to oppose them openly." Mademoiselle's best hope, she said, was to make the king so grateful to her that he would take it on himself to release Lauzun without consulting anyone, subsequently justifying his actions on the ground that his enormous debt to his cousin had made any other course impossible. In other words, Mademoiselle should inform the king of her intentions in favor of the duc du Maine, but not mention her expectation of a return. "Wouldn't you love to play a secret little game like that with the king?" Madame de Montespan coaxed. "Wouldn't it be wonderful to spring the results on an unsuspecting world? For my part, I confess that the very idea thrills me."

Mademoiselle agreed to proceed in that way. Madame de Montespan spoke to the king. The following day the king spoke to Mademoiselle. He thanked her for her intention. He hoped that the duc du Maine would prove worthy of the honor she was doing him. "As for myself," he said, "I assure you that I won't miss an occasion to give you tokens of my affection."

At that point, Mademoiselle still believed herself no more committed than the king.

There was a marked change in the behavior of Madame de Montespan.

"She was delighted that I had taken the step I had," Mademoiselle later wrote with perfect hindsight, "and she thought only of making me take a greater one. She flattered me, and I found pleasure only in her company. Even normally she is the most charming person imaginable, and now she went out of her way to please me. She came to see me more often than usual; we often drove together. The king, too, addressed me more frequently; but still there was no word about Monsieur de Lauzun. I urged Madame de Montespan to speak to His Majesty about him, but she always urged me to be patient."

But while the subject of Lauzun was still taboo, the royal lovers didn't fail to inform the ten-year-old duc du Maine of the immense inheritance he could look forward to, and like his parents he redoubled his attentions to Mademoiselle. One day they sent him to her with a gift of a certain gold goblet, set with diamonds, that they had seen her admire. "Such attentions are always pleasing," says Mademoiselle. "When you're dealing with a woman who's infatuated, it's easy to get her to swallow your bait."

Then, abruptly, Mademoiselle felt the hook: Madame de Montespan suggested that she make the duc du Maine a gift—a gift of her principality of Dombes and her county of Eu.

"But I'm going to leave them to him in my will!" Mademoiselle cried. "And I feel too well to want to keep talking about death all the time. I told you once that I'd do it: my word should be enough for you."

Madame de Montespan shrugged. "The king wants it to be a gift." And though she continued sugary with Mademoiselle, she sent harsher words by Barrailh. "The king isn't to be trifled with; when you've promised him something, you keep your word."

Mademoiselle, who had made, so she thought, a conditional promise of a bequest, and certainly no promise of a gift, was frightened by the sudden shift in the wind. But she still tried to preserve the fiction that she was a free agent, negotiating a bona fide transaction. "I want Monsieur de Lauzun's release," was the answer she sent back with Barrailh. "What guarantees do I have that they'll grant it once they've got what they want?"

The rejoinder was an ultimatum. If she failed to accede, came the message, not only would Lauzun continue to rot in Pignerol, but Barrailh—they knew she was fond of him—would be sent to the Bastille.

As before, in the matter of her father and her exile, there was nothing to do but give in. In a ceremony attended by Colbert, Barrailh, two notaries, and of course Madame de Montespan, who held the king's power of attorney in the transaction, Mademoiselle signed over to the duc du Maine two of her choicest possessions: the principality of Dombes and the county of Eu. The duke was to take possession only after her death; but his father, or more probably his mother, had greater faith in a deed of gift than in a more easily revocable testamentary clause. Why, indeed, should *they* have faith in anyone's word? The combined annual income from the donation amounted to 50,000 écus. After the signing, after the withdrawal of everyone except Barrailh, Madame de Montespan poured forth thanks, surpassed herself in honeyed words. "Everybody except the people who hoped to be your heirs will admire the cleverness and foresight of what you've just done," she said. "Quite apart from my own interest in the matter, I'm overjoyed for your sake." Mademoiselle would find herself the happiest woman in the world, she said; she'd see how magnificently the king would express his gratitude. "He'll have your house at Choisy decorated for you," she said enthusiastically.

"Whenever you go there you'll find something new—a room painted, a fountain installed, furniture, statues—he'll be as interested in it as he is in Versailles."

In her helplessness—everything now depended on the king's caprice—Mademoiselle thirstily drank Madame de Montespan's words. The speech about Choisy apparently seemed to her a metaphor—a figure of speech meaning that someday she'd find Lauzun there. "It intoxicated me: it filled me entirely." But only a few minutes later she was trembling. "As soon as I was alone in my room I dropped my rock-crystal mirror. 'It's an omen,' I said to Barrailh. 'I shall regret what I just did.' "

The next day the king echoed his mistress. "You're satisfied, I hope? I know I am. You won't regret your gift: nothing will ever come between us again. Monsieur and Condé will be displeased at the news"—one doesn't know whether this was the first Mademoiselle had heard of Condé in the role of would-be heir—"but have no fear, I'll stand by you."

Those words again raised her spirits. "I was in heaven."

Even Monsieur, who was indeed waspish as his brother had prophesied, didn't disturb her composure when he assured her that *his* love for her had always been disinterested, and expressed the dubious hope that "people would keep their promises" and that she would be "better treated than in the past."

Madame de Montespan kept assuring her that she was pressing for Lauzun's release. Then, one day, she switched to frankness, to brutality. "Don't fool yourself," she said. "The king will never allow you to marry Monsieur de Lauzun on your terms or let him be called the duc de Montpensier. He'll make him duke of something else, and if you insist on marrying him, he'll pretend not to know it. He'll reprove anyone who tells him about it. He'll permit no outward change in your position."

"What!" cried Mademoiselle. "Monsieur de Lauzun will live with me as my husband but won't be my husband publicly? What will people say and think?"

"No one will dare think anything bad. You'll have a clear conscience. Believe me, you'll be a thousand times happier. Monsieur de Lauzun will love you all the more. A little secrecy adds spice to things."

Weeks went by without news. Mademoiselle alternated between hope and despair. She had several violent altercations with Madame de Montespan. "Madame de Montespan told me twenty times, when we were both angry: 'I can scarcely keep from returning your gift.'

" 'Don't let anything stop you,' I answered her. 'I'd be overjoyed.'

" 'What does it amount to, anyway,' she said, 'compared with what the king can do for him?"

" 'The king is very powerful,' I admitted. 'He can give Monsieur du Maine commissions and governorships. However, an income of 50,000 écus as lord of domains, and the rank that goes with it—that takes a lot of money, and kings don't give away that much. Besides, no king has ever sliced up his estates for his bastards.' "

Then, one day in March, Madame de Montespan summoned her. It had become typical of Louis XIV's court that a royal mistress could summon a *fille de France*. Mademoiselle at first refused to go; then, urged by the king, she finally appeared. Madame de Montespan greeted her sharply. "You were in no hurry to come, though I was eager to see you. The king has asked me to tell you that he is ordering Monsieur de Lauzun's release from Pignerol. He's sending him to Bourbon."

Mademoiselle screamed. Bourbon was a watering place near Vichy, more than 150 miles south of Paris. "What! He won't come straight here, after everything I've done?"

"I don't know the details. His Majesty says you can choose his guards, if you like; but he wants it to seem like a prison." And Mademoiselle's tears brought a pretty jibe: "You're a hard person to please; whenever you're given something, you want more."

They went for a walk in the park; and there, as though it were an afterthought, Madame de Montespan gave her an additional item of news. "The king asked me to tell you that he doesn't ever want you to think of marrying Monsieur de Lauzun."

"At that I burst into tears," says Mademoiselle, "and reminded her that I had made my gift only on that condition, that all our negotiations had revolved around that point."

Madame de Montespan shrugged. "I never promised you anything."

This time Mademoiselle saw no further reason to control herself. "I told her straight out what I thought, and she made no reply whatever."

2

O N APRIL 22, 1681, Lauzun was released from Pignerol
and escorted toward Bourbon by a corps of musketeers.
After his more than nine years' incarceration in a dungeon, after Mademoiselle's more than nine years of striving, after
all her anguish and humiliation, it seemed that a new and serene
chapter was about to open in her existence. But what followed was
a nightmare that made everything that had gone before seem like
a happy dream.

"How fortunate is a career that begins with love and ends with
ambition!" writes the great Pascal, one of Mademoiselle's contemporaries.

And another contemporary, the duc de la Rochefoucauld, the
Frondeur whom she had seen bleeding from a head wound the
day of the battle of the Faubourg Saint-Antoine, and who was
later a frequenter of her salon, expresses a similar idea in one of
his famous *Maximes:* "We often move from love to ambition, but
there is no way back from ambition to love." Mademoiselle had
tried to reverse that order of passions which according to the two
great moralists is the most suitable to human nature. She had tried
to find her way back from ambition to love. In a way she had succeeded; but she had to pay a high price for being an exception.
Each step of her progress caused her increased suffering. Each
time she looked back, the preceding stage seemed a lesser evil.

The agitation and uncertainty that accompanied her falling in

[285]

love with Lauzun were bliss compared with the anguish that followed the king's breach of his word; that pain was more endurable than the bleakness of the years of his imprisonment; that long separation—she was now to find—was better than the news of his behavior on his release; and even that disillusionment was to pale beside the final discovery of his indifference—almost his hatred. Ambition had brought Mademoiselle much glamor, and even, for a brief time, glory; but she had never tasted its true fruit, which is power. And of love, except for her three days of deceptive happiness, she was fated to taste little but its asperities, its sorrows without its joys.

The year that elapsed between Lauzun's removal to Bourbon and his arrival in Paris brought her a series of cruel disappointments—disappointments in Lauzun himself. The one distress he had said he would never cause her was jealousy; but during this year, from Bourbon and from Châlons and Amboise to which he was successively removed, humiliating stories of his escapades came to her in a continual stream. Along with the thanks he sent her for accomplishing his release, he complained that his new "solitude" at Bourbon was worse than that of Pignerol, and he begged her to press for his final pardon; she, anxious to pave his way back to court, counseled sage conduct. "I wrote him, advising him to see no one at Bourbon; he should demonstrate by his behavior that he was thinking only of seeing the king, that nothing else interested him." The letters he wrote her in reply were charming, but the flattering and submissive words they contained were consistently given the lie by witnesses who had to be believed and, on occasion, by evidence supplied by Lauzun himself.

A tender letter he wrote to Madame d'Humières, the still beautiful forty-six-year-old wife of a general, who had been spending the season at Bourbon, and whom Lauzun claimed not even to have seen, fell into Mademoiselle's hands: "In it he spoke of a book she had given him, which he kissed a thousand times a day because he could no longer see the giver, etc." Mademoiselle, now fifty-four, burned that letter. "I pitied him for thinking that such a woman as that could be useful to him."

At Amboise, Mademoiselle learned, he was "never away from" the marquise d'Alluye, celebrated for her *galanteries,* although he wrote Mademoiselle that he "couldn't stand" the lady. "Everyone knew the way he was acting," says Mademoiselle, "and everyone found his conduct grotesque." During this same time Mademoiselle made him great gifts in recompense for the earlier bestowals that had been canceled. With the king's permission she gave him "the duchy of Saint-Fargeau, leased at an annual rent of 22,000 livres; the city and barony of Thiers, one of the jewels of the Auvergne, bringing an annual revenue of 8,000 livres; and a share of 10,000 livres a year in the taxes of Languedoc." The king refused to allow the title of duke to accompany this endowment totaling 40,000 livres a year—about as many dollars today—and Lauzun complained to several persons, who didn't fail to repeat his words to Mademoiselle, that "she had given him so little that he had to force himself to accept it."

So outrageously did he behave that by the time the king finally consented to his return to Paris, early in 1682, Mademoiselle found herself wishing that he would stay away. She feared his probable conduct; and indeed, even before he arrived, her fears were confirmed: "He didn't come as quickly as he should have. I had thought he would travel by post or relay; but he claimed that prison had ruined his health, and he couldn't be expected to act like other people."

Even now the king's favor was partial. He would receive Lauzun only once, he said, after which the court, though not the city of Paris, would be out of bounds to him. Lauzun made the most of his single audience at Saint-Germain. His appearance was a variation of his earlier return from the Bastille wearing a long beard, a variation of the marquis de Vardes' grotesque masquerade in twenty-year-old-clothes: Lauzun presented himself to his sovereign wearing, in Mademoiselle's words, "a tattered old *justaucorps à brevet* that he had worn before his imprisonment, much shorter than the present model, and a repulsive wig." Ten times he threw himself at the king's feet. But this time the king was moved to neither laughter nor pity, and the only result was a dry royal comment after Lauzun had left: "I see that his manners are as flattering as ever."

From the king he went to Madame de Montespan's apartment, where Mademoiselle was waiting. "He threw himself at my feet, thanked me over and over. He said that the king had received him well, and that he owed this to me. Only through me could good things ever happen to him, he said; he owed me everything."

The sight of him after ten years rendered Mademoiselle mute with emotion: "I couldn't say a word; I was paralyzed." Then he withdrew: Louvois, Colbert—there were many to whom he had to pay his respects.

But though he said the right things at that first meeting, his conduct since leaving Pignerol had made Mademoiselle wary. To others, she offered a charitable explanation of his escapades. "He has suffered so much, not even counting his imprisonment, that it's natural for him to have greatly changed." If that was the true reason, he might gradually regain his balance now that he was free. The only thing to do was wait and see.

She stayed at Saint-Germain four days, during which he made no attempt to see her. Only after she went to Choisy, pointedly failing to leave any message for him, did he see fit to call. Alas! So far, at least, freedom had wrought no magic: his opening words showed him to be the same new Lauzun. "It shocks me when I see the queen wearing all those colored ribbons on her head," he said abruptly.

The point of his attack on the new fashion wasn't lost on Mademoiselle. "Since I'm older than the queen, I gather you find it ridiculous that *I* wear them?"

He could have replied with any one of a dozen easy compliments, but he just looked at her and her ribbons.

Together they walked over the property, and he left her early, promising to return that evening after paying another visit to Colbert. But instead of appearing, he sent his excuses: he was no longer used to walking, he said; he was exhausted, and had to go to bed. The next day she learned he had spent the evening with ladies. He first denied it, and then, confronted with her evidence, complained of her nagging.

Though he constantly visited her in Paris, at Choisy, at Eu, time brought no improvement in his manners. There were constant *galanteries* with others, transparent deceptions, even complaints about her extravagant way of life. When the king paid him a sum of more than half a million livres, covering accumulated back wages and compensation for his commission, which had been sold to someone else, he reproached her with not having persuaded her first cousin to restore him to his post. Even Madame de Montespan, who seemed in some hidden way to have become his ally, chided him for that particular bit of ingratitude: "If it hadn't been for Mademoiselle you'd never have got out of prison or been given all that money: who else has ever been treated so well after falling from favor?"

He scolded Mademoiselle for having poured money into the house and grounds at Choisy—"All you needed was a cottage, where you could eat a chicken fricassee"—and then, after telling her that because of her stinginess he had no "decent place to live," he bought a mansion on the Ile-Saint-Louis full of sumptuous gilded chambers.

How deceived she had been in him! Madame de Montespan laughed at her. "If you'd known him better, you wouldn't have done everything for him that you did."

Mademoiselle recalled his own warnings to her during their days of happiness: that he wasn't easy to live with, that he liked to spend long periods alone. Courtiers who remembered him from those days were shocked by the change in his manners. No wonder: "Then he had shown himself only when he was in good temper; he knew his real disposition, and took good care to conceal it. Prison, far from improving him, had dispensed him for so long from the necessity of checking his bad disposition, that now he was no longer its master." Such was Mademoiselle's analysis. In prison he had turned rancid. He seemed no longer the man she had known.

Despite her gifts and his ingratitude, she still had a sense of obligation. She had failed to keep her promise to make him duke; she hadn't achieved his return to the king's full favor: in those things she felt her own prestige involved. But despite her best intentions and efforts his own meanness stood in the way. "Monsieur de Lauzun isn't conducting himself properly," Colbert told her one day. "The king doesn't like it. What angers the king particularly is that he doesn't behave toward *you* as he should." And, on another occasion: "Monsieur de Lauzun is digging his own grave," Colbert said. "I'm very sorry for you, Mademoiselle, having done so much for a man who is so ungrateful and disappointing. May God grant that he change! But I very much fear that he won't, and that you'll be driven to beg the king to exile him again, just as eagerly as you begged for his freedom. If so, you'll find one difference: your wishes will be granted more promptly this time than the last."

As the months went by, and he treated her more and more as a careless husband treats a despised wife, she realized that the situation was hopeless. She was nothing more to him—perhaps she had never been more—than a possible source of money and influence: he no longer made the slightest pretense of courtesy or consideration. He went so far as to blame her for all his misfortunes: had she not entered his life he would have continued to rise. He had thought that she would bring him even closer to the king than he had been; but she had lacked even the power to keep him out of prison. He was not indebted to her, but she to him.

Then, in the spring of 1684, Lauzun thought he saw his chance. Once again France was at war with Spain, and the army was being refurbished and restaffed for a new campaign—a campaign against Spain's northern possession, the duchy of Luxembourg. The king would be in the field himself. Surely by now, Lauzun felt, he had purged himself of his sins; surely this war must be the occasion for his restoration to rank and activity. Mademoiselle must help him. He wrote her a long letter. He demanded that she speak to the king. As former captain of the king's bodyguard in time of peace, he sought the post of king's personal aide-de-camp in the war; if the king wanted to do him justice, he said, he would not only restore him to his rank of lieutenant-general, but place him above all the other lieutenant-generals, since he was the oldest.

Mademoiselle received the letter. But for the first time she felt differently about Lauzun. She no longer took it for granted that because he asked a favor, she must do it. She wasn't sure how to proceed. In her perplexity she consulted Madame de Maintenon, the new favorite, who cared nothing for Lauzun. "You know how I feel about this," she said. "Please advise me."

"Write him a letter," said Madame de Maintenon, "and show it to me before you send it."

"As I recall," says Mademoiselle, "I wrote him that I thought I had given him plenty of proof that I hoped for his elevation and his restoration to the king's favor. I said I didn't think it was because of *my* conduct that these hadn't been granted him. I said that he ought to give a little thought to the difficulty, figure out where it came from, and behave in such a way that the situation might be remedied."

Madame le Maintenon approved the letter.

Mademoiselle was candid enough to show it to Madame de Montespan, who recognized it for what it was. "Would you be so cruel as to keep him down by not saying a word to the king in his behalf?"

Mademoiselle reminded her, too, of everything she had done in the past, of everything else she had tried to do, and of the thanks she had received.

"Do you want me to tell the king that you don't want Monsieur de Lauzun's commission restored?" Madame de Montespan demanded.

"On the contrary. I ask that it be restored. I humbly ask the king to give it to him."

But Madame de Montespan well knew the difference between such a reply to a third party like herself—whether it was ironic or merely formal, it amounted to the same thing—and a bona-fide direct request to the king. "I have spoken to the king as you told me to," she said the next day, "and I greatly pity Monsieur de Lauzun."

And indeed the king attached weight—or pretended to—to Mademoiselle's silence. As the day of his departure for Luxembourg drew near, he made no sign to Lauzun. On the very eve of his going, he spoke to Mademoiselle. "Madame de Montespan has been talking to me about Monsieur de Lauzun in a way I don't understand. Surely you don't want me to restore his commission unless you ask me yourself, do you? I have reasons for not seeing him. If I ever do anything for him it will be only for your sake: he should owe everything to you. But it's not yet time. Do you agree?"

His Majesty's goodness to her, Mademoiselle replied, left her wholly content.

The king set out for the north in the morning—April 24, 1684.

One can only relish the deliberate lightness with which Mademoiselle chose to break the news to Lauzun. "A day passed before Monsieur de Lauzun came to see me. Then he called. I went up to him quite gaily. 'Since you'll not be following the king,' I said, 'why don't you go to your château at Lauzun, or to Saint-Fargeau? It would be silly of you to stay in Paris. I certainly don't want people to think you're staying on my account.' "

Lauzun took it in. "I'll go," he said. "I'll go—and I'll never see you again in my life."

"It would have been a happy life if I had never seen you," mocked Mademoiselle. "And—better late than never."

His anger was growing; there were other guests who were watching and listening. "You've ruined my career," he accused her. "You've stabbed me in the back. It's because of you that the king didn't take me with him: you asked him not to."

"That's a lie; the king himself can tell you the real story."

Those last words were maddening to a man who knew that the king disdained to address him a word. "He was furious," says Mademoiselle, "and I remained very cool. I said: 'Good-by, then,' and went into my study. I stayed there a while, then went out again; he was still there. The ladies present asked me if I wanted to join them in a game they were playing. I went up to him. 'Stick to your intention,' I said." And Mademoiselle added what were her last words to Lauzun, "Get out."

He went to Monsieur and complained that Mademoiselle had thrown him out like a thieving lackey. Monsieur told Mademoiselle that she had done quite right.

3

B UT THE EXPULSION of the man she had loved, appropriate
and necessary though it was, brought Mademoiselle no joy.
No one and nothing entered her life to replace him. She
lived on in loneliness, with an ever-sharper sense of the injustice
of her fate. Only nine more years remained to her, and they passed
without hope and almost without event.

The entire court, the entire government, had moved definitively
to Versailles shortly after Lauzun's return from exile in the spring
of 1682. There, a year later, died the queen whom Louis XIV had
married at Saint-Jean-de-Luz; and after a year or so of widower-
hood, having sent Madame de Montespan into retirement, he married Madame de Maintenon, former governess of the royal bastards, in a secret midnight ceremony. The *mésalliance* he had forbidden Mademoiselle, he permitted himself. The marriage was
never announced; the bride was never called queen. She was forty-
nine, the king forty-seven; she was a prude and a bigot; for all the
grandeur of Versailles, the court became a place of gloom. The
revocation of the Edict of Nantes and the subsequent persecution
of the Protestants, which lost France thousands of her best citizens, were of course enthusiastically approved by the courtiers;
but they brought gaiety to no one except the soldiers given license
to rape, kidnap, and plunder in Protestant homes.

Colbert, the real genius of the reign, died in 1682. "Don't

mention that man to me," he said on his deathbed when he was told that the king had sent to inquire. "If I'd done half as much for God as I've done for him, I'd be more confident of my future."

Mademoiselle had her apartment at Versailles like everyone else, but she spent little time there. She had earned, she seemed to feel, the right to live where and as she liked. Chiefly she stayed quietly in the Luxembourg, shared now with one of her half sisters, and she summered at Choisy and at Eu.

Her old suitor Charles II died in London in 1685, and three years later his Catholic brother and successor James II—the young duke of York whom Mademoiselle had found preferable to Charles because he could speak French—was expelled from Britain by his subjects. Lauzun, unemployable in France, had gone to England to offer the beleagured king his services; and it was Lauzun who brought across the channel, to safety at Saint-Germain, the Italian queen of England, Mary of Modena, and her son James, prince of Wales (the Old Pretender). James II awarded Lauzun the Order of the Garter, and Louis XIV, in reluctant recognition of his services to a fellow monarch, re-admitted him to court. "He has found the way to Versailles via London!" marveled Madame de Sévigné.

Mademoiselle was indignant at his return to favor. "Is this my reward for doing what I did for the duc du Maine?" she protested. Louis XIV sent her a messenger to "explain." She never saw Lauzun. He soon disgraced himself by his incompetent command of the French army sent to fight for the Stuarts in Ireland; and after his return, though at the exiled James II's urgent request he was created duc de Lauzun, Louis XIV treated him coldly and never again employed him. From England he had brought Mademoiselle presents of Chinese porcelain, which she refused to accept although she "couldn't resist looking at them." Several times he wrote her, trying in vain to be reconciled.

More and more, as she grew older, Mademoiselle was called The Grand Mademoiselle, to distinguish her from the daughters of the king and of Monsieur, each one of whom was now a young lady, a princess of the blood entitled to the simple appellation "Mademoiselle." More and more she seemed to courtiers a figure from another age—an age when nobles had behaved with a reckless independence that was now unthinkable. "The king had never really forgiven her," writes Saint-Simon, who knew her only late in life, "for what she did at the Porte Saint-Antoine, and once I heard him reproach her at supper—in joke, but rather sharp joke —for having had the cannon of the Bastille fired at his troops. She was a little embarrassed, but got out of it very well."

Now it was no longer the distractions of brilliant society and travel that kept Mademoiselle from continuing her memoirs, but rather lack of purpose and lack of personal adventures to put into them. The manuscript still existing in her own hand breaks off abruptly in the middle of a sentence: "Monsieur de Lauzun lived obscurely, getting himself talked about nonetheless, often in ways that displeased me. When I returned from Eu in the autumn of 1688, my entire household staff was put into new liveries. One day, when I was driving in the park of . . ."

The last five years are an almost total blank. Then in the spring of 1693 she fell ill of uremia in the Luxembourg, and three weeks later, on April 5, she died there. She was almost sixty-six. "She died of nothing but the doctors' ignorance," Monsieur's German wife, who had been fond of Mademoiselle, wrote to her aunt the electress of Hanover, "for they didn't recognize her illness, and the irritating emetics they gave her caused a fatal inflammation of the intestines."

Mademoiselle had had at least one unmistakable sign that her end was near. The king visited her as she lay on her sickbed in the Luxembourg—visited her for the first time since his condolence call after breaking off her match with Lauzun twenty-one years before. How clear it must have been to her, when he appeared at her bedside, that this was his call of farewell!

Lauzun had tried to gain admittance to the Luxembourg as

Mademoiselle lay dying, but he had been sternly excluded. As befitted a good Christian, Mademoiselle assured the priest attending her that she "forgave everyone"; but it was clear that there was one person she did not forgive.

At the reading of Mademoiselle's will, it was found that she had left bequests to a number of charities, to all her servants, maids of honor, and ladies in waiting. She had been giving the comte de Charny an allowance of a thousand écus a year, and her will directed that it be continued for the remainder of his life: but by the time she died, he too was gone—he had died a year before, in Oran, the Algerian port that France had seized from Spain and of which he had been military governor. He was unmarried, and left an illegitimate son, named Louis like himself: Gaston d'Orléans still had no legitimate male descendants. Mademoiselle left her house at Choisy to the Dauphin. And everything else, all the properties that still remained to her after the donations to the duc du Maine and to Lauzun (they were still considerable, bringing an income of at least 200,000 livres a year) she left to—Monsieur. "I name as my residuary legatee Monsieur, Philippe de France, duc d'Orléans, whose first cousin I have the honor to be, and who has done me the honor of always showing me much affection." Whether or not Monsieur's affection for her had been, in later years, as disinterested as he claimed, Mademoiselle never forgot the spontaneous affection of an eight-year-old boy. And whatever Monsieur's qualities, he had never sent her into exile or kept her there, never blackmailed her, never broken his word, never betrayed her. In someone close to Mademoiselle—especially in someone called Monsieur, duc d'Orléans—those very negatives amounted in themselves almost to affection.

Just after the reading of the will, Lauzun appeared at court in mourning—the deepest mourning conceivable, the mourning of a member of the family—the mourning, everyone gossiped at once, of a husband! He had put his entire household into mourning, like the household of a widower. And clad in black, attended by his black-clad servants, he proceeded to give Monsieur and the Dauphin a brief scare. Monsieur's wife wrote her aunt in Hanover about it: "I must tell you of a trick of Lauzun's. In order to make people think he had been married to Mademoiselle, he immediately, after her death, asked for the hand of a lady whom he knew to be already promised to someone else, and whose marriage contract the king himself had already signed. Then he appeared before the king and the entire royal family in mourning clothes. After staying three-quarters of an hour with Monsieur, he left the room, only to return a moment later carrying a large folded document on which were six of Mademoiselle's seals. 'By the way,' he said to Monsieur, 'I forgot to give you this paper, which Mademoiselle gave Madame de Nogent to keep six years ago.' Monsieur said he couldn't open it, that it had to be sent to the executor. The document worried the Dauphin and Monsieur considerably, for if it was a different will, made within six years, they wouldn't inherit, since the one that had been opened just after her death was eight years old, dated 1685. But at midnight Monsieur learned that it had been opened and had been found to be dated 1670. Lauzun undoubtedly knew it all the time and just wanted to have a little fun, the wretched, ungrateful beast!"

There had always, of course, been gossip that Mademoiselle and Lauzun had been married. It had begun to circulate immediately after the announcement that the king had forbidden the match. "It was only my close friends who dared mention this to me," Mademoiselle had written, "and I didn't even take the trouble to deny it. I let them believe what they liked, convinced as I was that the king would never believe that Monsieur de Lauzun and I had acted against his orders."

It is scarcely a denial.

And then, when Lauzun returned from exile, there were *two* rumors: the old one, that they had been married in 1670, and a new one: that they married now, as soon after their reunion as possible. Only a husband, people said, would be allowed by the strictly virtuous Mademoiselle to visit her so frequently in Paris, to stay with her at Choisy and at Eu; their very quarrels seemed to friends and acquaintances the quarrels of a disenchanted married pair. In her memoirs Mademoiselle says that at a certain moment following Lauzun's return, there was a question of his marrying someone else. But that is something she might deliberately have said to mislead. The king, after first letting her know through Madame de Montespan that she could marry Lauzun only secretly, had later ordered her "never to think" of marrying him at all; and if she had disobeyed her sovereign, she might well have thought it wise to resort to a little deception.

No proof has ever been shown. Lauzun said nothing.

There is only the testimony of the abbé Anquetil, who fifty years after Mademoiselle's death undertook to write a history of the reign of Louis XIV. "In 1744," he says, "I was shown the apartment Lauzun occupied in the château d'Eu, just above Mademoiselle's, connected with her alcove by a secret staircase." And at the village of Le Tréport, a few miles from Eu, he met "a tall spinster, the same height as Mademoiselle and closely resembling the portraits of her that hang at Eu. She was said in the village to be Mademoiselle's daughter. She herself seemed to think that she was, and she lived on a pension of fifteen hundred francs that was regularly paid her by someone unknown."

The spinster of Le Tréport seemed to the abbé to be between seventy and seventy-five years old. As far as her age went, he figured, she might easily have been born in 1670—the year Mademoiselle was happiest.

But whether Mademoiselle had been married or not, whether or not she had a daughter, it is certain that after her will had been read, after Lauzun had had his little joke and revived all the gossip, there came a final shock. Mademoiselle, in death, was destined to be news once more.

Her funeral ceremonies had all the pomp due a *petite-fille de France*. For an entire week "her body lay in state," says Saint-Simon, "watched over perpetually, in two-hour relays, by a duchess or a princess attended by two ladies of quality, all veiled in black from head to foot, all chosen by the king."

But at the funeral service itself, the one held in the Luxembourg before the removal of Mademoiselle's body to Saint-Denis, the note of solemnity was hideously shattered. "A ridiculous misadventure occurred," says Saint-Simon. "In the midst of the proceedings, when the ceremony was at its height, the urn containing Mademoiselle's entrails exploded with a frightful noise and an intolerable stench. In an instant all the ladies were fainting with fright or fleeing the room. The heralds, the monks who were chanting the service, everyone made a rush for the doors. Everything was in confusion. Almost everyone sought the garden or the courtyards. The entrails had been badly embalmed; it was their fermentation that caused the fracas. Then everything was sprayed with perfume and restored to order, and everyone laughed at the scare."

The explosion of Mademoiselle was the sensation of Paris.

Little in her life except the last years of resignation had been accomplished quietly; and this noisy, irregular finale was almost like an involuntary return, at once ridiculous and pathetic, to the tempestuousness of her younger days.

APPENDIX

A SELF-PORTRAIT OF MADEMOISELLE

[THERE WAS A VOGUE in Mademoiselle's day for the writing of "*Portraits de Société*"—word-portraits of one's friends or oneself. Mademoiselle wrote this one in 1657, toward the end of her first exile in Saint-Fargeau. It was published in a volume called *Mademoiselle's Portrait-Gallery*, which contains portraits by herself and others—many flattering to the point of unrecognizability—of the king, the queens, Gaston d'Orléans, the chevalier de Charny, and others of the characters in Mademoiselle's story. Mademoiselle's own self-portrait is more realistic than most, even though on the subject of her judgment she perhaps goes slightly astray!]

Since I am asked to paint my own portrait, I shall try to do the best I can. I hope that my character may appear in its true light despite my lack of skill in depicting it: I am certainly incapable of concealing my defects. I shall, however, be frank and truthful about my good and bad qualities, and shall count on the kind indulgence of my friends. I don't ask for pity. It is something I dislike. I'd much rather be laughed at, for mockery usually reflects envy, and people without merit are seldom envied.

So, let me begin with my outward appearance. I am tall, neither fat nor thin, shapely and graceful. I have a healthy complexion, quite a good bust. My arms and hands are nothing special, but I have a fine skin. My legs are straight and my ankles trim; my hair is an attractive ash-blonde. My face is long and regular; my nose big and aquiline; my mouth neither big nor little, but well and pleasantly modeled. My lips are red; my teeth are not beautiful, but not horrible either. My eyes are blue, of medium size, but bright—soft yet proud, like my entire ex-

[303]

pression. I give an impression of dignity, but without conceit. I am civil and friendly, but in a way to make me respected rather than treated with undue familiarity. I am very careless about clothes, but not to the point of slovenliness, which I hate. I am very neat, and whether I am formally or informally dressed everything looks well on me. Not that I'm not immensely better when carefully groomed, but carelessness is less unbecoming to me than to others. If I may say so, I don't detract from what I wear; rather, I profit from it.

I talk a great deal, but I don't say silly things and I haven't an evil tongue. I don't talk about things I don't understand, in the manner of chatterers who are too conceited to listen to others. I could take pride in many things, but the one thing I am really proud of is being an excellent friend; and I am very constant in my friendships when I am lucky enough to find people of merit whose disposition is akin to mine: for I hate to suffer from the inconstancy of others. I keep secrets better than anyone else in the world, and the loyalty and consideration I show my friends are not to be surpassed. I like to have those same qualities shown me, and nothing wins me as readily as confidence, because confidence is a mark of respect—and respect is appreciated by anyone of courage and honor. I am a very troublesome enemy, quick to anger, impulsive; this, in conjunction with my high birth, serves to make my foes tremble; but at the same time I am high-minded and kind-hearted. I am incapable of any low or contemptible action; that is why I am given to mercy rather than to justice.

By temperament I am reflective. I like to read good and serious books; inconsequential things bore me, except for poetry, which I love in all its varieties, and surely I am as good a judge of it as if I were a scholar. I like society, and the conversation of well-bred people. Nevertheless, I am not too impatient of the rest, for persons of my rank must practice self-restraint, since they are born to serve others rather than themselves; and this obligation has become such a habit with me that I tolerate everything, even though I don't enjoy everything. For all that, I know a person of merit when I see one, and I love all those who are distinguished in their calling. Above all others, I like warriors, and hearing them talk about their art. And though I have said that I talk only about things which I understand and which fall within my range, I confess that I like to talk about war. I feel

that I am very bold; I am very courageous and ambitious; but since by
my high birth God has limited the scope of my ambition to the very
uppermost reaches, what would be overweening in another is in me
mere conformity to His design.

I am quick in my decisions, and adhere to them firmly. There is
nothing too difficult for me if it is a question of helping my friends
or obeying my superiors. I am not self-seeking; I am incapable of
any baseness; and I am so indifferent toward all worldly things, I care
so little about what others think of me, and I have so much self-
respect, that I would spend my life in solitude rather than submit to
the slightest humiliation, even if my fortune were at stake. I like to
be alone. I have no indulgence for others, and I demand a great deal
of it myself. I am skeptical, but self-confident. I like to give pleasure
and do favors. I also often like to criticize, and I don't fear to give
offense. Since I am not pleasure-loving, I am not eager to provide dis-
sipations for others. I like string-music better than any other; I used
to like to dance more than I do now, and I'm a very good dancer. I
hate to play cards, and I like active games. I enjoy doing all kinds of
needlework, as well as hunting and riding. I am much more sensitive
to grief than to joy, being more acquainted with the former than with
the latter; but others remain unaware of this, for although I am neither
an actress nor a hypocrite, and usually conceal nothing, I can nevertheless control myself when I want to, and show only the side of
myself that I want seen. No one has ever had more power over himself; never has the spirit been more the master of the body: this sometimes exacts a price in suffering. The great sorrows that I have experienced would have killed anyone else; but the qualities with which
God has endowed me are in good balance, and I have unparalleled
health and strength. Nothing dispirits me, nothing tires me; and it
is difficult to read the vicissitudes of my past, or my present sorrows,
on my face, for it rarely shows them. I might say that my complexion
is an index to my good constitution: it isn't delicate, but it is clear
and glowing.

I am not pious, although I should like to be, and have already
achieved a great degree of indifference toward the world. But I am
afraid that I remain attached to it despite my scorn; for I myself am
not among the things I scorn, and self-love is scarcely conducive to

piety. I take great interest in the administration of my property, and I am as mistrustful about it as about everything else. I like regularity and order even in the smallest things. I don't know whether I am generous: I know that I like magnificence and splendor, and I like to make presents to persons of merit and people I'm fond of; but since in this I often follow my whims, I don't know whether you would call it generosity. When I do good, I do it from my heart; no one does a favor more readily than I. I don't praise others easily, and I rarely criticize myself. I am neither malicious nor mocking, though I am as quick as anyone to notice people's foibles and enjoy ridiculing them. I am a bad painter, but I write well and easily. As for *galanterie,* I have no bent for it whatever, and I am even reproached for liking the most passionate poetry least, for romance doesn't appeal to me. But when I am accused of being as impervious to friendship as to romance, I protest strongly; for I love without reservation those who deserve my love or earn it: no one displays gratitude more warmly than I.

I am of simple tastes, and I find the pleasures of the table tiresome; it wearies me even to watch those who are enjoying them too much. Sleep I like; but when something claims my attention I can get along without sleep perfectly well. I am not at all an intriguer. I like to know what's going on in the world, but rather to keep away from it than because I want to meddle in it. I have a good memory, and don't lack judgment. I hope that if people judge me, they won't do so on the basis of the events that have befallen me; for my fate has been so unlucky up to now, as against what it should have been, that their verdict might be unfavorable to me. It is surely fair to say that fate has been more lacking in judgment than I, for had it had more sense it would doubtless have treated me better.

NOTE

"The courageous memoirs of Mademoiselle," as the French historian Michelet calls them, form the basis of the present volume. They are available in two principal versions. One, first printed in 1735 in Amsterdam, after an earlier, less complete publication in 1729, is based on a manuscript that Mademoiselle gave to President (we should say Judge) de Harlay, the executor of her will. In her narrative Mademoiselle tells us that because her own handwriting was well-nigh illegible, the portion of her original manuscript written at Saint-Fargeau was transcribed for her by her secretary, Préfontaine. Presumably this and its sequel are what was handed later to de Harlay. The latest important imprint of the 1735 edition appeared in 1824, as volumes 40 to 43 of the great *Collection des Mémoires relatifs à l'histoire de France,* edited by Petitot.

In 1858 a new version of the memoirs was published, edited by A. Chéruel, based in part on an incomplete manuscript in Mademoiselle's own hand in the Bibliothèque Nationale in Paris. The text of this version shows many differences as compared with the version published earlier. Some of these differences, particularly in its first section, are corrections of obvious errors; other differences, especially in the sections referring to Lauzun, are more thoroughgoing, though at no point are the two versions incompatible. In the second the wording is often altered, and sometimes a given dialogue is shorter or longer than in the first; but in neither case is the meaning affected. The story told by both versions is the same. I have felt free to use both versions, choosing, when they differ, whichever seems to me superior. Translations are by me.

I have also consulted, in addition to general and minor works, the two books by Arvède Barine on Mademoiselle and her period, and the duc de la Force's monographs on Mademoiselle and Lauzun. I thank the Columbia University Library, the Frick Art Reference Library and the New York Society Library for their many courtesies, and Mlle. Liliane Yacoël for her valuable researches in Paris and Versailles.

F. S.